SIDEWAYS ON A SCOOTER

RANDOM HOUSE

NEW YORK

Sideways
on a
Scooter

Life and Love in India

MIRANDA KENNEDY

Sideways on a Scooter is a work of nonfiction.
Some names and identifying details have been changed.

Published in the United States by Random House,
an imprint of The Random House Publishing Group,
a division of Random House, Inc., New York.

RANDOM HOUSE and colophon are registered
trademarks of Random House, Inc.

Grateful acknowledgment is made to The Random House Group Ltd., London,
for permission to reprint an excerpt from "Birches" by Robert Frost, from
The Poetry of Robert Frost, edited by Edward Connery Lathem, published by Jonathan Cape.
Reprinted by permission of The Random House Group Ltd., London.

LIBRARY OF CONGRESS CATALOGING-IN-PUBLICATION DATA
Kennedy, Miranda.
Sideways on a scooter : life and love in India / Miranda Kennedy.
p. cm.
Includes bibliographical references.
ISBN 978-1-4000-6786-2
eBook ISBN 978-0-679-60455-6
1. Women—India—Delhi—Social life and customs. 2. Women—India—Delhi—
Social conditions. 3. Women—India—Delhi—Biography. 4. Man-woman
relationships—India—Delhi. 5. Love—Social aspects—India—Delhi.
6. Kennedy, Miranda—Travel—India—Delhi. 7. Delhi (India)—Description
and travel. 8. Delhi (India)—Social life and customs. 9. Delhi (India)—
Social conditions. 10. Social change—India—Delhi. I. Title.
HQ1745.D4K46 2011
305.40954'56—dc22   2010020297

Printed in the United States of America on acid-free paper

www.atrandom.com

2 4 6 8 9 7 5 3 1

FIRST EDITION

Book design by Dana Leigh Blanchette

For my father,
who taught me
the love of reading,
and for Annie,
who illuminates

Contents

SIDEWAYS ON A SCOOTER

CHAPTER 1

Are You Alone?

Delhi's stale April air caught in my throat. Each breath had already been recycled through millions of Indian mouths, I imagined, growing hotter and thicker with each exhale. This is what it must feel like inside a burka: It was as though I was enclosed from head to toe in black cotton and inhaling the fabric that covered my mouth as I tried to scoop the dusty soup into my lungs.

"Natural air-conditionings, madam! Full breeze—open like a helicopter!"

When a three-wheeled auto-rickshaw slowed to a sputter alongside me, I was uncomfortable enough to pay attention to the driver's offer. I'd only been in India for a couple of weeks, but I'd already learned that most of Delhi's rickshaw drivers choose to nap away as much of the seven-month hot season as they can, sprawled across their backseats in a pool of sweat. When the temperature sails above a hundred degrees, they hike their fares to ensure that the predatory customers leave them to nap in peace. This driver must have been especially hard up. He gave me an exaggerated salesman's smile, disturbing the too-small pair of plastic glasses jammed onto his face, and agreed to a reasonable fare without arguing. I scrambled in, immediately grateful for the relief his rickshaw's flimsy canvas top provided from the sun, and for the slight breeze of his "helicopter" with two open sides.

The peppery smell of areca nut stung my nostrils as my driver dug a leaf-wrapped packet of *paan* out of a metal box and pulled it open with his teeth. *Paan,* a strong stimulant like chewing tobacco, reddens the teeth and lips of laborers, delivery boys, and shopkeepers across India. When my mother had first come to South Asia, she'd assumed the men were all dying of tuberculosis, spitting blood onto the streets. She had been only twenty-three—younger and even more naïve than I was when I first arrived, at twenty-seven. In fact, *paan* is a relatively innocuous vice, "the working man's way of getting through the day," as one friend later described it. If the middle class relies on air-conditioning and chauffeur-driven cars to endure the disorder and discomfort of Indian city life, everyone else blunts its frustrations with cheaper and more accessible aids, such as *paan,* hand-rolled cigarettes called bidis, and Bollywood films.

The rickshaw spluttered through Paharganj, a seedy district for low-budget tourists where British accents jostle with the guava sellers' Hindi cries and the shouts of the aggressive red-shirted porters at the railway station nearby. Adjacent to New Delhi Station, this area is the landing point for Israelis letting off steam after their mandatory military service, and for lost European souls in search of Afghan heroin or Russian prostitutes, or both. It's a little ironic that it is also where those in search of spiritual awakening come to lay their yoga mats. Paharganj isn't the "real India," but it was the version my parents would have seen when they made their way along the hippie trail to India back in the seventies. This, the spiritualized, photogenic India sought out by Western wanderers, didn't really parse with the globalizing India that I'd read about, of cable TV and McDonald's McAloo Tikkis.

Although I have been known to do yoga, I wasn't especially interested in a New Age-y ashram experience of India. However, there was no getting around the fact that I'd shown up in Delhi dressed the part. It took me longer than it probably should have to realize that outfits such as a long, wrinkled beaded skirt and tight black cotton eyelet top weren't doing me any favors in India, where neatness is sometimes the only way to tell the slightly poor from the desperately impoverished. Compared to Delhi's ladies—impeccable in freshly ironed silk saris and tiny beaded slippers, and radiating a fragrance of baby powder and palm oil—I looked like a sloppy hippie.

A few hours earlier, in the breakfast room of the Lord's Hotel, I had looked down at the strips of papaya and clumpy yogurt in front of me and tried to concentrate on my goals for the day. Half watching the translucent geckos skitter across the walls, I reviewed the list of interviews I wanted to set up, the apartment search I needed to embark on. It seemed overambitious and strangely irrelevant when I considered my surroundings: a cheap druggy traveler's hotel in a chaotic city that would seethe its way through the day no matter what I did with mine. I sighed in frustration and turned my attention to the geckos. Through their bodies I could see the cheery red and pink frescoes of Hindu gods.

I was determined to be more than a casual visitor to India. I'd been saving everything I earned at my job as a producer at a public radio show so that I could pick up and go overseas to try my hand at becoming a freelance foreign correspondent. The lack of transcendent, transformative experiences in my life so far had disappointed me: My days seemed a blur of headlines and deadlines. And even though it was a nineteenth-century idea, I couldn't help but worry that I needed to make a dramatic gesture to convince my New York boyfriend to stick it out with me. As much as I wished I could stride into the world without caring about such things, it wasn't that simple. I hoped that by taking myself off to the farthest, most exotic place I could imagine, I'd make myself more appealing to him.

There was never any question in my mind that India was where I'd go to do it. My family's fascination with the place dates back to 1930, when my British great-aunt Edith traveled there as a Christian missionary. My mother's side of the family is a small, close-knit group of wanderers, and I'd always expected that I would be like the rest of them. Going to India was like a rite of passage, entwined with my very idea of myself. Although the decision didn't make much sense to my friends, I had an idea that I would become my fullest, most interesting self there.

Moving around was also just a part of who I was. When I ask my mother to list the cities we lived in when I was young, she has to pull out a pen and paper to keep them straight. I think I went to four differ- ent first grades, beginning in England, where my mother comes from. Unlike some families, who are forced to change cities by circumstance or jobs, moving was itself the goal for my parents. Often, they would create the reason to leave. My father, a theater studies professor, seemed equally compelled by the drama of a life lived on the move as by practicalities such as career development or earning a good salary. Liv- ing in many places was important enough to them that they decided we'd never buy a new refrigerator or car. My mother was frugal by na- ture anyway; she'd half joke when telling us to eat our apple cores that this was how we'd be able to afford plane tickets to see her family in England.

My great-aunt Edith died when I was eleven, and all I have left of her is a family of brass elephants and a few leather-bound books of photographs carefully mounted onto wax paper. As a teenager in Pittsburgh—where my parents settled long enough for me to attend middle and high school—I would look at the three elephants lined up on my windowsill, each one slightly larger than the next, and imagine the life I would have. In every photo, Edith is wearing sensible black lace-up shoes and a dour Victorian expression. She and her mission- ary sisters look out of place, to say the least, under groves of South In- dian palm trees, or floating on elaborately decorated wooden Kashmiri houseboats on Srinagar's Dal Lake.

In one picture, Edith is being carried by several underfed Indians in a covered sedan chair through a mountain passageway. Transported through Kashmir like a princess in a palanquin to her summertime retreat in the cool hills! To my adolescent self, stuck in an utterly un- romantic postindustrial town, these images were reason enough to consider becoming a missionary. We rarely went to church and I didn't believe in God, so my mother had a good point when she suggested that

I might want to consider something that required less religion—such as being a foreign correspondent, perhaps.

Even if the grass isn't always greener, it is always worth checking just to be sure—that is my father's belief, and I inherited it. Early on, I learned that it was easy enough to make friends and not get too attached to any of them; it was okay, my parents taught us, because we had one another. Committing to a group of friends and learning to belong to a school or a neighborhood—we didn't do that in my family. I was the kind of teenager who kept a running tally of the European cities I'd visited and asserted my opinions about world affairs over the dinner table. When my father was offered a position in Ireland, at the University of Dublin, it seemed natural to transfer my college credits there and go along for the ride; I didn't want to miss out on any of my family's cool international adventures.

After college, I wanted to outdo my parents and crisscross the globe again, this time of my own accord. New York yielded me all the things I'd hoped it would: It helped me realize what I wanted to do with my life, and it gave me a boyfriend who believed in the poetry of adventure, as I did. I found a cockroach-studded apartment in a rent-stabilized building in Brooklyn that was cheap enough that after several years of working at magazines and radio programs, I could buy myself a ticket to India.

My friends were right to be skeptical about my tripping off. New York was full of opportunities for an aspiring writer, and my developing-world country of choice offered nothing in the way of career assurances. Although we knew plenty of journalists who'd decided to freelance overseas, they'd chosen higher-profile regions, such as the Middle East, where their reporting was actually likely to generate some attention. India's economy was booming, but it wasn't a major story. When I talked to editors about my plans, their eyes lit up when I mentioned Pakistan and Afghanistan. I said I was interested in reporting from those places, too, but I was quite sure that I didn't want to get slated as a war-on-terror correspondent.

When the September 11 attacks happened, I was at the radio studio, right below Canal Street, a few blocks away from the World Trade Center. I didn't leave for the next two weeks. We slept and ate and worked in the studio—afraid that if we left Ground Zero, the police wouldn't allow us back in. I spent every night down among the rescue workers. It was amazing to witness to such an important part of history, but it also helped me realize how difficult it was to burrow inside a major event like that and pull out the sad, quirky, and untold moments, as I like to. Part of me wanted to follow the story to Afghanistan; but I also wanted to get away from all the elbow-jostling of daily news reporters and go to the place I cared about most.

I got a small grant to train radio reporters in South Asia, which gave me enough money to get started. Other than that, though, I had no guarantee of work—just expressions of interest from editors at National Public Radio and a few other news outlets. My friends advised that if I stuck it out in the New York media world, I'd eventually work my way up to a job as a foreign correspondent. Even if they were right, I didn't want to wait. I thought I needed to kick my way out of the claustrophobia of normalcy and show the world that I could become a foreign correspondent on my own, rather than waiting for an employer to hand me the job.

I'd started to feel at home in New York, and that was exactly the problem. I'd lie awake at night working myself into a panic as I imagined myself ten years hence: working a slightly better job, living in a slightly nicer apartment—a scheduled, comfortable life that my parents would consider mundane. Now that I was a slightly rebellious, itinerant adult, resisting the urge to claim a community as my own, India had taken on an almost legendary aspect. Far away and unfamiliar, it had become a kind of resting place in my mind. On some level, I knew that it was where I would go to define myself as a journalist, an adventurer, a woman.

Before any of that could happen, I had to find somewhere to set up my laptop and improvise a recording studio so I could start filing my stories. Most important, I needed an address so I could print up business cards, which I'd quickly discovered were a mandatory accessory in India; without a card to present at the beginning of an interview, no one seemed to believe that I was real. I was already having enough difficulty convincing Indian officials and intellectuals to take me seriously as I made the rounds of their offices, trying to form intelligent interview questions about the opaque world of Indian politics and culture.

In status-obsessed India, my interviewees had reason to be skeptical of an unaffiliated reporter girl in inappropriate clothes. They were accustomed to meeting foreign correspondents of a different stripe— those who had been dispatched by their news organizations and lived a rather plusher Delhi life than I did. *The New York Times*'s correspondents, for instance, take up residence in a spacious colonial-era bungalow that the paper has owned for decades. Inside are the facilities they need to acclimatize and be as efficient as you can be in India— which is to say, not very, but every little thing helps: a full-time translator to lead them around the city, a car and driver, an imported washing machine. The *Times*'s bungalow is equipped with a permanent staff, including a gardener to beautify the outside spaces for entertaining.

When I found an inexpensive room for rent in the newspaper listings, the receptionist at the Lord's Hotel was emphatic in his recommendation of the area: "A-one neighborhood, madam, top class." So I was surprised when, looking out of the side of the rickshaw, I saw yet another Delhi neighborhood filled with vegetable vendors and the teeming impermanence of poverty. The smells of gutter rot and frying spices fused together into a heady brew. No wonder Indians laugh at Americans and Europeans who stroll across Delhi as though it were a pretty little New England town, I thought. The city is a flat outstretched plain of traffic and beggars; traffic circle after traffic circle, lush with hot pink bougainvillea bushes; and then this, chaotic markets choked with too many choices on which to settle your eye.

Outside the vehicle, I heard a squealing sound and cringed, convincing myself it was a monkey about to attack. Macaques have taken over the Ministry of Defence building in central Delhi, and stories about the "monkey menace" are not uncommon on the nightly news. Still, I had an outsize fear of being chased by rabid primates my first few months in the country. I turned to see that the noise was only a small boy shoving stalks of sugarcane into a huge metal grinder. As he cranked a squeaky wheel handle around, the white juicy foam squirted out of a funnel: pure sugar juice, two rupees. A decrepit, shirtless religious pilgrim limped up to the machine and was wordlessly handed a glass of the stuff. He looked as though he needed the calories.

A cow swished its dung-crusted tail across my face through the side of the rickshaw, wakening me from my reverie. The grit of its feces brushed against my lips, a textured wetness that tasted like soil. My rickshaw plunged bravely through a jumble of narrow lanes snarled with animals, bullock carts, and scooters. The houses leaned into the street, their contents spilling out onto rickety balconies—cleaning buckets and brooms, long swaths of saris and men's shirts hanging on laundry lines. The wobbly structures reminded me of the images of nineteenth-century tenements in the Lower East Side of Manhattan. Were these really the homes of the fast-growing middle class that I'd read so much about? Was this where the call center workers slept during the day when they were not transforming the global economy from inside new office towers?

After a quarter of an hour of bumping along the maze of streets, I realized my rickshaw wallah had retraced his steps more than once. He actually had no idea where he was going. He was just sputtering gamely down the center of the road, ignoring the lane divider. We both stared at the haphazardly numbered houses piled atop one another: "432-L" announced one house; "34-B" read the number on the building beside it. I groaned in frustration—"How could 432-L and 34-B be neighbors?"—but my driver was undaunted. He slowed near a boy pushing a cart of mangoes and shouted the house number we were looking for. The boy couldn't hear him above the engine's explosive stutter. He heaved his cart to the side of the road and sidled over as he scratched his groin absentmindedly through his polyester pants.

Only when my driver cut the motor did I realize that my head was pounding from its staccato clatter and the searing heat. My driver was suffering, too. He wiped his face with a corner of his grubby kurta, the long, loose shirt worn by both women and men in India. Then he reached below his feet, pulled out an old Coke bottle, the paper label long ago peeled off, and poured a stream of water into his mouth, making sure the rim didn't touch his lips. He offered the bottle to me, and turned back wordlessly, unsurprised, when I declined: Foreigners never drink Indian water unless they can vouch for its origins. The mango boy, however, took a grateful swig, using the same germ-free Indian technique. He had the sunken-eyed look of the hungry that I was becoming accustomed to on the streets of Delhi. Giving directions was probably a welcome diversion from the sapping blaze of a 120-degree spring day.

In the afternoons, when it is too hot to work, the solidly employed retire to their homes for lunch and a siesta, as they do in southern Europe, where lives have long been patterned around making the seasons livable. This civilized luxury is not an option for Delhi's underemployed immigrants, many of whom have no home to retire to. Some 70 million immigrated to Indian cities from the impoverished hinterlands in the decade before I moved to the country in 2002. Still more poured in from India's poorer neighbors, Nepal and Bangladesh. They come in search of urban wealth and opportunity, which, sadly, they rarely find. Instead, they take whatever bits of work they can get—serving *chai* or cleaning toilets. In the afternoons, they seek out fellow villagers, squatting in companionable clusters in scraps of shade, or walking together with their arms draped across each other's shoulders. Sometimes they hold hands loosely, in the village boys' sweet, casual gesture of friendship.

The undereducated village boys stop and stare at anything slightly out of the ordinary. Even if it is the capital of one of the world's fastest-growing economies, Delhi has a decidedly uncosmopolitan feel. It is, after all, a magnet for the rural poor. Eyes followed me everywhere unless I was safely ensconced inside a five-star hotel. *Feringhees*, or *goras*, as foreigners are called in Hindi slang, stand out in a city with little immigration from outside its national boundaries. The word *gora* is straightforward: It means "white." *Feringhee* stems back to the time of the Crusades, when Indian Muslims used the word to refer to Christians; the base of the word is *Frank,* once used for people of European descent. India has been home to dozens of ethnicities, skin colors, religions, and castes for centuries, but in spite of all the invasions and colonizations, the polyglot culture has still almost always been Indian.

The mango boy and my driver pondered our destination, and others strolled over to join the discussion, pointing here and there with lackadaisical arms. When one of them realized that the rickshaw contained a *feringhee,* they began popping their heads inside to peer at me: The effect was of a comic puppet show. Their expressions bore no hostility, just curiosity and surprise, as they took in the white face and platinum blond hair, which I'd dyed that color soon after college in an effort to stand out. The goal was easily achieved in India. After a couple of months of being treated like a freakish celebrity, inspiring turned heads and double takes on Delhi streets, I would decide to return to my natural brown.

From the backseat, I could see my driver nodding disinterestedly at the crowd of volunteer guides. He was getting comfortable, slipping off his *chappals* and folding his feet beneath him. I despaired that I would ever make it to the apartment viewing. Even with only three weeks of Hindi lessons, I could tell that my driver's conclave was more idle gossip than route planning. I hadn't learned enough of the language to ask directions for myself, though, and my driver was indifferent to my restlessness, so I just sank back to wait for the socializing to conclude.

We lived in semidodgy urban neighborhoods growing up; I wrote about gang violence for the newspaper at my public high school. I liked to think of myself as capable and street smart. During crises, such as the time I was robbed in Brooklyn by a neighbor wielding a gun, I'd been pleased with myself for staying levelheaded. But now, with the heat rising inside our steam box of a rickshaw, I had a fantasy of slamming my rickshaw wallah's head against the hot metal dashboard. Of course, then I'd probably destroy his already half-broken glasses, and I'd be not just a yellow-haired weirdo but a wild-eyed crazy one.

I took a deep breath and reminded myself what an Indian friend in New York had told me: If I was to make it in the "real," unsanitized

India, I had to be willing to surrender control and waste a lot of time. There was nothing for it but to swallow my impatience.

Eventually, the rickshaw wallah spat a trail of tuberculean red *paan* onto the road: "*Han-ji,* madam. *Chelliye!*" We were off, at the top auto-rickshaw speed of twenty miles an hour. Soon, we came to a halt again, beside an excited crowd of men. I craned my neck: A utility pole had collapsed, tipping a knotted mass of power lines onto the road, and a crowd of random guys was tugging the wires out of the pole, in the Indian spirit of any business is everybody's business.

When we finally arrived at the house, I peeled my legs off the ripped plastic seat. As I pulled myself out of the rickshaw, I caught a glimpse of myself in the side mirror: Strands of hair were plastered to my head with sweat, and the rest had been swept up into a bouffant by the wind. The rickshaw driver extended his hand—stained black from engine grease and red from *paan*—demanding double the fare because of the detours. He spun off in his Indian helicopter without returning my dollar-fifty change.

I threw up my hands and turned toward the house, where I thought I caught a flash of a woman peering at me before she dropped a lacy white curtain back into place. I rang the bell, trying to smooth out my creased skirt and wild hair with my fingers. A small, dark-skinned servant girl of about twelve came to the door, her face a mask of learned indifference. I could smell incense from the morning *puja,* or prayer session. Upstairs somewhere, there were young kids playing.

I was still blinking to adjust my eyes to the dimness of the unlit hallway when a Sikh man in a commanding blue turban strode toward me. He gave me a quick unwelcoming nod, and my disheveled clothes suddenly felt too tight, too hippie, too Western. I swallowed into my dry throat, hoping the servant girl would reappear to proffer cold water on a small plastic tray. I'd already become spoiled by the rituals of Indian middle-class hospitality: the servant who presents you with a glass of water and ushers you to the living room to relax for a moment. There, you will be served either a *cold drink,* as Indians refer to soda, or a small china cup of sweet *chai,* depending on the season. Yet the landlord met me in the hallway and didn't even ask me to sit down.

"Sorry I'm late. We had some trouble getting here—"

I stopped when I realized that his gaze was carefully averted from me and fixed above my shoulder. I turned to see whom he was looking at, but it was just the door frame.

"We?"

I could tell from the single word that his was the British-tinged English of India's elite prep schools. His brow was arched. I was unsure where to look.

"I mean, me and the rickshaw driver."

"Hmmm," he said to the door frame. "So, *are* you alone?"

I paused. The question, issued from this imposing figure in a gloomy hallway, seemed calculated to inspire an existential crisis. In fact, it was only evidence of how different the average Indian's attitudes to family and relationships were from my own. Most Indians I'd met found it incomprehensible that I would choose to live so far away from my family, which, at the age of twenty-seven, should have already included a husband, if not also a child.

At the very least, I should be able to rely on my parents and siblings for housing. Even in the new, globalized India, family governs most people's lives. Many upwardly mobile girls I'd met in Delhi had the appearance of independence—they wore jeans to college and went out to movies with their girlfriends on Saturday nights—but they didn't plan to move out of their parents' houses before they married. When that happened, they would stop working and move into their husbands' parental homes.

Over the next several years, I would be asked about my aloneness countless times in various ways—"Do you have your family here?" or "Do you have anyone?"—and I eventually became accustomed to the sorrowful looks my response elicited and learned not to be thrown off by the questions. I had close emotional relationships with my parents, my sisters, and my aunt—but it struck me now that we'd long lived in different countries and spoke only occasionally. My face flushed hot with embarrassment as I stood in front of the Sikh.

"My family doesn't live here, so I am looking for a place on my own."

The landlord straightened his posture.

"This flat is not for single girls. We are not interested in girls of your type here. Good day."

And he turned on the heel of his carefully polished shoe.

The servant stepped out of a shadow, and I realized she'd been there all along, waiting for the cue from her employer to usher me in or out of the hallway. She opened the door, her eyes following me impassively, as though I were of another species. I felt sure that even though she didn't speak English, she understood what had just transpired. I wanted to plead with her: "What can I do to be the right kind of girl?"

Months later, when I had made Indian girlfriends, they told me this was standard treatment for any woman attempting to rent a place without a husband in tow; there are even Bollywood films that show young women battling landlords when they move out of their parental homes before marriage. As I skulked back out into the heat, I could feel four eyes—those of the servant girl and the woman behind the lace curtain—boring into my back.

I should have known better, perhaps; after all, I had grown up hearing stories about the challenges of working in India as a single woman, though in a very different era. Aunt Edith, the missionary, lived in India from 1930 to 1966—staying even as the British Empire declined and India won its independence, through the bloody and tumultuous partition that led to the creation of Pakistan. Unlike most of their British compatriots, she and the other "lady evangelists" of the Bible Churchmen's Missionary Society, or BCMS, were urged not to leave. In spite of the "churchmen" in its name, BCMS boasted that "the toughest fields were served by women" in its missionary work.

Something like a million people died during the partition of India in 1947, killed in religious violence or by malnutrition or contagious disease as Muslims traveled west to Pakistan, and Hindus and Sikhs east to India. More than ten million refugees poured across the border in what is still the greatest mass migration in history, and during that time, many foreign missionaries risked their lives to run clinics at the dangerous border crossings between the newly divided countries. I don't know whether Edith was there, because she didn't like to discuss difficult matters with the family, which, according to the dictates of her proper British upbringing, included political turmoil and religions other than her own.

It seems improbable that the lady evangelists would have had any success in evangelizing the religion of the kicked-out colonizers, but Edith and the others "carried on" in India, as one former lady evangelist told me. They "wrestled with the strange Hindi characters, learnt to eat fiery Indian curries, and, ignoring aching joints, to sit upon the ground," according to a BCMS pamphlet. In the photographs of Edith's missionary days, the Indian women look shrunken beside her. She was over six feet tall, a disadvantage in her line of work: She refused to wear saris on her evangelizing missions for fear that villagers would think she was a man dressed as a woman, though I'm not sure why she thought wearing a shapeless ankle-length cotton frock protected her from making this impression.

In spite of Edith's fastidious English dresses, expressions of femininity were never appropriate among missionary ladies, who lived a life of self-denial and rigor completely unlike that of officers of the British Raj and their wives. Edith's hair was parted down the middle in a cruelly straight line and scraped back into a practical bun. Years later, my mother's sister, Susie, told me that their aunt's hair was actually her secret vanity. She would save the strands from her comb and wrap them into the bun at the nape of her neck, like some surreptitious storehouse of her femininity. Edith had few other indulgences: She spent her adult life in a rural mission with neither electricity nor running water. She would travel to villages on the dusty northern plains to distribute medicine, teach girls to read, and, of course, do God's work of preaching the Bible to the pagans.

They say every family has one black sheep, but almost all my mother's relatives were strong willed, rebellious, and independent. My mother and Susie did not share Edith's faith or her paternalistic missionary attitude, but her dedication and endurance had a huge influence on them both. Edith was in her late sixties by the time she retired. Until then, she continued making her annual summer expeditions north to Kashmir with missionary friends to rest, away from the heat of the plains. One year, they sent the porter ahead with their bedrolls and tins of homemade English biscuits and rushed through the train station to make their connection. After they'd leaped aboard, Edith's face went gray. She refused to interrupt the vacation by going to the hospital. When she returned to the mission, six weeks later, she discovered she'd had a heart attack.

As a sheltered child in rural England, my mother pored over the letters Edith sent each month on stationery printed with Indian birds. She dreamed of seeing the bulbul and the hoopoe, with its fan-shaped crest, and of experiencing the simple Indian village life Edith described. The opportunity came soon after she married my father, an American graduate student she'd met at Oxford University. He was working at a small college in a Michigan town they both hated. In the hope of escaping, my father decided to apply for a Fulbright scholarship. He didn't get India; instead, the committee offered him a lectureship at the University of Karachi, in Pakistan, a rather less appealing choice since it was reeling from a brutal civil war. Still, it got them out of Michigan.

As my mother anticipated, it was spending a couple of months in India, afterward, that had the greatest impact on her. After my sisters were born, she converted the whole family to Hindu-inspired vegetarianism, and stuck with it throughout our childhood. When my sisters and I complained that we didn't have name-brand clothes, she'd lecture us about the frugal lifestyle of India's independence hero Mahatma Gandhi. My mother always seemed to have Indian friends, and decorated every house we lived in with objects she and my father had collected in the East: leather safari chairs, antique tribal rugs, and a heavy brass statue of the god Shiva dancing in a circle of flame, which my father would complain he'd lugged all across India.

When I announced I was moving there myself, my parents didn't seem surprised.

"If I'd lived a different life and stayed single longer, I would have liked to do something like you did," my mother once said wistfully. "Just head off on my own."

She offered advice about how to clothe myself appropriately in India and how to avoid getting amebic dysentery, which she and my father had repeatedly suffered from in Karachi. She tried to prepare me for the harshness of life in India, telling me that what had shocked her most was the desperation, the bodies wasting away on the streets. I didn't pay much attention to all this, though. Even though my interest in the place was born of the family history, I was determined to make it mine. It was ironic that the most exotic destination was, for me, also the most conventional. I wanted to at least make my own mistakes.

I'd educated myself pretty thoroughly about India, I thought, having read obsessively about it for years. I knew that the country was yielding more nuanced stories in the U.S. and British press than it had for decades. It used to be that an assignment in India meant penning lyrical essays about starving men in *lungis*, exotic snake charmers, and the country's multiple truths and mysteries, but when India opened its economy to the world, it inspired a new level of engagement.

Now the press seemed to have arrived at a glowing consensus—that the country's transformation was social as well as economic. I read that millions of Indians were buying their first cell phones and upgrading from scooters to cars. According to the American papers, India's lowest castes were hoisting themselves out of their villages and hereditary occupations, couples were choosing their own life partners rather than being pushed into preordained parental arrangements, and women were buying microwaveable curries so they could develop careers as news anchors and lawyers.

Even these optimistic portraits couldn't neglect to mention India's poverty and grime, though. The average annual income was less than a thousand dollars a year. In China, the country whose economic rise was most often compared to India's, the annual income was almost three times that. The nation now produced more than enough food to feed its people and was growing a vibrant service-based economy; and yet its endemic inefficiency meant that millions of farmers and laborers struggled for one meal a day. Although my mother's warnings about lepers and teeming slums were based on an India of thirty years ago, little seemed to have changed.

I thought I was prepared for whatever would greet me off the plane, but India knocked the swagger out of my gait. The dissonant smells seeped into the aircraft before I even stepped onto Indian soil—a mix of burning plastic and metal that reminded me of the afternoon of the 9/11 attacks in New York. In Delhi, the smell of burning was mingled with other assaulting odors—the earthy fragrance of cow-dung patties leaching their odor into the streets, the tang of tamarind and lime from a roadside food stall outside the airport.

Who was in charge? I wondered as I looked around the airport arrivals hall that first, disconcerting night. It was a question I would ask myself hundreds of times in many different settings. The official who stamped my passport had dead eyes and food stains on his shirt. The roof was leaking. The baggage carousel screeched around with a frightening wail, and the passengers were shoving one another as though their lives depended on collecting their bags. One sari-clad woman pushed me aside with broad hands, and as I caught myself from falling, I clamped down on my tongue. The metallic taste of blood always reminds me of my first night in Delhi.

I'd expected a much more modern and globalized country than I found. I anticipated poverty, but I also thought I'd find a large, liberal-minded middle class that would approximate my own Western experience. I'd heard that a troupe of Indian actresses was staging *The Vagina Monologues,* Eve Ensler's graphic feminist play, and that gave me high hopes. In fact, I would learn, nothing in India is straightforward. It is home to highly educated entrepreneurs, and also to millions of illiterate villagers whose lives are guided by feudal principles and regressive social attitudes. India opened itself to me in ways I never would have thought possible of a culture so different from my own, and it also slammed the door shut on me like the Delhi landlord who assumed I was a whore because I wanted to live alone.

CHAPTER 2

Boyfriended

There is no word in Hindi for *boyfriend,* so the English word is dropped into Hindi sentences, and once there, it rings like a curse. Being boyfriended implies a depraved, decadent life; a girl with one boyfriend is sure to have many others. During my first year in India, when the language rang strangely in my ears, just a rhythmic patter of unfamiliar sounds, I would clutch onto the word as I did to other recognizable scraps inside speech. When non-English-speaking Indians use English words and phrases—such as *tension, operation,* and *by chance*—it is either to emphasize a point or to impress someone. The word *boyfriend* is different; it is always heavy with ugly connotations.

I'd been living in seedy hotels for several months while I made exploratory reporting trips around India, still waiting to find a landlord in Delhi who'd agree to rent an apartment to a single foreign lady. My unmarried status wouldn't have been a problem if I'd been able to afford a place in one of the city's elite enclaves, where the moneyed Indian classes stretch out in spacious colonial homes beside those of foreign diplomats and businessmen with generous expat packages. In lower-middle-class Indian neighborhoods, though, the landlords are unaccustomed to the wild ways of Western women who live by themselves or—worse—with a boyfriend. So I was scrutinized just as are Indian women when they try to break the grip of tradition.

The surges of electricity from Delhi's irregular power supply had decimated my laptop battery. I was living on cheap street food—fried potato patties with tamarind sauce, lentil dal in leaf bowls, thick *parantha* breads right off the iron griddle. It was all delicious, if not very good for my insides: I'd become accustomed to regular bouts of diarrhea. The drug-addled Europeans at the Lord's Hotel were getting to me, too, so I asked around for a hotel in a nontouristy part of town. At the New City Palace, a tiny single room was only four dollars a night, so I didn't mind that this hotel didn't live up to its name any more than the Lord's did. The only thing palatial about the New City Palace was the view: It faced directly onto the Jama Masjid, the largest mosque in India.

My first morning there, I was woken by the call to prayer before dawn, amplified through tinny loudspeakers projecting out of the building. I pulled on my clothes and ventured onto the hotel's balcony. Early-morning mist was floating across the red sandstone minarets, and the lanes echoed with the rough voice of the imam compelling worshippers inside. As I watched, the red sandstone steps were washed out with white, as men in flowing white kurtas climbed up into the mosque's great courtyard for morning prayers. The hotel proprietor sent out a wrinkled male servant in a Muslim skullcap to offer me tea. Even though the servant was over sixty years old, the proprietor called him a *tea-boy* to denote his low rank. He managed to take my order and refill my cup without once meeting my eye.

The New City Palace was undoubtedly a more authentic experience, as all the guests were Indian. It was also less comfortable, since they were all strictly observant Muslim men. I imagined that everything they knew about Western women they'd learned from reruns of *Baywatch*, which, to my bafflement and dismay, are broadcast daily on Indian cable even today. My fellow hotel guests treated me as though I were perpetually clad in a skimpy bikini, either completely avoiding

me or eyeing me with undisguised lust. The Sikh landlord's question—
"Are you alone?"—made much more sense now that I'd separated myself from other female *feringhees*. Women rarely live alone in India
unless they are for sale. Realizing this made me see that a girl alone in
Delhi is more exposed than she is in any of the other world capitals I'd
ever visited. It also gave me a rush of adventurousness; I liked believing I could fend for myself wherever I ended up.

One morning I hit upon the legitimization I needed. I would make
it known to the hotel staff that I had a boyfriend back in America and
prove, for once and for all, that I was no wandering prostitute. I strode
over to the hotel receptionist to deliver the news. He was the owner's
son, I'd gathered, and had a long, untrimmed Muslim beard and serious black eyes. With the conviction of someone on the right side of
moral law, I made my announcement in loud and ungrammatical
Hindi: "Soon, my *boyfriend* will be coming to stay in this place."

I gave the English word the emphasis I thought it deserved in the
sentence. For a moment, his expression was unchanged—he'd been
giving me the same disbelieving gape every time I came in and out,
since I'd first marched up to his desk and asked to check in to his
cheapest room. As my words settled in, though, they provoked a different response from the one I'd intended. A slow, sleazy smirk broke
across his face, revealing two terrible things: that his teeth were rot-
ting inside his mouth and that he was probably the same age as I was.

My arms prickled. I had just sexualized myself to him, I realized,
and in his almost certainly repressed world, it was even possible that I
had made him an offer. I walked back to my room, where I sat on the
edge of the bed cursing myself. That evening, I reemerged into the
small lobby—the rooms didn't have phones, so I couldn't call down to
the front desk—and asked for an extra lock for my door.

So much for the exhilarating reporter's life I'd envisioned for myself in India: I spent most evenings barricaded into my cramped hotel
room, afraid to venture into the lobby after dark. I'd pass the time
transcribing my interviews from underneath a mosquito net, watching
the insects pool greedily on its surface, and reading novels by Indian
writers, searching for clues to help me market myself to Delhi's land-

lords. I'm not sure why I was so slow, but it took me weeks to see my mistake. In India's realm of stark Victorian morals, what I needed wasn't a boyfriend but a husband. It was too late to redeem myself to the New City Palace, but from now on I resolved that Benjamin, my boyfriend back in New York, would become my unwitting husband in India. He'd be like the fake engagement ring some women slip on before they head out to a bar, except rather than warding off preying men, I hoped my husband lie would draw in those prying Delhi landlords. I decided not to inform Benjamin of this counterfeit change in our relationship status, since pretending we were married, even in a distant country, was liable to scare him off.

I began to take other steps to transform myself into a proper married lady, starting at the local tailor shop. The hippie-girl-in-India look wasn't doing anything for me, anyway—it was neither especially attractive nor useful at helping me fit in. I needed to get some *salwar kameez* outfits made for myself—the loose, pajama-style pants, or *salwar,* and knee-length tunic called *kameez* or kurta, which, along with a matching scarf, comprise the most common daily uniform of women across India. The costume is tailored differently depending on the region, religion, and modernity of the woman wearing it. A Muslim pulls the scarf across her head to completely cover her hair; a rural Hindu drapes the scarf across her face to demonstrate respect to her elders; and a middle-class city girl wears her tunic short and fitted over jeans, a gauzy scarf tossed over a shoulder.

It was dim and grimy inside the tailor shop. A silvery rendering of the holy Islamic city of Mecca lit one wall. The tailor, a tiny, exhausted-looking man, stood up from his stool when I came in. Wordlessly, he gestured for me to spread my arms so he could take my measurements. There was something deeply respectful in the care he took never to touch my skin or my clothes even as he inched his tape alongside my body. He beckoned, and a small boy emerged from a corner and began pulling bolts of material down from the shelves—sudden, energetic colors in the gloomy store. I made my choice: saffron and peacock blue.

When I showed up to my next apartment viewing, I wore my *salwar kameez* in a traditional village style, the scarf folded modestly across the chest so it functioned as what I called—to myself, because I had no one else to say it to—a "boob remover." I smiled shyly to emit what I imagined was a wifely aura and dropped an early mention of "my journalist husband" who would soon be joining me in Delhi. To my relief, the landlord accepted this without questioning. Achieving a façade of moral respectability turned out to be as simple as shedding my Western skirt and reciting the words *"Mehre patee aungi."* My husband is coming.

Now that I had my pick of lower-middle-class real estate, I started trying to make sense of the city's sprawling series of neighborhoods. It is impossible to know how many millions live in the slums. With no official addresses and no social security numbers, the vast majority of Indians cannot be tracked; they are chronically unaccounted for. There are somewhere between twelve and eighteen million residents in Delhi, which I could well believe when I looked out upon the heaving, flowing crush of humanity from the balcony of the New City Palace.

In the seventeenth century, during the Islamic Mogul dynasty, Delhi was said to be the world's most populous city. The Moguls built a settlement there in concentric circles, the inner core of which was a glorious walled city. After the British took complete control of India in the nineteenth century, they brought in their own architect, a man named Edwin Lutyens, to remake Delhi as "an empire in stone." He was to create a capital that would befit the jewel in the crown of the British Empire. Lutyens dismantled entire sections of the old Mogul city, replacing them with an inner core that looked more like Europe than India: monumental buildings, handsome white bungalows, and ceremonial boulevards laid out on a grid plan. But outside the colonial center that is still known as New Delhi, the British made no attempt to impose order. Subsequent planners have also failed to do so. The city quickly degrades from spacious avenues to narrow laneways crammed with Soviet-style cement apartment blocks. Farther out, the paved roads become dirt lanes, the sewer systems disappear, and shacks of cardboard and aluminum siding take over.

"Ostentation and wasteful extravagance" is how independent India's first prime minister, Jawaharlal Nehru, described the British-designed capital. Moral rectitude was the ruling sentiment in post-colonial India, as learned from the independence leader Mohandas Gandhi, universally referred to by the honorific *Mahatma,* or "Great Soul," by the end of his life. When Gandhi arrived in London to nego-tiate with world leaders for India's freedom, he was shirtless, a dhoti cloth wrapped around his waist and legs. British prime minister Win-ston Churchill scorned him as a seditious, half-naked fakir. To the India of the 1930s and '40s, though, Gandhi's traditional garb and scant vegetarian meals seemed to prove that he embodied the princi-ples of the nationalist struggle: nonviolent resistance, self-rule, and self-reliance. Even as today's materialistic India moves away from Gandhi's culture of self-denial, he is still canonized in school text-books as "the father of the nation" and extolled in biographies for his frugal lifestyle and commitment to India's high principles.

Gandhi was assassinated only five months after India declared its independence in 1947, leaving Nehru and other independence leaders to shepherd India into nationhood without their most beloved figure. Rather than revolutionizing the flaccid colonial culture of British rule, India's babus—its bureaucrats and civil servants—just took over where the elite imperial servants of the British Empire had left off. The new government simply moved into many of the existing British power structures. For instance, in spite of Nehru's distaste for British-designed New Delhi, he allowed it to become the seat of power of inde-pendent India. The magnificent 340-room palace that had been built as a home for the British viceroy wasn't torn down but rather reclaimed as the official residence of the president and renamed Rashtrapati Bhavan, Sanskrit for "president's house." In a rather unsatisfactory nod to Gandhian parsimony, Indian presidents are expected to occupy just a single wing of the palace.

Nehru faced bigger problems than these symbolic ones. The newly independent nation was deeply divided, impoverished, and uneducated. There were millions of homeless Hindu refugees from the now-Muslim Pakistan crowding into India's streets. At independence, only 16 per-cent of India's population could read and write—and only 7 percent of women.

Nehru was resolved to create a secular and equitable democracy out of what one historian calls an "unnatural nation." He devoted his early years in office to trying to pass social reforms, outlawing polygamy and increasing Hindu women's share of family property, although different laws applied to Muslims. The 1950 constitution is one of the world's most progressive and enlightened. But I would learn that all this enlightened reform had a negligible impact on women's lives. Now, as it did then, what determines acceptable behavior in India is not national law but thousand-year-old social customs. However fast the country is changing, this much is not: Nothing is sharper than the tug of tradition and family.

Eight months after I arrived in India, I moved into Nizamuddin West, a residential neighborhood just outside British-built New Delhi. It's a leafy little enclave, a world apart from the poverty and tumult of the area around the New City Palace. My neighbors were pilots, engineers, and government employees whose iron gates protected their carefully swept patios from stray dogs and beggars. A cobbler, an electrician, some convenience shops, and several press-wallah stands crowded the market, at which the concave-chested wallahs bent over the planks of wood that served as ironing boards. They used old-fashioned irons filled with hot coals. In Nizamuddin, as in the rest of the city, the *bustees*, or slums, are strictly segregated from the wealthier areas—but they are never far away, because they house the maids, sweepers, and drivers essential to the middle classes. Although I tried to ignore the servant and caste system as I set up my home in Delhi, I couldn't shut it out for long.

I moved into the top floor of an old house with lopsided floors, overlooking a quiet alley and a small park where the local kids played cricket every afternoon. The rent was less than one hundred dollars a month, shockingly low to my New York–trained eye. The landlord called it a *barsati*, after the Hindi word for "rain," because the top floor is considered the best place to watch the monsoon. The entire place was, in fact, a celebration of the great Delhi outdoors: To get to either the kitchen or bathroom, both separate outhouses, I had to go out onto the patio and *into* the rain, or whatever was going on outside. During the hot season, which is interrupted only by a brief monsoon and a cursory cool winter fog, dust blew in through the cracks in the windows. There was no point in installing an air conditioner since the cold air would have just leached back out. In monsoon season, the walls of the dank cement staircase literally perspired moisture. The plaster peeled off my apartment walls in giant chunks, and the doors and windows swelled up, so I had to shoulder them closed.

I'd made sure to check that the bathroom outhouse was fitted with a Western-style toilet: The ad had boasted of a pukka—which means "real" or "genuine"—toilet, meaning one including seat, cover, and flush. After months of adopting an athletic squatting stance over Indian-style toilets—holes in the ground lined with ceramic—this felt like a great luxury. It had not occurred to me to make sure there was a tank to heat water in the bathroom, so it wasn't until my first morning in my new place that I realized there was neither shower, bath, nor hot water—just a single tap of cold running water. Standing on the cement floor of the bathroom, I tried to mimic the bathing technique I'd witnessed at public taps: Fill a plastic bucket with water, scoop it out with a smaller bucket, dump it over you, and scrub furiously. Within minutes, the whole thing was over. Washing, I decided, is one of the few activities consistently more efficient in India than in the United States.

My apartment was invaded by critters as well as the weather. Geckos claimed corners of the rooms; multicolored bugs and cockroaches scuttled across the floors; sparrows sometimes landed, confused, on the tiny kitchen counter. In the mornings, I'd take in the cacophony of Delhi life from the patio as I drank my milky instant coffee, the only thing approximating the stuff that I'd found in the local market. The hoarse cries of the vegetable sellers competed with the screech of the trains pulling into the nearby station; there were always chanting and drumming at a temple somewhere. Much closer were the intimate sounds of my unseen neighbors in the next house over, performing their ablutions: the woman hawking into the sink, her husband hollering at their maid to heat up water for his bath. Layered over their human noises was another rich bed of animal sounds: the cartoonish squeak of the jewel-green parakeets dancing through the trees; the persistent, head-knocking cuckooing of the aptly nicknamed "brain-fever bird"; the Hitchcockian cawing of the wicked black crows who ruled the neighborhood. One morning I watched an aggressive flock of them intimidate two chattering monkeys out of a neighborhood tree.

I hadn't been in my *barsati* long before word of a new tenant spread to the nearest slum and the first aspiring maidservant tripped up the stairs in plastic *chappals*. I opened the door to an underfed woman, her hands already folded at her chest in respectful greeting, her face twisted into a plea. She launched into a fast-paced Hindi description of her skills. I could pick out some familiar words—*clean, fast*—from the torrent, but I couldn't imagine trying to talk to her every day. In any case, I wasn't yet convinced I needed a maid, despite everyone telling me it was inevitable.

Every middle-class household I'd seen had at least a couple of part-time servants. The idea still made me uncomfortable, though: Not only would I lose my prided American privacy, but I imagined that the acute imbalance of power might quickly transform me into a haughty duchess. So I shook my head apologetically, chanting no at the woman—"*Nahin. Nahin.*"—until she gave up and flip-flopped down the steps, leaving a frustrated trail of Hindi behind her. By sundown, I'd had half a dozen depressingly similar interactions with aspiring employees: drivers, gardeners, and garbage collectors.

A few days later, I heard male feet stomping up the stairs. A short, dark-skinned man paused to catch his breath before he announced himself as "Joginder Ram, building caretaker." He used the English words with relish, although his responsibility extended only to myself and one other tenant—a senile old lady I'd seen through her open door on the floor below mine. As proof of his stature, he handed me a business card with his name printed across it, and the words WORK PAINT, POLISH, PIOPE REPARING ETC.

Joginder's self-satisfied smile revealed a wad of *paan* lodged, chipmunklike, in his cheek, spreading a red stain from his gums to his lips. He sported a proud paunch over his carefully ironed trousers, and his hair was henna dyed to hide the gray. All of this imbued him with an energetic and self-congratulatory air. He occupied the back porch of the house next to mine, which was also owned by my landlord, Arun Mago. Since Mr. Mago lived seven hundred miles west of Delhi, in Mumbai, I couldn't understand why he had granted Joginder squatting rights to no more than the tiny back porch of the house. Later, the landlord told me he was reluctant to surrender more space because city law favors the tenant, and he was afraid he'd never be able to evict him.

The landlord was "Mago-sahib" to Joginder, in an unsettling throwback to colonial times, when masters were sahibs and their wives were memsahibs. Joginder didn't begrudge sahib's lack of generosity, because the landlord was his savior in his tale of impoverished migration. Joginder was born in Bihar, India's most rural state and one of its poorest. His father owned no land, so he worked as a daily wage laborer for those who did. In Bihar, as in much of feudal India, land is power, an inherited right, reserved only for certain castes. Joginder's village didn't have decent schools, nor did it have factories to employ the unschooled.

Like millions of other Indian fathers, Joginder's had no option other than to dispatch his only son to the city to find work. Joginder was ten years old when he clambered aboard the bus. He remembers receiving two instructions: Seek out fellow Biharis and send home money every month. He worked on construction sites and in tea shops, the kind of day jobs at which employers never ask the age of a willing worker. Child labor is technically illegal in India, but no one cares. At night, Joginder would stretch out in a public garden, or on the floor of the tea shop if his employer let him. When he met Mago-sahib and was offered the porch in exchange for keeping an eye on the two houses, Joginder felt as if he'd finally made it. Now that he had his own cooking area, he sent a message back to his family that they should find him a wife.

Two decades later, five of them shared the hot, cramped porch: Joginder, his wife, Maniya, and their three young children. The blue plastic tarp draped across the entrance may have kept out the rain and the monkeys, but the cockroaches and rats were undeterred. Because

their only other choice would be to live in a chaotic *bustee,* Joginder
stayed put, and his family stretched their living space out of the porch
and into the alley. After Maniya sent the kids off to school, she'd do the
laundry at the tap at one end of the lane. During the hottest hours of the
day, she'd pull the family charpoy, or string cot, into a shady patch in
the alley and sit cross-legged staring into space, the flies collecting on
her damp forehead.

Joginder was not one to while the day away on the charpoy. He always seemed busy: From my patio, I could hear him negotiating with
his laborers or shouting into his cell phone from the square of shade
cast by the buildings in the alley, which functioned as his office. Once
the day's heat abated, he'd hurry over to the market to negotiate with
the electrician and plumber. Joginder was endlessly resourceful,
which made him an important resource for the neighborhood's Bihari
community; in the evenings, there was often a line of immigrants
squatting patiently on their haunches in the alley, waiting to talk to him
about their troubles.

The next time I heard Joginder scaling the stairs to my apartment, I
knew he must have important business.

"Miss Mirindaah madam!" he bellowed through the door. Like
many Indians, he transmuted my name into a popular soda brand,
Mirinda, which, I'd discovered, was available in both lemon and orange flavors. The TV ads for the drink featured an enthusiastic Indian
making the open-mouthed exclamation "Mirind*aaahhh*!" And as a result, I was destined to have the last syllable of my name dragged out,
and to be asked which flavor I was. I opened the door and stepped back
a pace: Joginder had the villager's habit of addressing everyone as
though they were several fields away.

"You must take minimum-minimum one maid!" I tried to beckon
him inside, but he shook his head, determined not to stray off message. He continued his monologue, repeating the key words in both
Hindi and English, sometimes rhyming them for added emphasis.
"Minimum-minimum *ek kumaari.* One maid minimum. For *jaroo-
pocha,* sweeping, swabbing, dusting-shrusting. It is top important for
Indian lady or pukka English madam."

I felt bombarded by his aggressive pitch.

"I'm not sure I want to, actually. I'm used to cleaning up myself. No one has maids in the U.S."

I thought of my mother's frustrated stories about how she couldn't make a cup of tea in her Karachi kitchen without insulting the servant, who referred to himself in the third person as "memsahib's bearer," even though it was decades after the end of British rule. My parents had been instructed by their neighbors that they were to pay part of the costs of six servants shared by their compound. Each performed discrete tasks: a cook who doubled as a bearer, meaning he brought them "bed tea" in the mornings and did the grocery shopping; an inside sweeper and an outside sweeper; a *dhobi* to wash the clothes; a *chowkidar*, or guard; and a *mali*, or gardener, whose sole job, as far as my mother could tell, was to squat on the patch of grass in their compound and squirt a hose at it.

Joginder peered past me into the living room and made a similar appeal about the importance of hiring help.

"Indian houses very dusty-dusty, madam. And so many problems. You are needing to replace gas tanks for stove. You doing *dhobi* work by hand, washing dishes by hand. No machines. All hand to hand."

The list of chores was daunting. Joginder gave me the classic wobbling Indian head nod when I acquiesced, the only possible outcome.

"Very good, Miss Mirindaah. I have good maid lady for you—my cousin-sister Radha. She is also coming from Bihar. She is trusts. She is coming tomorrow."

Aha, I thought. So that's why he wanted me to hire a maid so badly: It meant a job for a fellow Bihari, and a relative to boot.

Radha showed up right at eight. In the doorway, she gave me a long, hard look. I peered back with equal curiosity. I had no way of guessing her age: She seemed around forty, but probably would have appeared younger if she'd lived an easier life. She was wearing a freshly ironed pale blue sari, and her hair, neatly smoothed into a bun at the back of her head, was partly covered by her sari's *pallu,* the scarflike fold of material at the end of the garment. An overbite sent her top teeth skidding out of her mouth. As she kicked off her *chappals*, I noticed that the skin on the soles of her feet was thick and calloused, and her heels were split by deep cracks. In spite of these outward signs of poverty, though, Radha was straight-backed and dignified. She had none of the pleading desperation of the women who'd crept to my door asking for work.

"*Namaste, deedee,*" she said, calling me by the Hindi name for "elder sister." Although she was clearly the older of us, the term was a way to demonstrate respect without using the matronly term *auntie,* generally reserved for married women, and without the sycophancy of memsahib. I don't know how she made the calculation, but hearing her refer to me as family warmed me to her immediately.

"I am Radha, and I am Brahmin," she continued. Apparently, my new employee considered it more important to inform me that she was born into the highest caste on the Hindu social hierarchy than to tell me her last name. Later, I realized that she was actually interpreting her name for me; Indians would know instantly that she was a Bihari Brahmin when they heard her last name, Jha.

I could tell Radha was disappointed in my meager furnishings as she walked through the apartment. I hadn't yet invested in much more than a set of tin plates and cups, a desk and chair, and a daybed with polyester fibers poking through the mattress. She raised her open hands and looked at me quizzically, as if to say, "What gives?" When she'd heard she'd be working for a *feringhee,* Radha had probably envisioned rooms of Western extravagances—or, at the very least, a television set and more than one chair. I didn't have any cleaning implements yet, either, beyond a couple of scrub pads in the sink. But Radha was a take-charge type, with much of the confidence of her "cousin-brother"—although I found out later that Joginder was neither her brother nor her cousin. They considered themselves related because they came from the same region of Bihar and because Radha had married a man from Joginder's village.

My new employee was eager to ensure that I bent to her will whenever she could manage it. In this case, her priority was making me purchase the correct tools. She'd lean in close, until her face was only an inch from mine, and holler a Hindi word—I guess she thought I'd be more likely to comprehend it if she raised the volume. Then she'd squat back on her haunches and release her breath in an audible sigh as she waited for me to understand.

At first, I'd just stare back at her, blank-faced, thinking again how impressed my yoga teacher would be with her flexibility. Clearly, Radha's comfort in the squat was due not to twenty-dollar New York yoga classes but to years of sitting in fields and alleyways in the posture adopted naturally by so many impoverished Indians. I'd already seen ample evidence, in Delhi yoga classes, that this wasn't a preternatural national trait, because the middle-class Indians—who, like me, had grown up sitting on chairs—struggled as much as *feringhees* to lower themselves onto their haunches.

Radha continued to toss words in my direction, and eventually I played along, miming a game of charades for my solemn audience of one. When I'd demonstrate the task—sweeping or mopping—to match the word she'd used, Radha would nod imperiously and repeat it, so I could later recite it at the store. I'd dreaded having to order around a meek, simpering maid, but Radha turned the master-servant relationship on its head. She seemed not to suffer from the all-too-common postcolonial ailment that still afflicts many Indians: the belief that all things foreign are better. Radha knew full well that her American mistress did *not* know best.

My maid had strong opinions about a startling number of things: how I should store food in my kitchen, how I should arrange my furniture, what I should eat for breakfast. If I was in the bathroom when she wanted to ask me something, she'd push open the door like an exceptionally intrusive relative. She'd ignore my protests at being observed in my nakedness at the tap, and linger to chuckle as I scooped and poured.

"I know it's hard for you *feringhees* to learn how to do Indian things correctly, like bathing and eating with your hands," she'd say.

Radha pretty consistently treated me like a dim and slightly wayward daughter. No Indian employer would have stood for it, but I found something comforting and motherly in her bossiness. I sometimes wished I had the Hindi to confide in her about my troubles with adjusting to a culture so different from my own. Even though I couldn't express this, I liked to believe she understood something of my loneliness and also felt responsible for my welfare.

It was Radha who found me lying on the cement floor, trying to cool my fever after I'd ingested some nasty waterborne bacteria. I'd been sick from both ends for a couple of days, and I shook with weakness as Radha sat me up. She poured lemon water with salt and sugar into my mouth. One friend called this the "Indian slum tonic"—a cheap way of restoring lost salt and minerals.

Radha must have told Joginder I was sick, because sometime later he was standing over me, speaking rapid Hindi. He had to repeat himself several times before I got the gist: There was a problem with the water tank on the roof that pumped unfiltered municipal water into my taps. The lid of the tank had blown open in the wind, and one of the neighborhood crows had drowned in there. I'd been drinking rotten crow remains for days. My jury-rigged filtration system clearly hadn't been sufficient to conquer the bacteria emitted by a bird carcass. After a while, the neighborhood plumbers arrived. They clambered onto my roof and cleared the crow remains out of my tank. When I recovered, I went up there myself and wired the tank shut with a clothes hanger.

Joginder had suggested I pay Radha twenty dollars a month, the shockingly low industry standard for three hours of hard manual labor each day. Even though Radha was inside sweeper, bearer, *dhobi,* and *mali* all in one, and even though Joginder was her advocate and sort of relative, he urged me not to pay her much more than the going rate. He had a keen understanding of market economics: Overpaying her would skew the wages of other maids in the neighborhood, he pointed out. He also knew that Radha ranked pretty low in Delhi's maid hierarchy. She was an "Indian-style maid": She neither spoke English nor cooked Western food nor understood the lifestyle and expectations of non-Indian employers.

Radha was accustomed to cleaning without electrical appliances like washing machines, and also without much more basic tools such as upright mops with handles. She swept the floors and then mopped them on her hands and knees, using a cloth and a natural cleaning fluid that smelled of fennel. It was hard to believe this weird stuff made my floors gleam. She pounded my clothes and sheets against the bathroom floor and swished them around violently in buckets, as *dhobis* do against the rocks in riverbeds across rural India.

Over the years, I gradually doubled Radha's pay in increments of guilt-induced generosity. When I'd hand her the monthly fold of bills, her supercilious attitude would briefly disappear as she tucked the wad of rupee notes into her *choli,* the blouse women wear under their sari. Nevertheless, money meant nothing to her compared to caste. My maid's place at the top of the ancient social hierarchy was pretty much the only source of her pride and confidence. I'd read that Indians were choosing their own professions and marrying people from different strata on the hierarchy; this didn't jibe with Radha's world and the world of many Indians, in which the caste system still determines occupation, rank, and karma. It is the unseen hand guiding most social interactions, ingrained into behavior patterns and expectations, with innate rules that need never be discussed.

These days, many of the globalized middle class are embarrassed by caste; like child marriage and underperforming bureaucrats, it's a symbol of the old, preglobalized India. Radha, however, felt no compunction about asserting its primacy in her life. She knew deep in her heart that her Brahmin caste made her intrinsically superior. She'd remind me of it often—that Brahmins are at the top of the pecking order, the highest among the Hindu castes. There are literally thousands of castes and subcastes separating Brahmins from the bottom end of the hierarchy, the group called *dog-cookers* in ancient times because they were believed to be so low as to eat dogs. The British called them *untouchables* because the higher castes considered their touch, even their shadow, polluting.

Brahmins are traditionally priests and teachers, and for centuries, education was their exclusive right. In ancient times, untouchables were forbidden from hearing the recital of the written word, because the higher castes believed that they would sully any sacred text they spoke or even heard. Until the British took control in 1857, India's government was hereditary and run by Brahmins. Even today, the upper castes overwhelmingly dominate the professional world; the country's two hundred million untouchables are disproportionately represented in poverty, malnourishment, and illiteracy. And yet, as though to prove that no rule is without exception in India, here was my maid: a completely illiterate Brahmin who lived in a slum and swept my floors like an untouchable.

Radha was painfully aware that it was beneath her to clean other people's houses. She tried to make up for it by drawing lines around the tasks she considered unacceptable: taking out the garbage, cleaning the bathroom, and doing the outside sweeping, meaning the staircases, hallway, or street. Dealing with animals was out of bounds, too, I discovered. The highest ranking in Hinduism's hierarchy of the animal kingdom is reserved for cows, which are venerated as symbols of nonviolence, motherhood, and generosity; Gandhi went so far as to call the cow "a poem of pity." Next come horses, snakes, and monkeys. When cats appear in ancient Hindu texts, though, they are shown as religious hypocrites. Even rats rate higher; Ganesh, the powerful elephant-headed god, is often depicted riding one.

Urban educated Indians have started keeping purebred dogs as pets, as a sort of symbol of upward mobility, but cats have not benefited from the trend. The only ones I saw in Delhi were brute-faced, prowling the alleys, the recipients of regular kicks from neighborhood guards.

Eager to root myself in my new life, I looked for an animal shelter from which to adopt some of Delhi's beleaguered felines. The closest I could find was a *gaushawla,* a sanctuary for abandoned, sick, and dying cows rescued from Delhi's streets. Cow slaughter is banned in most parts of India, and the untimely death of one is liable to spark a furious riot. When a cow blocks the road, drivers descend from their vehicles to move the beast aside with great care. Yet Indian cows do not all receive treatment befitting the sacred. During their milking years, city cows are cared for so they can supply small dairies; once their milk dries up, though, their owners often abandon them to wander the streets and forage in garbage. The vet at the *gaushawla* told me that these old cows sometimes ingest so many plastic bags in the garbage that their stomachs explode.

She gave me a strange look when I said I wanted to adopt a cat, but she obliged by dispatching a boy up to the roof, where she said she'd seen some. He returned grasping an orange tabby with feral eyes, an infestation of lice and worms, and ears black with dirt. I took her home and gave her three baths. By the time Radha came in, the kitten was curled sweetly on a cushion on the floor. Nevertheless, Radha recoiled with such exaggerated horror that I had to struggle not to laugh. She'd never seen a domesticated cat before; to her, it was as though I'd brought a wild possum into the home she was responsible for cleaning—except worse, because to righteous Brahmins like Radha, animals are considered spiritually impure.

When I brought home a second one, from a litter my vet had discovered on the street, Radha took it as a personal insult. I struggled to calm her: I'd grown up with cats in my home in the United States, I said, and they were meticulously clean. My *feringhee* naïveté forced Radha to revert to her most dramatic invocation of God: "*Ay, bhagwan, deedee.* You don't know. I know. No Indian would bring this dirty creature into their home."

I'd filled a box with grimy sand, bilked from a nearby construction site, since the only cat litter I could find in Delhi was imported and heavily taxed under some obscure government pet tariff regime. I put the litter box out on the patio, but that did not stanch her fury. Her eyes darkened at my betrayal, and my nervous Hindi became muddled. Afraid she might quit, I assured her she wouldn't have to touch the litter box; I would clean it myself.

Taking care of my own garbage presented a new set of problems. A few days after I'd started carrying the used cat litter to the neighborhood garbage dump, I heard Joginder tromping up the stairs again.

"Why you are doing this, madam?" His customary bellow was softened by disappointment. Apparently, people in the neighborhood were making jokes about the crazy foreign girl who carried her cat crap to the garbage dump. "Garbage collecting is not good work, *deedee*. Only certain people touch it."

I sighed, wondering whether the complex Indian protocol for caste and pollution would ever make sense to me. Indians rarely discuss such matters forthrightly, but my building caretaker decided it was time to set me straight. He folded his arms, leaned back against the door, and dedicated several minutes of his morning to explaining the complex system for dealing with garbage in Indian cities. The city doesn't pick up trash cans from the curb, he said, so the job is outsourced to India's lower castes.

"Garbage is a job for the sweeper caste, madam. But no problem! I have arranged."

And just like that, I became an active sponsor of the caste system. Uncomfortably, I recognized that by agreeing to pay my untouchable employee just over a dollar a month to do the dirtiest work in the house, I was tacitly agreeing that I and my Brahmin maid were too good for such chores. But if I wanted to fit in to India, I'd have to go along with India's ways.

When the garbage collector rang the doorbell, I greeted her hesitantly, wary of being too personable and sticking my elbow in the eye of yet another Indian tradition. I'd witnessed Radha shooing away low-caste women in the alley with the same disdain with which she treated my cats. But the untouchable smiled widely as she held out her plastic bag, the identifying tool of her trade, and introduced herself. Maneesh was scrawny from centuries of malnutrition, the kind of thin I had never seen before coming to India. Her *salwar kameez* was grubby and wrinkled, a sure sign of someone on the bottom rung, since India's ubiquitous press wallahs charge only a rupee—about two U.S. cents—to iron a piece of clothing with their antiquated coal-fired appliances. She'd taken some care in her appearance, though, wearing rings on her toes and colorful metal bracelets right up to her elbows—symbols of a married woman. They clattered up and down her arms as she went from room to room collecting the trash. Without a twinge of shame or indignation, she stooped to sift through the litter, picking out the cat poop with her hands inside a plastic bag.

Later, Joginder told me that Maneesh's husband was a drunk who beat her; she supported him and their two sons by collecting garbage, cleaning bathrooms, and mopping the floors at half a dozen houses. As an uneducated untouchable, her job options were limited. Few families would hire her to work in the kitchen. My servants represented the extreme ends of the caste system, and that was always apparent—even when they sat gossiping together, squatting on their haunches in the kitchen. Once, I overheard Radha asking Maneesh in a low voice whether she came from the Valmiki subcaste, one of the groups of untouchables that traditionally dispose of human excrement. Maneesh assented amiably that indeed she did; her family had collected garbage for generations.

I came to look forward to Maneesh's midmorning ring of the bell. I'd linger to chat in the doorway after she arrived. Even before my Hindi improved, these conversations weren't a struggle, because she almost always said the same thing: "How are the cats, *deedee*? Is the black one still acting crazy?" Sometimes Maneesh even stroked the cats, giggling nervously at their purring sound; but Radha never came around to them. To her, they were always *shay-tann,* the Hindi word for "terror," which was all the more amusing to me because it sounds like the English word *Satan.* When the black one—whom I'd named Kali, after the Hindu goddess of destruction—slinked near the folds of Radha's sari, she'd give it a vicious swipe with her broom.

I'd been trying to work out how to tell my maids about Benjamin. He'd emailed that he was coming to stay with me for three months, and I knew I needed to ensure that my domestic workers not judge me a boyfriended woman. So I resurrected that useful Hindi phrase *"Mehre patee aungi,"* my husband is coming.

"Wow, *deedee!*" said Maneesh, breaking into a grin, which exposed a mouthful of wonky teeth. "We didn't know you were married! Did you know, Radha-*deedee*?"

"No, *deedee* didn't tell me, either!" I tried to organize my features innocently as I turned to Radha. She was shrewd, and I wouldn't have been surprised if she'd sniffed out my lie, but she looked pleased, not suspicious. I think it's because I was easier to place now. I was part of the club of married ladies, a recognizable element, no longer a girl alone.

Within days, my maids had passed word along to the neighborhood: The *feringhee* lady has a *patee*. When I walked through Nizamuddin market a few days later, I was surprised to receive a nod hello from the pock-faced electrician in his shop; although I walked past him every day, he'd never directly acknowledged me before. Later that week, when the tailor and his twin brother greeted me with a respectful *Namaste*, I felt inexplicably proud.

As my neighborhood began to accept me, I promised myself I'd figure out how to belong here. The morning smells from my patio—chapatis cooking inside kitchens, incense burning in the local storefront shrine, the sour rush of sewage—were not so overwhelming if I made an effort to differentiate each one from the others. It was easy to ignore the staring, if I resolved not to care.

There was magic in Delhi's many newnesses: the paper boys, squatting on the empty streets at dawn in a long row to sort the sections of the newspapers. The way K.K., my favorite driver at the local taxi stand, would twinkle his eyes at me in the rearview mirror when he informed me that the roads were blocked, again, because "a V-V-V-V-I-P is zipping through"—Indian English lingo to describe a government minister so important that he warranted three extra "very"s in front of his "very important person" title. We'd chuckle in the stalled traffic—he in the driver's seat, me in the back—as we waited for the minister's clunky white Ambassador car to pass, its red light on top blinking importantly. I loved the care that my local press wallah took with my clothes, stiffening out every last crease with her flatiron filled with hot coals. They still smelled slightly acrid when her teenage daughter delivered them to me in a tidy, compressed cube. If, in order to belong here, I needed to play the part of a good wife, then that was what I would do. I wrote Benjamin to tell him that a little family awaited him in India: two scrappy street cats, two maids, and one fake wife who had laid a very real claim on her adopted city.

CHAPTER 3

Pious Virgins and Brave-hearted Heroes

The set of car keys dangling in her hand caught my attention. Women are rarely seen behind the wheel in Delhi; usually, they get dropped off at the office by a male relative or are chauffeured around town by a family driver. My new neighbor, Geeta Shourie, was a modern girl—and although the phrase is often used as a pejorative, to me it was a sign of hope. My neighbor's brown hair was stylishly highlighted and cut in long layers. I noticed right away that her *salwar kameez* was not the standard shapeless kind that I'd come to associate with housewives, but the close-fitting, thigh-length tunic and tight-fitting leggings preferred by college and professional women.

She shot me a sympathetic smile as she stepped into the alley, over-hearing my meek attempt to bargain with Ram, the vegetable wallah who sold his wares from a wooden cart he wheeled around the neighborhood, crying out *"Sub-ziiii!"* to announce himself. I was pretty sure that Ram had been ripping me off for the vegetables I bought from him—the sweet bloodred carrots and the studded, lumpy squash that I thought of as the "skin-disease vegetable" because I'd once seen a woman on the New York subway with similar eruptions on her face, neck, and hands.

The housewives from the neighborhood who clustered around the cart never accepted Ram's first price. Sometimes, they'd even toss his vegetables back at him in dramatic displays of disgust. When I tried to do the same and reject his prices, Ram would make a big show about his meager earnings and drop the price a mere rupee or two. Since even his inflated prices were a fraction of what I would have paid for vegetables in New York, I'd always concede. I was reluctant to prolong these interactions, mostly because I couldn't keep my eyes off the seeping boil growing out of Ram's forehead. Had it leaked onto the vegetables; did I need to disinfect them? Did he notice me staring at the thing? I didn't understand how the other women could ignore his festering third eye. They bargained as if they were staking their lives on getting him down, and they always walked away with more vegetables for their money than I did.

"How much is he asking for those tomatoes?" Geeta asked, with an Indian ease about intruding on the problems of strangers. She flashed me a shy smile, which dimpled her cheeks, making her look even younger than she already did. With her petite frame, she could have passed for a college student, though I guessed she was in her late twenties.

"Sorry for the interrupting, I just thought you might like some help."

Right away, I could see that Geeta was blessed with the kind of smile that made other people want to smile back. When I told her how much Ram was charging me, though, the sweetness drained out of her face.

"He thinks he can overcharge because you're a foreigner. This gives our country a bad image. I'll fix him."

Although her English was fluent, it was slightly stilted, with awkward Indian English phrases; I imagined she mostly spoke Hindi at work and among her friends. She turned to Ram, her features hardening, and for a second, I felt sorry for him. Even though he'd been overcharging me for months, it probably cumulatively amounted to less than fifteen dollars. Like everyone else from the slums, my vegetable guy was just a chancer, as they'd say in England—running whatever little scam he could, on the chance of improving his lot against bad odds. In Delhi, you charge what you can get; there are few chain stores with fixed prices to provide a solid point of comparison. In the ad hoc world of informal shopping, the worth of goods and services is slippery, decided more by the urge to best the other guy than anything else.

Like any good bargainer, Geeta knew how to feign anger without getting agitated; that would have revealed her hand. Ram played his part, too—displaying righteous indignation, holding out for as long as he could. They both knew they'd eventually compromise and one of them would walk away feeling that he'd tipped the scales a few rupees in the right direction. This time, it was Geeta. After several minutes, she wheeled around triumphantly.

"You only owe him thirty-two rupees. He was trying to charge you double that."

She hurried down to her little Indian-made car parked at the end of the alley, saying she had to get to work. Ram handed me my cut-rate vegetables, his forehead boil throbbing angrily.

A few days later, I stopped by to thank Geeta. Although we hadn't met properly, I knew who she was from Joginder, my primary source of neighborhood information. He'd told me Geeta had just moved to the floor below me with Nanima, an old woman known universally in the neighborhood not by her name but by the respectful term for grandmother. The door to her apartment was slightly ajar, and I caught a strong whiff of urine as I pushed it open. Even in the dim evening light, I could tell it was grungier than my *barsati*.

"Hello? Is Geeta here?"

"Oh God!" came a melodramatic howl from the sofa. "Geeta hasn't come yet! Neither has my servant girl. Everyone is gone. Even my children have abandoned me. And I am starving!"

Her theatrics made me smile, because the woman spoke with the quaint accent of someone who had attended a colonial British school, an accent which would have been familiar to my great-aunt Edith. And she scarcely looked like she was dying of malnourishment.

"Can I get you something, Nanima? Some toast?"

"Yes please, *betee*," she said enthusiastically, calling me the affectionate term for child.

I went upstairs to my place to scrounge something together. I didn't do much cooking in my outhouse kitchen, since it was invaded by bugs and lacked electrical appliances of any kind. I'd come up with a toaster replacement, though, using my little space heater, which approximated toast more successfully than the Indian frying pan method. When I reappeared with a plate of Anglo-Indian toast—thinly sliced white bread spread with butter and a red fruitless paste that passed for jam at the local store—the old lady beamed at me.

"How I love toast. Lovely, buttery British toast—"

She froze, hearing Geeta's heels on the floor.

"Nanima, did you make our neighbor bring you food? You know you're not supposed to have toast." Geeta's hands were on her hips moments after she clip-clopped to a halt inside the apartment.

Nanima looked briefly ashamed, but when she realized Geeta wasn't going to take the toast away, she dug into it. Nanima was diabetic, Geeta said resignedly, and always breaking her diet.

"Must be quite a job to take care of her," I sympathized.

Geeta frowned and lowered her voice, though Nanima was focusing on her toast, not on us.

"It isn't actually supposed to be my job. There's a full-time maid who is off today. But it's still always exhausting. Her kids basically just left her here. They send money and that's it. She relies on me for everything."

I'd assumed Nanima was Geeta's relative, but the old woman was actually the grandmother of a family friend. Geeta had moved in with her because her mother wouldn't let her get an apartment by herself. A girl living alone, as I well knew, carried almost as much stigma as a girl with a boyfriend. Still, Geeta had taken a drastic measure by moving in with Nanima. It obviously curtailed whatever social life she might have had in Delhi: The old woman was so emotionally unstable that if Geeta went out for more than a couple of hours in the evening, she was likely to cry and pee all over the sofa. I wondered whether Geeta's mother had calculated this when she had her move in with Nanima.

Geeta moved to Delhi three years before I did. Before then, though, she'd scarcely left her hometown of Patiala, a small city in the North Indian state of Punjab. Her father, a doctor in a government hospital, was a progressive man. He'd urged her to go to college and even agreed to let her move to Delhi and take a job at a public relations firm after graduating. Many families would refuse to allow their twenty-something daughter to head off to another city to "live alone," she said.

"My father spoiled me. He always calls me a Punjabi princess, and it's true. I am their only child, which is rare in India . . . I guess I got used to having my own way."

She grinned unself-consciously. Still, she added, her parents had allowed her only a couple of years in Delhi. In fact, their deadline for her to return to Patiala to get married had long passed. Her smile turned sour at the edges. There was more to Geeta than the bubbly, easygoing exterior. She seemed to miss her family—not just the comfort and ease of living at home, but also the knowledge that she was living in the correct, traditional way. I was struck, though, by how much she wanted to emphasize her identity as an independent city girl, at least to me.

I could sympathize. In Delhi I was, for the first time in my life, completely free: I had no boss, no friends, no family, and scarce contact with my boyfriend. I was no longer limited to a schedule of any kind. I'd set off on reporting trips, having spoken briefly to an editor about an idea, and no one would notice whether I was gone for two days or ten. I would hire a translator and travel through villages, just looking for story ideas, stop and report on one of them for a few days, and continue on by local bus, staying in inexpensive guesthouses in temple towns.

I'd come to India with the idea that here I could remake myself into the person that I imagined my family wanted me to be—a brave adventuress and chronicler of cultures. I anticipated that I would embrace the expatriate life in the romantic way that Isak Dinesen, the Danish author of *Out of Africa,* described it: "Here at long last one was in a position not to give a damn for all conventions. Here was a new kind of freedom which until then one had only found in dreams!"

Of course, I rarely felt that liberated. Often I felt suspended in midair like the mosquitoes that hovered over my bed. Now that I was no longer surrounded by the outward things with which I had previously defined myself—friends, work, activities—it was as though my life had come to a pause. I'd think about how overwhelmingly busy I'd felt in New York just a few months before, rushing from work to yoga class, perpetually late to dinners with friends, falling asleep on the subway on the way home. Now I struggled to fill the hours. Reporting and writing didn't take up enough of them, and interviewing strangers could scarcely satisfy my need for human interaction. In India, I was a bizarre white ghost whom no one knew.

When I started feeling sorry for myself, I'd remind myself that restlessness was my inheritance. That made me feel better about it—as though it was fated or something. My mother's sister, Susie, had also refused to take the expected straightforward path. She defied her father's wishes and trained as an opera singer when she was young, and spent much of her twenties and thirties touring Europe. In my childhood imagination, she was a glowing mezzo-soprano sweeping onstage in a diaphanous gown, her hair swept into a dramatic updo. Susie had only sometimes mentioned the hardships of her time as a performer. I knew that after she'd done it for years—traveling for months at a stretch, steeling herself for another concert, winding herself up about being successful enough onstage—the stresses of the performing lifestyle became too much for her. She'd believed since she was ten years old that she was born to be an opera singer, but by the time she turned forty, my aunt had started to realize that this might be more of a self-imposed image of her identity than anything else.

I've always loved recounting this next part of Susie's life, the part where she set off to work out who she was. She established a second career as a psychotherapist in London, but a bout with cancer changed that. When she recovered, Susie traveled to Hawaii to work with alternative healers—which turned into a multiyear odyssey. After selling her London apartment, giving away her beloved dog, and surrendering her therapy practice, my proper British aunt started acting completely out of character. She rode Harleys and shot guns in Yuma with a biker boyfriend and his gang, practiced somatic meditation, and learned to decorate cakes in a bakery out west. She changed her name from the frumpy Susan to Susannah, which seemed much better suited to the soulful and sophisticated aunt I knew. At the age of fifty, she married a poet in Santa Fe.

I was chaotic and impulsive, but I hadn't expected my life to be as iconoclastic and freewheeling as hers. Still, I'm sure that something about Susie's determination to find her own way in life gave me the nerve to move to Delhi. Once there, I'd found myself wanting to know more about what she'd felt in Europe during her opera-singing years, away from everything she knew. I remembered her describing a sense of dislocation that she thought made her more susceptible to romantic propositions from pianists and conductors she met on the road. Susie didn't follow through on most of these offers—nevertheless, my semi-invented picture of her glamorous European years stirred me to seek my own experience of that traveler's stereotype, the spontaneous overseas love affair.

Benjamin and I had been together for only six months when I'd decided to move to India for an indeterminate length of time; I bought a yearlong ticket and warned I would stay longer if things worked out. I would have liked him to come with me, to package him up into a tidy, portable boyfriend format, but he wasn't willing to surrender to my bossy urges when we lived in the same city, let alone tag along on my adventure with me. I knew, of course, that he wouldn't come, that he shouldn't come, that taking off to India was actually my way of asserting my independence.

In the days before I left, I remember us agreeing that we wanted to stay together, and him quite calmly suggesting that if we did so, it would be better not to be monogamous. It seemed unadventurous and cowardly not to agree. Experimenting with the idea of free love also felt like a kind of postfeminist rebellion. By separating myself from society's expectations, I imagined, I would free myself and my relationship, and Benjamin and I would be able to be our honest selves. Having affairs also seemed like a natural step in the life of a woman of international intrigue. Still, this "arrangement" felt awkward to both of us. We only discussed it once more before I left, and when we did, it was as though the idea had quotes around it—we didn't really believe it was going to happen. Surely, I was aware that an open relationship was bound to be hurtful, but I preferred to focus on the fantasy, that we'd be able to have our separate adventures and still trust each other enough to come back together again.

In India, I was determined to abide by our relationship code, which decreed that we be independent, undemanding, and not jealous. I refused to undermine the image Benjamin had of me as brave and strong, certain that he wouldn't love me otherwise. I emailed him with funny stories and exotic anecdotes about my new life and never called him when I was lonely or afraid. Instead, I'd spend dull nights in the heat, holding staring contests with the translucent-eyed geckos in the corners of the ceiling and willing myself not to think about him. That was always a bad idea, because my longing for him would inevitably turn to jealous imaginings about what he might be doing. Eventually, I resolved to put an end to the pining and distract myself by leaping into affairs with other men. I was just holding up my side of the agreement, I told myself when I felt sad about my disloyalty. But part of me welcomed the chance to have affairs while holding on to my boyfriend. Benjamin was little more than the idea of a boyfriend, but he provided an important link for me to my life back in New York.

There was another reason that it made sense to have affairs in India. It was the most passionate, emotive place I'd ever been, though I still cannot clearly articulate why. There's something about the swoony film music blasting out of the little *chai* stands; the vivid saffron and crimson of women's clothes; the sun saturating everything. There's the crackling excitement of the festival season in October and November, which slides into the season of weddings, when there is gold everywhere: jewelry on the brides, streaked into the women's saris. There's something about the sentimental way Indians talk about their mothers and grandmothers and husbands, so their voices grow scratchy and their eyes well up with tears. And something about how present and human the Hindu gods are in daily life in India, their names coupled off into mythical pairs and recited like mantras—Sita, Rama, Radha, Krishna. Their sensual, sometimes even lusty images, full breasted and well toned, leap out from billboards, mantels, car dashboards, and shop windows. Alone in front of their bedroom shrines, or in groups inside temples, women chant prayers to the gods, and they sound more like love songs than the words of the devout:

The god of love never hesitates!
He is free and determined like a bird
Winging toward the clouds it loves.
Yet I remember the mad tricks he played,
My heart restlessly burning with desire
Was yet filled with fear!

Still, it was rather ironic that I decided to pursue my saucy side in Delhi, where boyfriends are only to be had on the sly and even married couples do not hold hands on the street. Love affairs are complicated by the fact that most young people live at home with their families until marriage. "Doing a live-in," the Indian phrase for cohabitating before marriage, is only acceptable in the most progressive families. Such is the poverty and close proximity of family life in India that intimacy is often impossible even for married couples. As a result, public spaces are precious real estate for lovers. Strips of beach, coffee shops, shopping malls—all highly desirable locales. One Indian official was right when he denounced malls as "havens of hand-holding"; they are full of snuggling teens and married couples. In Mumbai, one highway overpass has become infamous as a make-out spot; there are invariably two dozen scooters and motorcycles parked along the side of the road at dusk, the couples tangled over each other on the seats. The residents in the apartment buildings overlooking the highway can do little more than complain to city authorities about their "indecent view."

In Delhi, the favored spot for lovers is Lodhi Garden, a public park filled with verdant flower beds and sixteenth-century monuments. One evening a few months after I arrived, I noticed that the blooming shrubs on the lawn were a little too dazzlingly colorful. Peering closer in the fading evening light, I saw that the bushes were actually spread with women's saris. From under the fabric came the murmurs of Indian

lovers on the evening grass. I couldn't suppress my curiosity. I loitered
nearby until I spotted a couple emerging from one of the bushes. The
guy stood up first, glancing self-consciously around him as he tucked
his shirt back into his jeans, which were tight and stonewashed, in a
style I called "slum-cut" because they are so pervasive among the poor.
A minute later, the woman darted out behind him—tousled, though
completely clothed. It was a "boyfriend bush"! She smoothed back her
hair and folded up the sari with crisp, humiliated efficiency, staring at
the ground. There was no playfulness between them. No smile lin-
gered on her lips. I felt inexplicably sad as I walked away from the
scene of their secret lovemaking.

My own Delhi affairs were infused with a similar sense of wrongdo-
ing and embarrassment. Even when I got involved with fellow *feringhees*, we sneaked around behind the backs of the coterie of servants
that surround you in India; having successfully propagated the myth of
my so-called husband to my new community, I didn't want to destroy
it. Rafi, a young Indian journalist I met through a mutual friend, was
the first of my Indian relationships. We had coffee and dinners together for a couple of months, which, I realized, qualified me as his
girlfriend. Dating in India is sort of like in middle school. We'd have
inexpensive dinners of South Indian *dosas*, and he'd drive me home,
weaving through the Delhi traffic on his scooter. He showed me how to
perch behind him so that I wasn't straddling the seat, which is considered unseemly for proper Indian ladies. After a couple of months living there, sitting astride a scooter behind a man started to feel obscene
to me, too. I tried to get comfortable sitting sideways, my legs dangling
into the street, even though it gave me the sensation that I was about to
tip forward into traffic.

In fact, no matter how I sat on his scooter, Rafi thought of me as
anything but a proper lady. I don't think he considered telling his
friends about me, let alone his family—especially not after our relationship moved out of the virtuous Indian realm and into Rafi's rented
room. He lived separately from his family, in a crowded block of tenements near the campus of Delhi University, one of the city's largest, in
a dank cement box of a room with a single window. I learned to hold my

breath while using the squatting toilet. There was no stove on which to brew tea, so we'd go out to a shopping complex near the university and bring it back in plastic cups. At night, we'd lie on his mattress on the floor and curl sadly into each other under his bright block-printed bed sheet. Being with him made me realize how lonely I was for home. And although the rules of my relationship allowed me to do as I wished, and I'd told myself this was the adventurous life I wanted, Rafi made me miss Benjamin all the more. In the mornings, I felt as though I was crawling out of a boyfriend bush. I'd want to fold up the sheet quickly and leave the room.

Rafi said he was getting nervous that his neighbors would see me coming and going from the apartment. He suggested I cover my head with a scarf to disguise that I was a *feringhee,* so that he could say I was his sister. If someone reported that he, an unmarried boy, was spending nights alone with a girl, he could actually be evicted. I didn't know how to respond when he told me that. After a while, we decided we'd be better off being friends. I think I missed the idea of him more than the person he was; but it was hard to know, because all my interactions in Delhi during those first few months seemed somehow unreal. I'd never struggled like this to form bonds with people.

In the meantime, I had Geeta. Although we had little in common other than our proximity and our loneliness, I'd remind myself of the Indian families I saw who seemed content simply sitting together, even if they didn't talk at all. With my own friends and family, I'd always felt I had to be dynamic and funny, and to prove myself by announcing fantastic plans for the future. Geeta and Nanima freed me from that pressure: We rarely did more than sit around watching TV. Since my hippie parents had essentially banned TV during my childhood, this was a great luxury in itself.

I'd join Geeta downstairs in her apartment when she got home from work, relieved to escape my dusty *barsati,* which by the end of the day often felt like an isolated prison cell. When I wasn't traveling, I worked alone up there. One night Geeta whipped up a batch of frothy Punjabi milkshakes called *lassis*, and we settled in on Nanima's sofa to channel surf. Geeta flicked past a CNN report, a grave-faced mullah on a Pakistani prayer channel, and a hyperbolic anchor on an Indian news show.

"Look at all this. It's amazing how much India has changed in my own lifetime." Geeta seemed to consider it her duty to impress on me the breadth of her country's advancement in the last two decades, as if she was doing her bit to ensure that the transformed India would no longer be ignored by the developed world. India had only one TV channel when she was growing up, she said. The state-owned Doordashan network had held a complete monopoly on the airwaves since the first television broadcast in India in 1959.

"It was just endless footage of government ribbon-cutting ceremonies. You wouldn't believe how dull." As a child she'd lived for Wednesday evenings, when Doordashan would broadcast a half-hour show of film songs.

It wasn't until 1995 that the Supreme Court declared the government monopoly on broadcasting unconstitutional and private broadcasters flooded in. By the time I moved to India, you could watch hundreds of shows—news, reality TV, and prime-time soap operas—in dozens of Indian languages, all for a cable fee of four dollars a month. But even in its improved state, television takes a secondary place in Indian pop culture to film. Some twelve million people a day go to the movies, whether to a multiplex in a big city or to a village temple where new releases are projected on a sheet on the side of the building.

In India, the movies mean Bollywood, the film industry whose name conflates Hollywood with Bombay, where the first Hindi-language film was made. Even after Bombay was renamed Mumbai in an effort to free the city of its colonial legacy, Bollywood stayed Bollywood. It churns out at least two hundred films a year, each costing less than a million dollars—a sixth of the average price tag of a Hollywood film. Prolific, popular, song-filled, and sentimental, Bollywood films almost always swoon over the three-hour mark. As a result, they all have intermissions, during which theater concession stands rake it in selling spicy veggie burgers, samosas, and "American snacks" such as caramel popcorn.

Movie soundtracks are Bollywood's best promotional tool. In the weeks before a big studio release, music videos of the songs take over the TV channels. The songs are recorded by an army of unseen "play-back singers" but are associated in perpetuity with the actors who have lip-synched them. I'd hear Geeta humming a new film tune, and later that day, Joginder's cell phone would announce itself with the same song. India's star culture is even more obsessive than our own. Hollywood has the celebrity website TMZ, but in India, Bollywood gossip isn't relegated to the niche media: it is often a top story on the nightly news. Many movie stars have actual, real-life shrines erected to them, and when they are not literally being worshipped, their faces are everywhere, from well-produced TV ads for toothpaste to hand-painted movie billboards on rural unpaved roads.

Bollywood's biggest romantic hero, Shah Rukh Khan, is best known as "King Khan," though Geeta preferred to refer to him by the less obsequious nickname "SRK." He's produced a stunning five dozen films over his career of almost twenty years. When he was named one of *Newsweek*'s fifty most powerful people in the world, the Indian media treated it like a national accomplishment; when he was invited to present a Golden Globe Award, Indian announcers said it spoke to the country's growing might; when he was detained at Newark airport in 2009, presumably because of his Muslim last name, the TV channels called it a "national humiliation."

The Bollywood phenomenon puzzled me at first: Hindi films have very little of the stuff Westerners expect from movies—realism, cynicism, sex. They are medieval morality plays made entertaining through melodrama, song, and spectacle. The villains are always villainous, and goodness almost always triumphs. "Pageants for peasants" is how the early Indian filmmaker S. S. Vasan described his movies. But watching Bollywood helped me come to terms with Indian culture. It also helped me understand Geeta, which made things easier for both of us: Instead of having to explain her parents' expectations, she could use film plots as shorthand. Bollywood has three archetypes for its heroines, she informed me: the beautiful pious virgin, the pure Indian wife, and the seductress-vamp. Until very recently, an actress who was typecast as the latter would have been shut out from mainstream success.

Geeta acknowledged that SRK's films were overblown and fantastical, but that didn't make her any less of a Bollywood-ringtone-downloading fan. If I scoffed that Bollywood's lavish houses and pristine streets looked nothing like the India around us, she'd get defensive.

"You have to simplify things to get people into theaters, Miranda. That's how it works here. Why would some poor rickshaw driver want to go and see his slum on the big screen? People go to the movies to escape reality."

The 2008 film *Slumdog Millionaire* garnered eight Oscars in the United States, but its gritty portrayal of poverty led to angry protests in India. In fact, the industry's most famous actor, Amitabh Bachchan—universally known in India as "the Big B"—disparaged the film for projecting India as a "third-world, dirty, underbelly developing nation." This caused "pain and disgust among nationalists and patriots," he said.

This evening, after channel surfing a while, Nanima begged us to watch part of an old film with her. Even today, almost all Bollywood films are musicals; but in the 1940s and '50s, the songs were the focus, and sometimes as many as forty of them interrupted the plot. When Geeta reluctantly agreed, Nanima clapped her hands with a joy matched only by her response to my space-heater toast. She scooted forward to the edge of the sofa as the first love scene got going. This one had a long buildup in a wheat field, the stalks quivering in the wind. The carefully groomed, fair-skinned hero gazed soulfully at his plump heroine, her eyes darkly lined with kohl, which has been used in India for centuries. The music crescendoed. They leaned closer in the soft-focus light, and the music peaked again. Nanima was holding her breath. Just when it seemed certain that the lovers would kiss, the camera darted away to focus on a wildly shaking tree branch, a classic Bollywood substitute for an on-screen kiss; a bee pollinating a flower is another one. When the camera cut back to the lovers, their lips were parted, their hair was tousled, and they were about to sing.

Geeta and I cracked up laughing: "We missed all the action, Nanima."

"No, no. We had the passion, only, and none of the bad parts," she said primly.

Until the late 1990s, the sexiest Bollywood scenes featured the heroine "caught" under a spontaneous spray of water in a clinging wet sari. Even today, on-screen nudity is banned by the Indian Censor Board. Although kissing on-screen is not officially illegal, many stars and directors self-censor displays of passion to avoid angering India's vocal and powerful Hindu conservatives. As a result, Shah Rukh Khan has never once delivered a movie lip kiss—much to the chagrin of fans such as Geeta and me. He's just as careful about maintaining a culturally acceptable, wholesome persona offscreen. Like 1950s Hollywood studio stars, SRK is a symbol of manhood—although unproven rumors about his sexuality persist.

It follows that Bollywood starlets are expected to be emblems of chastity, though this struck me as especially incongruous in today's sexualized Bollywood. I thought it strange to see heroines dance suggestively in hot pants and bustiers even as they acted the parts of virginal characters. On TV shows such as the popular Saturday night program *Koffee with Karan,* starlets regularly disavow affiliations with various actors. The host of the program, Karan Johar, is further proof of Bollywood's double standard about sex: He's stylish, good looking, and significantly unmarried, and theories abound about his romantic life.

"What toss!" the otherwise uncynical Geeta would jeer when she heard top Bollywood actresses disavow that they'd ever had romantic relationships. In spite of the industry's famously chaste image, gossip shows and magazines spin vicious stories. One of Bollywood's top actresses, Aishwarya Rai—or Ash, as everyone in India calls her—was long pursued by the media. She waited until she was thirty-three to marry, and even that didn't quiet the rumors about her character. Although that's late for a normal Indian girl, it's acceptable in Bollywood, since wedlock traditionally signals the end of an actress's career.

Industry wisdom has it that audiences do not find it believable to watch a married woman play a virgin, and, of course, audiences want to continue to watch their top stars for as long as they can. The restriction applies to male actors, too: When SRK first started getting cast in Mumbai, producers suggested he keep his marriage a secret so as not to spoil his budding career as a romantic hero. After Ash was arranged into a marriage with the son of Amitabh Bachchan, she did continue acting—unlike previous generations of Bollywood starlets—but found herself offered more matronly roles. She even went so far as to start wearing flesh suits under her saris when she performed. Hiding the real skin of her arms and stomach was a sign of respect to her husband and her in-laws.

In spite of all this, Indian audiences were changing. With only-slightly-edited reruns of *Sex and the City* now on Indian cable, some Bollywood producers worried about keeping up. They started producing a wave of sexy films. The first and riskiest of these was *Khwahish* (Desire), in which the lead actress, Mallika Sherawat, delivered seventeen carefully counted kisses, spawning a new mini-industry in editorials and op-eds opining the loss of morality in the new India. But although it was predicted that the movie would be career suicide for an aspiring starlet, the opposite happened: It shot Mallika to stardom. The theaters were packed with gleeful boys having the most sexual experience of their lives; nary a man in India under the age of sixty missed the film.

Mallika took her image as a bombshell seductress-vamp and inhabited it with full force, dressing seductively for every public appearance. She took to the stage in a red miniskirt for the hundredth performance of Eve Ensler's *The Vagina Monologues* in Mumbai. During interviews, rather than fluttering her eyelids modestly at the camera, as do Ash and the other pious virgin types, she makes suggestive comments about her "male friends." Mallika will never be cast as the innocent girl in a moralistic coming-of-age blockbuster—Bollywood audiences definitely wouldn't find that believable—but she doesn't need such roles. She's proved that it's possible, even in Bollywood, to be a vamp and be successful.

Although Geeta complained about Bollywood's limited female characters, Mallika's multiple on-screen kisses and steamy videos were a bit much for her. She preferred a more moral school of movies, a subgenre of Bollywood blockbusters aimed at upwardly mobile Indian audiences and the Indian diaspora. The female characters in these films are often college students or professional women; SRK usually plays the hero, successfully negotiating the complications of contemporary sexuality. His characters often move overseas, where they struggle to maintain Indian traditions or battle with love that precedes marriage. I think Geeta found these films comforting. In the end, the hero always recovers his fundamentally Indian sensibility; the heroine always proves her noble character. When we watched SRK's blockbusters together, I could see her scanning them for clues about how to resolve her own struggles over identity, love, and marriage. Geeta wanted to live a modern life, at least in theory, but she worried that her identity as independent Delhi girl could overshadow her other identity as pious virgin.

I learned a lot about Geeta those nights in Nanima's apartment. She'd sometimes bring me into her bedroom, where she'd rifle through boxes of her photographs. I could tell that she was proud of her highly educated Brahmin family. Her home state, Punjab, has relatively liberal attitudes toward women, she told me, and her grandmother sent all five of her daughters to school in an era when that was anything but common in India. Geeta's mother had worked as a schoolteacher when Geeta was young, though the vast majority of Indian women—even today—quit work after marriage.

Marriage is a topic on which Geeta's family had more traditional views—but that's only to be expected in India, where some 90 percent of Indian partnerships are arranged, either by the family or by matchmakers. Most marriages are still a merger between two families of similar caste backgrounds and religious beliefs. Euphemism abounds inside the institution of Indian marriage: Parents talk about finding "a mutually agreeable match," meaning one that meets a set of religious and astrological specifications. Geeta told me that her family had been looking to arrange her into marriage for years already with a "boy from a good family," meaning a Punjabi Brahmin from a family of equal status to theirs.

In the vocabulary of arranged marriage, potential mates are referred to as *larke* and *larkiya*, boys and girls, because for centuries marriages were formalized at puberty. Mahatma Gandhi was betrothed at the age of seven and married at thirteen. As far back as 1929, the Indian government raised the legal age of marriage to twenty-one for boys and eighteen for girls, but no one paid much attention. According to the United Nations, in 2007, 47 percent of Indian women had been married before they were eighteen years old. In rural areas, it is 56 percent. Modern-minded, middle-class Indians in cities are marrying later than ever before, though. Geeta said that in her community it was acceptable for a girl to hold off until her mid-twenties. She was veering uncomfortably close to the age of thirty, though, and I couldn't help but wonder about the delay.

When Geeta showed up at my door one evening clad in a denim miniskirt and heels, I found it hard to hide my surprise. The skirt wasn't actually that short, in retrospect, but at the time, I was under the full sway of Delhi's prudish fashion sense. Wearing a Western skirt at all, but especially a knee-length one, was a freighted decision. Geeta noticed my eye on her hemline.

"I'm going out dancing with my friend from college tonight. We always wear skirts." Her confidence faltered. "Do you think it's too short?"

I raised an eyebrow, unsure how to answer. Just the other day, she'd told me that although she liked wearing the comfortable *salwar kameez*, she was treated more respectfully at work when she donned a sari, the more traditional garb of older women. Geeta would sometimes "wear Westerns," as she referred to jeans and blouses, but only in restricted places, such as malls and upscale movie theaters. In these kinds of settings, it's common to see girls in revealing tank tops and short skirts—that is, the kind of girls who can limit their dealings with the rest of India. If they are chauffeured from coffee shops to nightclubs in five-star hotels, they limit the risk of getting eyeballed or grabbed. That wasn't Geeta's world, but she aspired to be a part of it.

"I have worn this skirt out dancing many times already. It's becoming quite normal for girls to wear dresses in Delhi. There's just a few people who are stuck with those old views."

She flipped her hair with forced nonchalance. I tried to wipe away my skeptical look so as not to make Geeta any more defensive—either about her reputation or about her country as a backward place.

Geeta's defiance was only skin deep, though. In fact, she admitted, she'd stopped by to ask me to walk her out to her car. No one would bother her at the club, she said, but she wanted moral support on this end—just in case some of the people with old views happened to be hanging around the neighborhood tonight. An elderly man on the street had once yelled at her for wearing a miniskirt, she said, chiding her that she should be ashamed of herself for dressing in such a way. I thought about Joginder in the alley, and the rest of our neighbors, and found it hard to imagine that any of them *wouldn't* judge her for her outfit. I hoped selfishly that none of the Nizamuddin market guys would see me escorting Geeta around the corner; I had my own image to maintain, after all.

I found it hard to navigate between Geeta's two identities—the naïve, closed-minded girl and the savvy, globalized woman. She grumbled about playing nursemaid to Nanima, but I think it also made her feel virtuous to martyr herself for this old lady who had been abandoned by everyone else. Her mother believed that the living arrangement would be appealing to potential in-laws. "Isn't it ridiculous, the things mothers think of?" Geeta laughed. Still, I sensed that part of her agreed that it was a good idea to present herself as a conventional wife-to-be.

I found it hard to know what to say to the conservative girl from Patiala, though I could talk to her fairly openly when she was in her miniskirt mode. Still, I had no intention of informing her about my Delhi affairs—she would have been horrified to think of me kissing Indian men. When I told her that I'd be doing a live-in with Benjamin for a few months, though, she was refreshingly unsurprised.

"I've watched *Friends,* Miranda: I know you do things differently in America."

I didn't know what to think about having my life compared to an

oversimplified sitcom, but outdated American shows were an important point of reference for Geeta. Sometimes she presented them as
evidence of her globalized savvy, and sometimes to prove to me that
her life was more complicated than mine. Whether or not this was the
case, this much was true: Everything she did was carefully scrutinized
and outlined with the thick black marker of social custom.

The more I got to know Geeta, the more I saw that her life was
poised between two very different possible outcomes. She hadn't yet
chosen her modern Delhi identity over marriage, but neither was she
making a move toward the conventional option. In the Bollywood
movie of her life, Geeta wanted to be Ash, forever a virginal bride; but
I think she was afraid she'd be seen as Mallika. There was a sadness to
her face sometimes that made me wonder whether there was more to
the story than she was telling me.

Her parents had sent her on dozens of arranged marriage meetings,
or parentally approved blind dates, even before she'd graduated from
college, and she'd gone along, because it was easier than refusing.
She'd always managed to find something wrong with the boy, though.
On the verge of the high-water mark of a girl's marriageable years,
Geeta now seemed frozen. It was as though she was waiting for an indi-
cation about which version of herself she should be.

Fate was very real for Geeta—she saw its hand in almost everything.
What seemed to me a series of normal coincidences Geeta read as destiny; anecdotes about an unseasonable rainfall or running into an old
colleague were transformed, in her telling, into small miracles. Like
many Hindus, she believed the events of her life were guided by
dharma, the eternal order of the cosmos, meaning everything could be
explained by events of the past. These beliefs only seemed to heighten
the fear that she was too modern to be marriageable.

The same conflict is at the heart of the Bollywood classic *Dilwale
Dulhania Le Jayenge* (The Brave-hearted Will Take the Bride), a mouthful of a title that everyone avoids by using the Hindi acronym, *DDLJ*.
When the film came out in 1995, Geeta saw it several times in the theater with her college friends, and she still watched it every time it came
on TV—which was often, because it is one of the highest-grossing and

longest-running Bollywood movies of all time. There are still daily screenings in one Mumbai movie theater; the schedule wasn't even disrupted by the 2008 terror attacks.

The brave-hearted hero of the title is played by Shah Rukh Khan, in what is undoubtedly his most famous role. His character, Raj, is a rich second-generation Indian immigrant in London; to prove the extent of his Westernization, he is depicted strutting around in a motorcycle jacket and playing soccer and the piano, rather than having Indian hobbies such as playing cricket and the sitar. In an early scene of the film, Raj bullies a London shopkeeper, a fellow Indian immigrant, to give him a six-pack of beer. This all proves that he is, in Bollywood-speak, a "crooked character" who has moved too far away from Indian traditions. But, in typical Bollywood style, he's given a chance to reform, and it comes in the form of a beautiful pious virgin. Among the first things we learn about our heroine, Simran, is that she prays at the family's Hindu shrine before dawn. Her father considers her the very essence of Indianness. When he tells her he's accepted an arranged marriage proposal for her and she runs out of the room in horror, he misinterprets her reaction: "Ah, she is shy. That's our etiquette, our culture. In the heart of London, I've kept India alive!"

Even before the intermission, Raj begins to resurrect himself from Western depravity, having realized that he is destined to be with Simran and must better himself to deserve her. According to traditional Hindu beliefs, if the priest, the community, and the astrologers approve of a match, it proves it is fated and should last for the next seven lifetimes. So, in the hope of proving to her family that he should be with her, Raj follows Simran to India. I assumed the film was approaching its climax when the two reunite in a field of swaying yellow mustard seed in Punjab. They clutch passionately at each other—though they don't, of course, touch lips, because the hero is played by the chaste SRK. Simran begs Raj to elope with her, but he refuses.

"I haven't come here to steal you. I'll take you only when your father gives me your hand. About our lives, they can decide much better than we can. We have no right to make them sad for the sake of our own happiness."

It is not for another hour into the film that Simran's family finally comes to terms with fate. Our hero is standing in the door of a moving train, literally streaked with blood and tears, by the time Simran's father tells her to go to him; only then does she leap from the platform onto the accelerating train. This movie is Bollywood at its most melodramatic and sentimental; still, its message about society hit me hard. I'd always wanted to believe that love would be unassailable if it was true and right. I cried my way through *DDLJ*'s whole drawn-out final scene the first time I watched it.

I thought that if I followed my urge to set off on my own, I'd eventually find my place in the world—the city, job, friends, and man that I loved. But *DDLJ* made me wonder what I was trying to prove and why I needed to leave everyone who mattered to me to do it. Perhaps I was just doing as my family always had and trying to escape the conventional, driven not by my adventurous soul but by my fear of normalcy. If there was a Bollywood movie version of my life, I'd certainly be the seductress-vamp, unwilling to sacrifice my own goals for either love or family.

I was pretty sure that, as lost as she sometimes seemed, Geeta would find her way back to the girl she'd always expected to be. Someday soon, she'd project pure Indian virginal side of herself to her Patiala audience again—because if she didn't, the consequences would be dire: A modern girl is one thing, but an aging spinster without a family is a pitiable specter in Delhi. I'd never thought about my actions as having such stark consequences—in my world, being a single woman wasn't ideal, but it didn't automatically brand you as a spinster, either. I knew my mother would be sad if I ended up alone, but it wouldn't make her write me out of the script altogether.

Still, as I watched *DDLJ,* the thought filtered into my mind that the decisions I'd made to leave New York and my boyfriend might have an impact on the kind of life I would end up leading. If this sounds as if it should have been obvious, let's just say that it wasn't. I'd been raised to think of my life as a series of disparate events, not as a straight line working toward a happy ending. It was impossible for Geeta to ignore the consequences of her choices, though they echoed around her all the time, in her mother's warnings, her friends' decisions, and the films that she watched several times a week. Bollywood tells us that love is spontaneous and all consuming, but that it is worth nothing without community. When heroes fall in love, they stretch their arms open wide as though to say "Now I feel a part of this beautiful world." In the next scene, they lower their heads and touch the feet of their elders. Only then do they earn the right to marry the person they love.

CHAPTER 4

A Whiskey-drinking Woman

My stomach was churning as I pushed my way to the front of the barrier at Delhi airport's international terminal. The place was packed with uniformed hotel boys displaying handwritten signs as they waited for the early-morning flights to land. They joked around between tranches of arriving passengers, but when a flight cleared customs, they would focus intently on the rumpled crowd, elbowing one another aside to achieve prominence for their sheets of paper. They paid the most attention to the foreign passengers, whose slightly panicky eyes skipped among the unfamiliar brown faces, searching for their names.

I felt briefly and irrationally envious of these unknown foreigners, many of them businessmen making initial trips to India, optimistic about the potential it offered their companies. They were tired and overwhelmed, but soon they'd find their sign. The hotel porters would ask them the standard questions as they delivered them to their chauffeured cars—"Which country? How many days in India?" In the morning, they'd dine in the carefully sanitized five-star-hotel buffet. Their transaction with India would be clean and simple—or so at least it seemed, compared to the arrival of my not-husband, maybe-boyfriend in this country that had already drawn me in more deeply than I had anticipated.

I would have been ashamed to admit at the time that Benjamin was one of the reasons I left New York. Not because I was trying to get away from him, but because I hoped that by setting off to India, I would prove that I was just as carefree as he. He'd spent his postcollege years hopping illegal rides on freight trains, staging theatrical protests to save community gardens in New York, and living in an artists' commune in Brooklyn, a lifestyle he supported by working at magazines and writing travel articles. In the six months we'd been together, I'd discovered to my dismay that just because I shared his ideals and his wanderlust didn't make him believe I wouldn't suffocate him.

In the weeks before I left, the decision seemed to have the desired impact. Benjamin started hesitating about whether he shouldn't come with me, after all. He initiated discussions about our relationship. We set limits on our "arrangement," promising we'd only have affairs when we were in different countries. When we were together, we told each other, we'd wipe all of that away. He promised to get writing assignments in India, so he could spend a couple of longish stints with me each year. After we'd both had our adventures, I'd move back to the States, and we'd fill a rambling house in Vermont with kids and animals.

The vagueness of this plan suited us both. We thought we wanted to be together—although neither of us was sure we wanted to get married—and this seemed like a good way to bookmark the idea. Plenty of women I knew were starting to settle down at my age of twenty-six or twenty-seven, but I had no such urge. I'd always been ambivalent about marriage and kids; I'd certainly never drawn up a plan to make them happen by a certain stage of my life. I just wanted to have my experience of India, without having to worry that I'd severed myself from New York altogether.

When Benjamin emerged in the airport terminal, he was taller than I'd remembered, even hunched under the weight of his pack. My first thought was that Radha was going to be very impressed by my American husband. For a moment I saw him through her eyes: fair skinned and well built, with dark hair and light eyes, like one of the actors she'd seen on *Baywatch* reruns. Watching him walk up the arrivals hall, I felt suddenly distant from him and my life in New York. My year in India had already changed me in ways I hadn't figured out yet, and I was, for a moment, not at all sure that I wanted my old life to catch up with me so soon. There was nothing for it, though; he was here.

When he leaned to kiss me, he became familiar and wonderful again—the self-confident grin, as wide as the curve of a banana, the slightly unwashed smell of his clothes. As we drove to Nizamuddin, the taxi breezing through the red traffic lights in the empty streets, his face shone with a small-town boy's wonderment at Delhi in the gray smoggy dawn. Benjamin was the best of companions in India. He didn't mind the hassle, dirt, and discomfort. He didn't care that the guys in the market stared at him in his baggy shorts, which made him look goofy and half naked—men in Delhi almost always cover their legs. To him, India was just another in a lifetime of adventures. That freed him from the pressure of trying to fit in, and seemed a welcome break from my own obsessive concern about what my neighbors thought of me.

Soon after he arrived, Benjamin bought a clunky Indian-made bicycle, thinking it would be an efficient way to avoid bargaining with Delhi's notoriously unscrupulous auto-rickshaw drivers. I warned him that he'd be the only cyclist in the city who earned more than a dollar a day. India has a caste system for the roads, as for everything else, and bicycles rank lower than bullock carts and camels.

Benjamin came home sweaty and grimy after an especially trying afternoon ride. An aggressive "jingle truck," so called because the hand-painted vehicles are hung with jingling ornaments, had edged him off the road. He'd walked the bike home along the freeway.

"If I'm going to spend any time in this insane town, I'm going to have to pull myself up a few notches on India's transportation hierarchy," he asserted. After all, he reminded me, with a touch of the bravado that I found so charming in him, he drove a Honda Nighthawk 750 in New York. A few days later, I heard a honking in the alley and stepped out on the patio to see an ebullient, bareheaded Benjamin revving a silver motorcycle: a Royal Enfield Bullet Machismo, aptly named for restoring his manhood.

In the morning he ran down to Joginder's house, full of the enthusiasm of the virtuous. He knocked on the aluminum siding door and presented the bicycle. Joginder was not impressed by the offering.

"I am superintendent. I am not for bicycle, sahib. Even sahib should not have been cycling-trykling." The most Joginder would deign to do was donate the bike elsewhere. He gave it to the Bihari boys who worked at the local grocery, and for years afterward, I'd see them swinging up onto its thick frame, a canvas bag of supplies slung across a shoulder.

It didn't take long for word to get around Nizamuddin about the generous foreigner who'd made an unexpected donation. Now when Benjamin walked down to the market, the neighborhood boys would gather around him. There was something in his confident amble and the awe he inspired in the Bihari immigrants that called to mind a movie star. He'd sometimes buy the Nizamuddin guys a round of Thums Up—a harsh Indian-made cola that is considered a manly drink in villages and comes in returnable glass bottles. They'd drink it in companionable silence, standing in the street outside the shop, because the shopkeeper insisted that customers return the bottles right away. One of them would light a bidi, and they would pass it between them like a joint.

In the weeks before he left Delhi, Benjamin talked about how much he would miss the camaraderie he'd established with the neighborhood guys. In spite of their limited interactions, he'd developed a wordless attachment with them, the kind that blooms quickly in South Asia. He was especially enamored with the youngest of the shop delivery boys, Arjun, who was newly arrived from the village and didn't yet have the dead-eyed cynicism of many of Delhi's older slum dwellers. When he appeared with the day's milk and bread, Benjamin tipped him excessively. The affection was mutual, so much so that I dreaded ordering things from the shop after Benjamin left. Arjun would peer hopefully over my shoulder from the doorway, as though hoping my husband would pop out from behind me in the apartment. When he realized it was just me, he'd pocket the few rupees of my comparatively meager tip and turn back down the stairs, his face bereft.

Everyone says that India desensitizes you to human misery. During my first year in Delhi, I eagerly awaited that change, but it was a long time coming. Just driving through the streets, I routinely felt a low-level sadness that exploded into horror, or even nausea, at the sights around me—limbless beggars, children eating garbage, the desperate abusing the desperate.

During Benjamin's stay, we went to Mumbai and visited the Haji Ali shrine. Attracted by its whitewashed minarets perched on a tiny islet off the coast, we followed a procession of pilgrims across a long causeway, lined on both sides with supplicants asking for alms. It was a veritable nineteenth-century freak show of misery that reminded me of the Chamber of Horrors at Madame Tussauds museum. Among the gallery of beggars sat a bloated balloon of a woman, her body expanded wide with elephantiasis, and a man with a hole in his chest, through which, I swear, you could see his left lung. Stacked in front of each of them were piles of coins—when I looked more closely, I realized they weren't rupees but paisa coins made of tin. Each coin was worth one-hundredth of a rupee; the donations they'd received probably totaled no more than several American cents. At the end of the causeway, four legless and armless torsos were writhing on the ground. The heads attached to the torsos were chanting fervent prayers to Allah. My own legs were shaking by the time we got up to the mosque, and for years afterward, I wondered how a man can lose all four of his limbs and still survive. The Indian government cites endemic infection, arterial disease, severe burns, traumatic injury, deformity, and paralysis as some of the reasons that ten million people in India have lost limbs.

Geeta instructed me rather harshly that I would have to "get over" my "Western oversensitivity" if I was to live in India. I tried to follow her advice and get better at inuring myself. I learned to skip over the almost daily newspaper articles about traffic accidents and natural dis-

asters—"82 Dead in Bus Mishap"; "Hundreds Washed Away on Flood
Plain." Even with death tolls that would have been front-page news in
the United States, these stories were relegated to the inside pages of
the Indian papers; there were simply too many of them.

I always read the reports about caste-related violence, though,
drawn to the topic with horrified fascination. Not long after I moved to
India, the papers got hold of a story about several untouchable villagers
in the North Indian state of Haryana. They were leather tanners, a job
reserved for the lowest of the low because it involves working with
dead cows. The police stopped the men when they were on their way to
the market to sell a cow hide, accusing them of killing the cow to tan it,
which is illegal in most Indian states. The villagers insisted that the
cow had died naturally, but the police brought them in, and rumor
spread fast. A mob gathered outside the police department, rushed
into the building, and dragged the five men out. They were beaten to
death in front of the police department.

The English-language press ran articles with headlines such as
"Five Men = One Cow." Television talk shows pondered whether caste
inequality had improved at all in India's sixty-plus years of independence. One fierce and poetic newspaper op-ed began: "Thanks to my
upper caste credentials, I don't have to skin a dead cow for a living. Nor
are my 'community members' not allowed to enter temples or stopped
from drinking water from village wells, or forced to use a 'marked' cup
in the local tea-shop, or made to eat human excreta as divine punish-
ment."

I went to see the journalist who'd written it. Vijay Mukherjee had
the brooding look of an aging Marxist—furrowed brow, receding hairline, string bag of books over a shoulder. It's not an uncommon style in
today's India, where communism remains a potent force in politics
and attracts millions of followers. Still, Vijay seemed out of place in the
sleek office building in central Delhi where he worked as a senior
writer for one of India's top-selling English-language papers. That impression was only exaggerated when he sat down in front of my microphone and his account of the caste system morphed into a furious
hour-and-a-half-long monologue. He worked himself into a sweat in

spite of the air-conditioning, pounding on the table and rendering my radio recording unusable.

The word *caste,* he told me, is actually a conflation of two Indian concepts: *jati,* which describes the community, clan, or tribe that you marry into, and *varna,* the place this group occupies on the hierarchy mandated by Hindu scripture. There are four main *varna*s, topped by the Brahmins—traditionally the teachers and priests—who are followed by the kings and warriors, the merchants and farmers, and the service people. Inside each of these four categories are thousands of *jatis,* or subcastes. And below the lowest category are the untouchables, literally outcastes from the system.

Indian scholars think caste stratification evolved gradually, as the idea of religious purity became central to Hinduism. Unlike Christianity and Islam, Hinduism has no one single canon laying out the principles of the religion. There are books of mythology with morals and stories; for the rules, Hindus turn to the *Manusmrti* (The Laws of Manu) from the first century B.C. It records in meticulous, cruel detail the Hindu caste code that came into practice during the Vedic period, from 1500 to 200 B.C. Manu, the book's author, was naturally a Brahmin himself, since they were the only educated caste. He is careful to preserve the preeminence of his own tribe in his taxonomy of the social order. The jobs of the untouchables, he says, should include disposing of corpses and carrying out executions; they should wear the clothes of executed convicts and live outside the boundaries of villages.

Manu is still considered the best authority on the social and religious duties of dharma and caste. And although it is not known how closely or widely the rules were followed in his era, it is indisputable that he formalized caste divisions. Today's Hindu marriage code is still based on his principles. Then, when the British took over India, they only entrenched the caste system further. The British slotted the educated Brahmins into the colonial institution to serve as imperial bureaucrats and religious advisors to judges.

When Mahatma Gandhi launched a long-overdue movement to reform the caste system, in the 1920s, he linked the issue to the bid for

India's independence, accusing the British of exploiting caste as part of its policy of divide and rule. Gandhi forced the issue into the open for the first time. He declared that untouchables should be called Harijans, which means "children of God." The media photographed him eating from banana-leaf plates among untouchables in their slums, a shocking image because he hailed from an upper-caste family. Interdining between the castes was extremely rare.

The untouchable leader B. R. Ambedkar thought these gestures patronizing, though. He was an unusual man: Born into a family whose hereditary work was cleaning toilets and guarding the bodies of the dead, he became the first untouchable to be educated overseas. On his return to India, Ambedkar rose into national politics, advocating radical social revolution and hoping India's new democracy would itself overthrow the caste system. Ambedkar shared Gandhi's goals of self-rule and self-reliance for India, but he didn't believe it would happen within the Hindu framework. Gandhi, as a privileged caste Hindu, had no right to speak for untouchables, he said—or to name them. He rejected the name Harijan, preferring to describe himself as a Dalit, which means "downtrodden" or "broken to pieces." His is the term that stuck.

Ambedkar, a lawyer, was the lead author of India's 1950 constitution, which made it illegal to discriminate against untouchables. More than fifty years later, when I'd moved to India, I still saw caste everywhere. Intercaste marriage was officially legal, for instance, but it was regularly prevented or punished by families wielding their own system of justice. In ancient times, high-caste Hindus believed there were terrible mental and physical consequences to being touched by the people who cleaned toilets and skinned cows. One scholar of Hinduism compares this fear of pollution to Americans' terror about people with HIV at the height of the AIDS panic. Hindus who defile their high-caste status—by killing an animal of any kind or sharing a drinking vessel with a low-caste person—were supposed to purify themselves with what Manu called "expiatory penances" such as begging for food and bathing three times a day.

At school, Ambedkar was forced to drink from a separate untouchables cup, into which water was poured from a height to protect the server from being contaminated by the vessel. Dalits still drink from a separate well in some villages. In ancient times, they were obliged to announce their arrival by clapping together the soles of their shoes to avoid contaminating the higher castes. In some parts of today's India, Dalits are forced to hold their *chappals* in their hands when they walk past high-caste houses, so as not to pollute the path. Although interdining is now common in cafés and restaurants in Delhi and Mumbai, the highest and lowest castes almost never share meals in rural areas, let alone align their lives in any more intimate ways, such as marrying into each other's families.

Ambedkar was the first to warn that good laws alone wouldn't end caste discrimination. India would "enter a life of contradictions" when the constitution came into effect, he said, because "in politics we will have equality. . . . How long shall we continue to deny equality in our social and economic life?"

It's a question that could be asked today. India's new economy makes merit-based social mobility possible as never before, but caste discrimination is old and deep. It is built into every institution and impulse in India, as was racism in the pre–Civil War American South. If it is difficult for an outsider to have an honest conversation about race in the Dixie states, the same is true about caste in India. It's not that these conversations don't take place, but even in private they are veiled in platitudes and spoken in hushed tones.

When I brought up caste, progressive-minded intellectuals, economists, and politicians would fiercely resist the comparison to slavery and racism. In the mainstream narrative of India's economic and social uplift, there is no room for India's deep-rooted system of discrimination based on birthright.

"Caste was a problem in the old India, but now things have changed," they'd say, or "It's been solved in the cities. It is only an issue in villages now." I'd usually keep quiet, for the sake of holding on to a source or avoiding an argument about a topic I was scarcely an expert in, but I didn't believe them. Globalization and urbanization just paper over caste—they haven't eradicated it. In my own apartment in the capital city of one of the world's fastest-growing economies, my two servants lived out the most basic inequities of the caste system every day.

As I packed up my radio equipment, Vijay apologized for barely allowing me to get a question in.

"I get *too too* passionate about this subject. We should have a calmer discussion sometime. Why don't you come and meet some friends at the Delhi Press Club this weekend. I think you'll like my friend Parvati."

I didn't need convincing. I was so starved for social activity that I didn't care whether he ranted all night about caste, cricket, or Bollywood dance moves. Nighttime activities had proved surprisingly difficult in Delhi. Everyone from Joginder to my taxi driver, K.K., recited the same foreboding counsel: "Single ladies should not be venturing outside after dark." The newspapers regularly chronicled incidents of "eve-teasing," the Indian euphemism that has its root in the biblical story of Eve and that makes sexual harassment sound much less serious than it is. In fact, government statistics show that violence against women has actually risen since 2003. Probably due to more women entering the workplace and other public spaces, rape cases rose by more than 30 percent; kidnapping or abduction cases increased by over 50 percent. Geeta had her own stories of being "harassed by village boys," as she put it, on public buses and even in temples.

When Benjamin was in Delhi, he provided a certain amount of protection from Delhi's butt pinchers. Nevertheless, the city offered few nightlife options even for a couple, other than expensive cocktails at five-star hotels or late-night house parties and family gatherings that we weren't invited to. Bars are still a new enough phenomenon to be a focal point in India's culture wars. In 2009, a group of women was physically attacked in a college-town bar by members of a conservative Hindu group who accused the women of acting "un-Indian." Government officials condemned the attack, and then, a few days later, India's health minister held a press conference to urge national prohibition, declaring, "The pub culture must end. It is not our culture."

Over the years I lived in Delhi, the city's public life improved dramatically as it opened up to more global influences. But even if young
people are hanging out more in malls and bars than ever before, family
remains the core of social life in India. Gatherings tend to take place
inside the home, and alcohol is not usually the focus since it is forbidden by both of India's major religions, Hinduism and Islam. In Manu's
Hindu codebook from the second century, drunkenness is listed
among the four worst sins—along with stealing gold, "defiling the bed"
of a religious teacher, and killing a Brahmin—and women are forbidden to drink.

After independence, several Indian states banned the sale and con-
sumption of liquor. It's still illegal in Gujarat, Gandhi's home state, out
of deference to his principled teetotaling. The ban has spawned a dangerous industry of bootlegging booze; a bad batch of illegal liquor
killed more than 130 people in Gujarat, in one of several such incidents in a single month in 2009. Home-brewed arrack—distilled from
palm, rice, or sugarcane—is cheap and easy to get. I'd see the slum
dwellers lining up outside the liquor stall a few streets away from my
apartment to buy plastic pouches of booze called *thaili,* which look like
snack-size potato chip bags. When the shop opened, at noon, the place
quickly became a frantic throng of shrill voices and skinny arms wav-
ing ten-rupee notes, the equivalent of twenty cents, at the hooch dis-
tributor. They'd put the pouches down the legs of their skinny pants
and then knock them back inside their rickshaws while waiting for
customers.

Delhi's middle classes buy their spirits at different stalls, known as
English Wine Shops, although wine is rarely on offer. Imported wine is
heavily taxed in India, and the domestic industry has been slow to take
off, partly because Indians typically drink before, not during, dinner.
More to the point, a bottle of whiskey costs a third as much as a bottle
of wine, even an Indian-made bottle, and it has three times the alcohol
content. *English wine* is actually a catchall term for *Indian-made Foreign
Liquor,* clumsy Indian bureaucratese that is commonly shorthanded to
"IMFL" by English-speaking Indians. It is branded under familiar
names, such as Smirnoff and Gordon's, but it pretty much all tastes the

same because most of it is distilled from molasses rather than the grain or juniper berries that are used in the West to make vodka and gin.

Delhi's discerning drinkers can either pay ten times the standard U.S. price for imported booze, or they can procure an exclusive membership at a place such as The Delhi Golf Club, whose wood-paneled bar features a view of the Mogul-monument-studded golf course. Here, uniformed waiters serve Bombay Sapphire gin, a brand manufactured outside India. Its name refers to the popularity of gin among the British Raj in India; they drank it with tonic water, which contains quinine, to protect against malaria. Club memberships are as highly coveted in today's India as they were among British officials, passed down from generation to generation of industrialists and military officials. One of my neighbors liked to joke that her parents would use her Delhi Golf Club membership as part of her dowry, the money or goods that women in India are expected to bring to the groom's family in marriage.

The Delhi Press Club, Vijay's favored drinking joint, attracts a rather less exclusive crowd: Indian journalists, almost all of them male and as hard-drinking, chain-smoking, and cuss-mouthed as American newspapermen of the 1950s. They throng the bar in crumpled button-downs, tossing back whiskeys and handfuls of spicy fried Bombay mix, and trying to best one another with tales of political scandal. The place is windowless, run-down, and raucous, with TV sets blaring Hindi news channels. When I walked in, a half-beat of silence fell across the smoky room as a number of the men paused to take note of the unlikely sight of a *feringhee* girl in their midst. It was worth just that—a glance—before they returned to their stories.

I wandered outside to the patio and found Vijay in the falling dusk. He was with the only other woman in the bar, whom I took to be Parvati. She was wearing a white *salwar kameez*, a wool shawl pulled around her shoulders against the late October chill. Her makeup was the traditional kind that Geeta disdained for Western-style colored eye shadow and lip gloss. For centuries, Indian women have lined their eyes with dramatic black kohl and painted a black or red *bindi* dot on their foreheads—women from upper-caste maharanis to 1930s Bollywood heroines. Parvati was dressed like a pious virgin, and yet, lined up on the table in front of her were a pack of Gold Flake cigarettes, a bottle of soda water, and a shot of amber-colored whiskey.

Vijay introduced her with a grand sweep of his hand. She was one of Delhi's best political reporters and one of the few women who'd been asked to join the press club, he boasted, then added, "She also really cares about issues, which is unusual among most of the journalist *choots* you see in here." Vijay's words slurred together boozily, and his English was peppered with Hindi profanities that he must have restrained himself from using during our interview; I soon learned that Hindi curses are an essential accessory among the Delhi Press Club set.

Parvati rolled her kohl-lined eyes at his effusive praise.

"*Arre*, boss, maybe so. But you know I was too lazy to fill out the form." Turning to me, she added, "We've been coming here for years, but I still use Vijay's membership. So much for the great honor of being asked to join."

She caught sight of the waiter scuttling among the rowdy tables in a gray Mao suit—the working man's uniform, a holdover from decades of socialism in India.

"Dev!" I was startled by the sudden power in her voice. Dev appeared swiftly beside our table, and I faltered, unsure what to order. Parvati waited half a beat before she commanded: "Start with some vegetarian snacks. How about *aloo chaat,* the potato stuff. And to drink?"

"What are you drinking?" I asked her.

"A peg of Seagram's Blenders Pride with soda." She used the Anglo-Indian term for a shot. "It's the best Indian-made whiskey. Or rather, it's the only drinkable one."

"That's not real Indian whiskey!" Vijay exclaimed, shoving his glass across the table. "This is. Royal Challenge."

I looked doubtfully at the two glasses lined up in front of me. Parvati stepped in to explain: Her brand, Seagram's, was one of the few Indian whiskies that was distilled with grain rather than molasses.

"In foreign markets, my brand, Royal Challenge, isn't even considered whiskey," Vijay continued. "Can you believe it? They can't sell whiskey made from molasses in Europe unless they call it something else."

Taking a sip, I wasn't surprised: The sweet, pungent stuff tasted nothing like what I knew as either scotch or bourbon. I smiled politely and decided not to get involved in the competition, since Vijay seemed as strong willed and passionate about whiskey as he was about caste. I ordered a beer.

As the waiter plunked our glasses down on the plastic table, Parvati leaned toward me like a practiced storyteller. She seemed eager to explain herself. Perhaps she could tell that I was trying to sort out her place in conservative Indian society; or maybe, because she considered herself something of an outsider, she felt a kinship with me.

"There are lots of people who immediately assume I'm a certain kind of woman when they see me smoking and drinking. But I don't give a crap about this pure virginal Mother India bollocks. I'm not even very Westernized or anything, but I don't see why I should have to act a certain way—"

"She doesn't give a damn what these judgmental Delhi wallahs think of her!" Vijay interrupted.

"It's true that I've learned not to care," Parvati said with a smile. "People are always surprised when they find out that I am not raised in some upscale Delhi household, because those women are much more likely to break away from society's expectations. In fact, I am a village girl. Really. I come from a tiny place in the Himalayan foothills." She scanned my face to make sure I was listening. Her eyes were more complicated than the brown I'd first taken them to be. Flecked with yellow-green and hazel, they glowed like a cat's when the light hit them.

"We didn't have any money—my father worked for the government—but mine was one of the few upper-caste families in the village. My father wore his sacred Brahmin thread under his clothes every day of his life, like every good Brahmin is supposed to. Everyone in the village knew it was there. His last name, my name, is clearly a Brahmin name, Pande."

According to Parvati, her teachers tolerated her bad behavior as a child because of her family's high standing in the village, punishing other kids more harshly. She grew up believing she could get away with almost anything and still achieve whatever she wanted.

"I wasn't a good student, but I had my family name, which made it easier to get into universities. My father taught me English and helped me apply to college. I wouldn't be here otherwise; I wouldn't even be able to talk to you like this, in your language."

"Also, her father thought that his daughter should have ambitions beyond marriage," Vijay added. "But how did he get that way, to have those beliefs about women?" He looked at me as though he was really quizzing me. When I shook my head, he flicked his hand impatiently and answered himself. "Because her father was also educated, that's how. In these small villages, it's still true that only the high castes are well educated."

For centuries, Vijay said, high-caste Hindus have dominated Indian institutions. At the time of India's independence, Dalits accounted for as much as 25 percent of the population in some provinces and were represented by a sole untouchable minister in parliament. Brahmins, who made up only 2 percent of the population, held fully two-thirds of the seats. The vast majority of India's prime ministers have been Brahmins, leading British prime minister Winston Churchill to scorn Indian politics for being dominated by "one major community."

In recent decades, affirmative action policies and better education opportunities have broken the upper-caste stranglehold on Indian politics and helped create a small but substantial Dalit middle class. In 1997, a Dalit was named president of India, a position with great symbolic significance if little actual power. One of India's most powerful national parties, the BSP, rose to prominence on a platform of dignity and self-respect for Dalits. The leader of the party, Mayawati, is instantly recognizable across India by her single name. She styles herself as a defender of the oppressed—at her early rallies, she famously urged fellow Dalits to beat higher-caste people with their shoes. She has repeatedly been elected chief minister of the largest state in India, Uttar Pradesh.

Parvati pulled her shawl around her shoulders.

"This cold weather reminds me of the hills where I grew up." She gave Vijay a moony look.

He ducked his head shyly.

"Parvati's name means 'she of the mountains.' Isn't that nice? We both love it in the hills. If only it wasn't so bloody restrictive to live there . . ." His voice trailed off.

Not for the first time that night, I wondered about their relationship. They had the natural ease of a couple who had heard each other's stories many times. But I hadn't seen his hand on hers all evening, and despite their tipsiness, their chairs remained scooted a prim distance apart. It seemed unlikely they could be married, either to each other or to anyone else. But Parvati was a couple of years older than me, and Vijay was approaching forty, so if he was her boyfriend, they were even more unusual.

I didn't have to wait long before Parvati solved the mystery for me.

"Stay at my place tonight. I'll drop Vijay home, and we'll be able to chat in the morning."

Apparently, she not only lived separately from her boyfriend but also drove him around; when we got outside, she slid into the driver's seat of the small white car parked outside the club. I folded my feet up in the tight backseat, trying to process all the ways that my new friend broke Indian norms. Parvati seemed unusually self-assured about her decision to defy Indian stigmas against women drinking and smoking. I thought of how Geeta occasionally donned a miniskirt and flirted with boys, and those rebellions seemed trifling in comparison. Sometimes, she'd allow one of her male friends to buy her an Old Monk rum and Coke, the sweet and not very alcoholic drink of choice of many Delhi college girls. She always claimed to get tipsy on the first sip, as though to emphasize her daintiness. Parvati, on the other hand, had imbibed multiple pegs of whiskey and at least a pack of cigarettes over the course of the evening. At least in my own boozy state, this seemed an apt symbol of her break from tradition; it was as though Parvati occupied her own moral universe, outside mainstream values and norms.

I was so absorbed by these thoughts that I didn't consider that a night ride with the whiskey drinker might not be prudent. During the day, Delhi traffic operates according to its own organic logic. Streams of cycle-pulled rickshaws, street-vendor carts, and imported BMWs meet and glide seamlessly between lanes; they rarely honk when they cut one another off, nor do they move fast enough to inflict major damage when there is a collision. At night, the unwritten rules of this traffic ballet expire. Vehicles pick up speed in the empty streets and new obstacles assert themselves. Parvati seemed not to notice the roaming packs of dogs, the steaming piles of the homeless stretched out to sleep on the medians. She cruised through the red lights, chattering away with one eye on me in the rearview mirror.

I gasped: Out of the gray nighttime fog rose the lumbering rump of an elephant, indistinguishable from the night air. High above it was the red bobbing turban of its rider. Parvati swerved, waking Vijay from his passenger-seat nap. In the beam of her headlights, I saw a hand-painted sign strung on the elephant's tail, the size and shape of a license plate: I LOVE MY INDIA, it announced.

Parvati guffawed with relief and adrenaline.

"I don't even have a license!"

"Are you serious?" I gulped, and fished around the backseat for a seat belt, surrendering to my stereotypical *feringhee* fear of Indian driving. Parvati cackled at my alarm.

"There's no belt in the backseat of Indian cars. Welcome to India, my friend. No one wears a seat belt, and hardly anyone has a license."

I noticed that like many Delhi taxi drivers, she'd pulled her seat belt loosely around her chest but hadn't clipped it in. She said she did so to avoid the fines the cops had started enforcing on drivers who didn't wear them.

"They don't stop you if you look like you're wearing it. Anyway, if they do, it's no big deal. You just hand over a hundred rupees baksheesh."

I decided not to tell her that my concern was whether we'd get back alive, not whether she had to pay a fine.

We were headed for Trans-Yamuna Delhi, the distant suburbs east of the river. On the other side of the bridge, the cityscape stretched into pocket-sized fields of crops that were cultivated between small factories and low-income housing blocks. Vijay stumbled out of the car at his apartment complex, and Parvati drove us around the block to her place. As she led me up the open staircase of her whitewashed concrete building, I realized that they live in the only acceptable way an unmarried couple can in Delhi: separate apartments in adjacent buildings. Parvati said they hung out together most evenings, sometimes spending the night together, "if the circumstances are right." That sounded foreboding, but I couldn't be sure; I'd become accustomed to hearing a different meaning from the spoken one.

"I like having my own space so my mother can come stay with me. It's tiny, but unlike Vijay's place, it is very, very clean." That was definitely the adjective that came to mind as I looked around her box of an apartment. Lit by fluorescent tubes, the three rooms had the sanitized glare of a hospital. "My mom comes to stay with me for six months of the year, and she is obsessed with purity. Some kind of Brahminical austerity."

She handed me a white Victorian-style nightgown, so crisply ironed that it felt starched, and we passed out on the large daybed that took up the bedroom's entire floor space.

When Parvati tugged open the curtains the next morning, the sun was already searingly bright, even at seven A.M. and close to winter. She brought *chai* in china teacups, steaming with cardamom and ginger, and a thick roll of several newspapers to flip through. Hardly anyone savors India's tabloid-style papers slowly; most of the stories are no more than a couple of paragraphs long and have little context or history. Parvati was an especially speedy news skimmer. She peeled past the entertainment and sports headlines that so often litter the front pages and found a story she was looking for inside, an update about a politician caught on video accepting wads of rupee notes. She guffawed as she read out details of his political humiliation.

A wrinkled brown skin formed on top of my *chai* as it cooled. I pushed it to one side. Its steam, rising in a slot of sun, made me feel comforted and much less alone than I'd felt in many months. I'd first spoken to Parvati only twelve hours before, but I already hoped I'd be able to talk to her as I would to my girlfriends back in New York. I had an instinct that she shared something of my own values.

I wondered for a moment whether it was wise to bring up her relationship with Vijay so early on in our friendship. I've never been especially subtle or oblique, which I liked to excuse by saying that those traits do not suit the job of a journalist. From what I'd seen, Parvati was even blunter than I was. Because she'd talked frankly about one of the greatest Indian taboos—caste—I hoped she would be as easy about discussing another—sex and love.

She looked up sharply at the question, though.

"That is a difficult question, Miranda." She returned to her paper. I raised my eyebrows in mild surprise. It was several minutes before she spoke again. "You know, I haven't ever been to the U.S.—or anywhere outside India, actually. But from what I can tell, you have many acceptable kinds of relationships there. In case you haven't realized, there is really only one way in India. And I've decided to opt out." There was a finality in her voice that referred not just to the decision but to our conversation.

Later that morning, as she was dropping me off at home, Parvati pulled over at a roadside tobacco stand. She rolled down the window and shouted to get the attention of the kid working at the stall: "*Han-ji!* Hello!" He was maybe fourteen, his bony brown shoulders jutting high out of his white tank top. He stared at Parvati dolefully. She lifted her hand out of the window at him in a questioning gesture, but he didn't move. She cursed under her breath.

"*Gaand ke dhakan.* This happens half the time I try to buy smokes in this town. These village boys land up in Delhi and act like it's bloody illegal for women to smoke."

She pulled herself out of the car. She was wearing another conservative *salwar kameez* set, complete with a matching scarf looped across her chest. The boy gummed a wad of *paan,* sizing her up as she approached, as though trying to place her in the hierarchy of the world as he knew it.

"Ten Gold Flake cigarettes," Parvati demanded in Hindi. Like everyone else, she pronounced her favored brand of cigarettes "Gold

Flack." He didn't move. She raised her voice to full volume, drowning out the horns and cow moos of the market: "Ten Gold Flack!"

I watched nervously from the car window, half expecting her to grab a pack from the shelf and throw it at him. After a long moment, the teenager leaned over, disgorged his mouthful of *paan* into the street, and set a pack on the counter. Parvati let it lie there for a moment. Then she snapped it up.

"Thank you, *ji*," she said, her voice full of irony as she used the term of respect. She pulled a cigarette out and lit it with the lighter that was tied to the boy's counter with a piece of string. The lighter tube flashed red and blue, and I could see the colors reflected in his blank eyes. Parvati slammed her money on the counter and marched back to the car, her lit cigarette dangling from her mouth.

CHAPTER 5

Cooked by Brahmin Hands

The crows were cawing anxiously in the top branches of the *gulmohar*, a tree with fire-red blossoms that Indians call "the flame of the forest." The tree arched gracefully over the apartment building I'd just moved into, though it looked anything but graceful now, as the winds stripped it of its fleshy blooms. They landed on the concrete with pregnant thuds. An August monsoon storm was coming. The skies darkened, the birds disappeared, and the air became heavy and silent, like the interior of a mangrove swamp. Then the rain came, lashing and slanting viciously at the windows. The drains quickly clogged, filling the gutters with rainwater and stinging my nostrils with the putrid sewage smell.

I saw Joginder dash toward the market, his head covered with a plastic bag. A delivery boy teetered through the stalled traffic on a bicycle, precariously balancing large metal canisters of gasoline on each side. A taxi swayed through the flood, the driver poking his head out the window to navigate, his hair slick with rain. He couldn't see through the wall of water on the windshield; his wipers must have been broken. By evening, the last of summer's *gulmohar* blossoms were bloody smears on the pavement.

I'd moved around the corner from my old *barsati* in Nizamuddin, and although my new apartment was fully indoors, we still couldn't stave off the ooze and creep of the humid season. The spices disintegrated into a soggy mash in their leaky jars. The chapati bloomed with fungus just hours after Radha made it. Brilliant green mold rose up in a shimmering line along the windowsills. Millipedes scuttled along the walls, and hordes of mosquitoes hovered around the sink. The transparent geckos gorged themselves all day on the insects in my kitchen.

My second Delhi apartment was four times as expensive as the *barsati,* which horrified Geeta. Until she saw the place, that is. It was "family sized," she gasped—three bedrooms, three bathrooms, each with Western-style toilets and actual showers—with an air-conditioning unit in almost every room. It was definitely not the kind of apartment typically occupied by a single girl. I'd justified it to the landlord by saying that my husband would be spending half the year there, but I didn't really expect Benjamin to be around that much, which meant I'd have a lot of space to myself.

The thing that I loved best about the apartment was the inverter that came with it. I don't know how I made it for two years in India without this particular luxury: a device that stores up battery power and switches itself on when the electricity goes out. Because Delhi's electricity supply is so unreliable, an inverter is as essential as a ceiling fan or a window screen, even though only those in the upper middle class can afford one. For all the discomforts that Delhi's masses endure, the chronic power cuts seemed the least bearable to me. The inverter is rarely robust enough to power an air conditioner, but it can sustain a couple of fans—and during the almost-daily power cuts of a Delhi summer, a fan's breeze was air from the flapping wings of a blessed angel.

In my *barsati,* the chronic blackouts meant I'd spend my nights awake, sweaty and helpless to do anything other than pray that the Delhi electricity board would get its act together. After an hour of such frustration, I'd flee downstairs to Nanima's slightly cooler apartment, where she and Geeta were inevitably up, too; without any air circulating, sleep was not an option. Geeta and I would push open the windows in the hope of a breeze and watch the neighbors filtering onto their patios. Often, they'd join Joginder and his family on charpoys in the alley, where the pitch darkness was unrelieved by even the narrow beam of a streetlight.

In my new apartment, I realized, I might sleep straight through the power cuts. I tried not to rub it in to Geeta as I showed her around, because I could tell she was already jealous of the new place. I think she would have loved to move into the spare bedroom, but she couldn't leave Nanima. Nevertheless, Geeta made it clear that she intended to spend a lot of time there. She decided that this was a good time for me to learn how to manage my household better than I had in my *barsati*, which she considered chaotic and understaffed. Geeta appointed herself a sort of household advisor for my new Nizamuddin life. It wasn't a position I'd realized I needed to fill, but Geeta was determined that I'd be a proper Indian homemaker yet.

The first step was finding me an Indian woman to show me how it was done. That was easy enough: Geeta quickly got a friend from work, Priya, to move into my extra bedroom. Like Geeta, she was a modern girl from a middle-class family who had been "living alone" in Delhi for a couple years. Her parents were only two hours' drive from the city, and she spent most weekends with them. During the week, Geeta tasked her with showing me how to run an Indian household. This arrangement had multiple benefits, as Geeta saw it. I wouldn't be as lonely in my huge family-sized apartment, and I'd have someone to contribute toward my rent, which, at four hundred dollars a month, she considered irresponsibly profligate.

Radha and I walked over together the day I moved in. The skinny neighborhood boys skittered past us with boxes of my clothes on their heads, perspiring through their polyester shirts to earn their three-dollar moving fee. Radha lumbered beside me, scowling occasionally in the direction of the steel cage in which I carried my howling cats. She was grumpy: She'd lost an argument that morning in which she'd ordered me to leave my cats behind, on the premise that I should not allow them to dirty a second apartment.

When we stepped inside, her disgusted incomprehension fell away. She stood in awed silence, as though taking in a Gothic cathedral. Then she walked through the empty rooms, exclaiming softly to herself. The place seemed bigger than I remembered, now that I considered that my maid would have to sweep and mop the long stretches of white tile. After she'd peered inside every closet door, Radha sank down on her haunches to digest.

"It's going to be lots more work, *deedee*"—I was about to apologize when she looked up at me, and I saw that her eyes were shining with pride—"but it is so beautiful. I've never seen a more beautiful house, *deedee.*"

Radha took my apartment upgrade as evidence that I was moving up in the world, and according to the traditional master-servant equation, this meant she was advancing, too. Maybe she'd brag to her friends about the mansion her rich *feringhee* employer had moved into, I thought; perhaps it would ease some of the humiliation of cleaning someone else's floors.

The news that I'd have an Indian housemate blunted Radha's glee, though. She knew that with an Indian employer around, her reign as head of my household would come to an end, because no Indian woman would endure her imperious behavior. Geeta had long suspected that Radha took advantage of me because I didn't know how to manage her. She also thought I was crazy to have so few people working for me. It was high time to correct both ills. Like the stereotype of the bossy Indian housewife, Geeta began piling on unasked-for advice about how I should supervise my new home. Under the pretext that Priya wouldn't be comfortable there without some semblance of middle-class living, Geeta instructed me to expand my employee roster.

"Having people to do things for you is one of the advantages of India, Miranda. No need to feel guilty about it; just start hiring."

With Geeta's help, I soon had Asma to wash the staircase, Ajay to do odd jobs around the apartment, and K.K., my favorite from the taxi stand, as a part-time driver. Finding people willing to serve your needs, however specific, is never difficult in a city full of the chronically underemployed.

Learning how to oversee them was more of a challenge. Even with Geeta and Priya's help, it only seemed to make my life more complicated to have servants around. I'd never managed anyone before, let alone negotiated the complex caste hierarchies among Indian employees, and I was surprised at how much patience and skill it required. For the first time, I could sympathize with Indian housewives' complaints about how overworked they are—not from doing the chores themselves but simply from managing the servants. I could also understand why expats often hire from embassy-approved lists. Such employees have had a police check, can cook fettuccine Alfredo, and are supposed to take a professional attitude toward their work.

Most Indian servants behave like poorer cousins who have agreed to be your slave for a year. To Geeta and Priya, who'd grown up with full-time cooks, maids, and drivers, the employer-servant relationship seemed perfectly natural. Both hailed from middle-class Brahmin families, so it went without saying that others would do their dirty work for them, but since both came from the low end of the middle class, they had relied on underage workers from the villages: easily available, cheap, pliant labor. In many Indian homes, servants are essentially indentured. They are kept on call day and night, housed in a tiny slit of a room in the back of the house, and granted meals and vacation time only on their masters' whims. Yet these relationships are often affectionate. Geeta's childhood cook, for instance, had witnessed all the major events of her life—always present, never participating—and she considered him part of her family. Of course, she still had to keep him in line.

"You give a finger and they'll take an arm," Geeta informed me. "Even the best servants. You need to show them who's in charge." She couldn't help but add, "Which you have not done with Radha." I protested that Radha was a good worker, but my self-appointed household advisor was unmoved. "Many things are difficult in India, Miranda, but finding a good worker is not one of them. You're paying Radha what she'd earn working for a whole family. She knows you aren't going to fire her, because you let her get away with anything."

It was true; I'd failed to play the role of chiding memsahib to Radha. Now that Geeta had urged me to hire K.K. part-time, I was finding it similarly awkward to manage him. Still, having him around was a panacea to many of the hardships of being a single lady in Delhi. He saved me hours I would have spent bargaining with rickshaw wallahs; he could understand my American-accented Hindi; and he knew Delhi's streets, which was important because I had to drive all over the city for interviews, and the geography of the city still flummoxed me. K.K. also lent me protection from late-night eve-teasing dangers. When I stumbled out of a bar into the hot glow of a Delhi midnight, he was always waiting for me outside. I'd rap on the car window, interrupting his sleepy cell-phone prattle with his wife back in his village. He'd twinkle his eyes at me, never judgmental or annoyed, no matter how late it was.

"I am paid for the waiting, madam," he'd say when I apologized.

If Radha knew the color of my underwear and what I looked like in the morning, K.K. knew me in other intimate ways. He knew how late I stayed out and in whose company; he could tell when I was frustrated or sad, and when I was, he'd sometimes crack jokes at me in the rearview mirror to cheer me up. K.K. and I had quickly bonded over the fact that we were the same age. I kept up a running commentary on this simple alliance between us—"You have three children and I have none!" and "You own two houses in the village, and I own nothing more than a bicycle back in New York!"—because it would win me a flash of his charismatic smile in the mirror, and I would feel myself soften into his reflection.

No matter how much I asked him about his wife and kids, there was no way I could ever know K.K. as well as he knew me, or make our relationship more equal. Still, he made an effort to open up his life to me, unlike Radha, who seemed scarcely able to endure my lists of questions. Once, when my mother was visiting, K.K. drove us three hours outside Delhi to his village—"the most best village in India!"—and put us up for an entire weekend in his family's farmhouse. He stocked up on bottled water, because he knew *feringhees* couldn't drink from the village well, and whiskey, because he knew Western ladies drank alcohol, although the idea of my mother—however adventurous—downing shots of Royal Challenge is in the realm of the ridiculous.

When we arrived, K.K. sent his wife off to bring us fresh buffalo milk in grimy metal cups. There isn't much point in drinking bottled water if you're also drinking unpasteurized milk in cups teeming with bacteria, but my mother and I forced it down, warm and frothy and animal-smelling. The satisfaction on K.K.'s face when I complimented the beverage was worth the resultant days of diarrhea, though I'm not sure my mother would agree. She was grayish green for most of the weekend.

In his farmhouse, K.K. was the confident master of his own domain, receiving foot massages from his wife and ordering his younger brothers to take us on a tour of his fields. But to show his respect for us, he would eat only after we did; he and his brothers sat with us, overseeing each bite. K.K.'s wife waited behind us—her strong body tensed, her hand on the serving spoon—to dish out more *matter paneer* or egg curry when one of the men saw space open up on our plates. When my mother heard the buffalo baying outside the window, she'd lurch to the pukka Western toilet that K.K. had proudly shown us— complete with toilet seat and lock on the door. I forced myself to eat for both of us.

In the morning, after stuffing us with his wife's *paranthas*—thick, fried breads filled with cauliflower or potato—K.K. swallowed a few mouthfuls of *chai* and nodded a formal farewell to his family assembled at the gate of his feudal farmhouse. Then he opened the car doors for his two memsahibs, and I was no longer the guest in his domain, but once again his employer.

When I reported from Pakistan or Afghanistan, my drivers would join me in casual restaurants for kebabs, but that isn't acceptable in class-obsessed India. K.K. insisted he preferred the drivers' canteens to sitting at a table with me in a restaurant. I can remember us eating together only once in public. Even though it was a cheap roadside café, so deeply entrenched are India's hierarchies that the tea-boy actually scoffed when my driver sat down beside me and ordered *chai*. I wanted to smack that boy, but K.K.'s lowered eyes spoke of such shame that I quieted myself. It wouldn't have helped his case to have a *feringhee* girl trying to defend his manhood.

Geeta and Priya had been conspiring. One morning, Priya informed me that she and my household advisor had decided it was time to present Radha with her own key to the apartment.

"We've decided it's the best way to give her a sense of her responsibility to the household," she said.

I'd long ago decided to surrender to the two of them when it came to household stuff. When it came to managing the staff, they were almost always right. When I handed Radha the key, a rare smile escaped as she tucked it into her *choli,* as though her smile had been released with a puff of air from inside her sari blouse.

"Now I won't have to wait for you to wake up and let me in," she said.

Priya didn't allow Radha to linger in the moment, though. She and Geeta had a precise, multistep plan of action, and she'd reserved this morning for informing Radha of her new status and the accompanying duties. Next up was to inform Radha that she was to be responsible for buying the vegetables and dusting the bookshelves and tables. She was to adopt the role of press wallah as well as *dhobi* and iron our clothes after washing them and hanging them to dry. No more would our clothes smell of the press wallah's hot coals; Priya had an electric iron, and she dedicated several mornings to showing Radha how to plug it in and work the buttons.

Last of all, Priya informed our maid that she would have the honor of cooking for us. Upper-caste Hindus consider the kitchen the most sacred and pure part of the house, and, Priya reminded Radha, many do not like non-Brahmins to even set foot inside the kitchen. Priya made a real effort to impress on Radha that she should be flattered by this new chore.

"I grew up with a Brahmin cook, and I prefer to eat food cooked by other Brahmins. So it is only because you are Brahmin that we want you to cook for us. Geeta will be having meals here too, and she's traditional like me. In fact, she will prefer to take her meals here now, because Nanima's maid isn't a Brahmin like you."

Radha's expression was solemn. She knew well how momentous this occasion was: being handed Brahminical responsibilities by her new Brahmin employer. My maid already proudly adhered to the strictest upper-class rules about maintaining the purity of the kitchen. She'd only eat food she'd cooked herself or that had been prepared by Brahmin hands on the grounds of a temple. After her husband died, years before, Radha had restricted her diet further; Brahmin widows are supposed to live a life of deprivation. Even on the hottest of days, she would refuse a glass of water from my apparently impure kitchen, preferring to go thirsty until she could drink water from her own. It didn't make any sense, because her water came from the same filthy municipal source as the water in my taps, and, unlike mine, was not filtered. But I guess she believed her Brahmin sink somehow made the city water more pure.

I had to hand it to my household advisory committee: Radha actually thanked Priya for adding to her workload. I'd never have guessed it would happen, but the new tasks seemed to make my uppity servant feel more important: She started arriving to work earlier, humming to herself as she set the day's vegetables on the counter and planned out our meals.

We invited Geeta over for our first Radha meal: a creamy spinach dish called *palak paneer*, slightly sweet tomato chutney, and hand-rolled chapatis. Although it was pure vegetarian North Indian food, cooked by the immaculate hand of a fellow Brahmin, Geeta just picked at it.

"It's hard for me to get used to Bihari cooking." She curled her lip as she said the word Bihari. "My mother taught me our family recipes. That's real food—the Punjabi dishes I grew up with. Not too spicy, not too oily. Priya will tell you. She's just as particular as I am about having her own kind of regional cooking."

Priya nodded sympathetically, though I was relieved to see that she'd made more progress than Geeta had on her plate. I dreaded having to explain to Radha in the morning why so much of her food had gone uneaten. I didn't really understand how they could have such a problem with Radha's cooking—to me, Punjabi vegetable dishes tasted scarcely different from Bihari ones—but I'd learned that many Indians have exacting palates. Radha was honored to cook for us, for instance—just as long as she could cook the dishes she'd grown up eating. She would argue fervently that Bihari food was better than Punjabi food, as though it were an objective matter.

Food has long been the custodian of regional, religious, and caste specificity in India. It is only in the last three decades that globalization has started to take its uniforming toll on Indian cuisine. In the years that Geeta had lived in Delhi, her friends and colleagues had started eating out more regularly. Even in restaurants that advertise themselves as "pure veg" or "pure Brahmin," they cannot know the caste of the kitchen workers. Geeta had made it clear that she considered this a negative side effect of India's modernization; still, she wasn't a purist like Radha, who claimed she'd never once been spiritually polluted by "taking a meal outside."

Parvati had little in common with Radha other than her preference for traditional home-cooked vegetarian food. She and Vijay would happily "take whiskey" at the Delhi Press Club, but rarely would they eat there, because they considered restaurant food inferior in quality and cleanliness. Parvati went to extremes to keep globalization out of her kitchen. Like Radha, she shunned store-bought and packaged ingredients. She made her own yogurt out of fresh milk, and chapati out of wheat she bought in bulk; the vegetables she prepared were all fresh and locally grown. Her kitchen was as low-tech and traditional as Radha's: She cooked exclusively out of three tin pots and had no electric mixers or processors.

Parvati was also particular about doing the cooking herself—she only occasionally outsourced *sous*-chef duties to her part-time maid. She never used a cookbook; she'd memorized dishes by watching her mother as a child. And yet each of the North Indian dishes she made—lentil dals, bean dishes, vegetable curries—required half a dozen spices to achieve a subtle complexity of flavors. Even though she used the same spices night after night, somehow each dish tasted different from the other. She'd begin by roasting them in a pan, then grind them with a mortar and pestle; she'd fry them in a specific order to achieve the right blend of flavors. Parvati measured in pinches, handfuls, and lidfuls and seasoned the dishes instinctively, by taste and smell.

It was intimidating, watching these two very different women roast, grind, fry, and stir. Although my mother had cooked fairly complicated vegetarian meals for us growing up, and a lot of Indian food, it didn't compare. A Western kitchen inevitably includes canned and processed ingredients to save money and cut down on cooking time. In any case, I hadn't picked up my mother's skills in the kitchen. When friends had stopped by my Brooklyn apartment, I'd offered them a glass of wine and some nuts.

In Delhi, I was alarmed to discover that no social call is complete until a hot meal is offered. Of course, this is less of a burden in a city where almost everyone employs a cook, but starting the day out by planning major meals with Radha was more than I wanted to take on. It was easier to plead American ignorance and let Parvati entertain me.

Because Vijay's apartment was larger, we'd spend a couple of nights a week there. I loved staring out into the dusk from his window at the glowing white dome of the sixteenth-century Humayun's Tomb, far away in the center of the city. We'd replace our outdoor shoes with clean plastic *chappals* from the pile Vijay kept by the door, and Parvati would exchange her *salwar kameez* for a T-shirt and a pair of his knee-length shorts. She'd only expose her legs if it was just the three of us, but even so I found it disconcerting—that's how quickly I'd become accustomed to women's lower parts always being covered.

One night, Parvati stuck a cassette of 1950s Bollywood songs into the tape deck—they both refused to buy CD players, let alone iPods. We headed into the kitchen to start dinner before Vijay got home from work. Because his kitchen windows didn't close completely and there were no storage cupboards, my task was to rinse the dust off the pans while Parvati took a blunt knife to an onion. I found myself thinking of the fancy tools most Westerners rely on in the kitchen, and considered how different my own experience of food was from hers. She was surprised when I said that most urban Americans grow up eating many different types of cuisine and buying vegetables without any idea where they are imported from.

"I guess we are still a very insular country compared to the U.S. or Europe," she mused. "Maybe it's because India was colonized for an entire millennium: first by Muslim invaders, then by the British. We held on to whatever we could of our regional and religious specificity. Most Indians don't think a meal counts unless it involves rice or chapati."

"But that's totally changed now," I prompted.

"It's true. We are in love with your American fast food. College kids rush to McDonald's after class to eat their McAloo Tikkis and all. But you know what? I guarantee you they all go home and eat rice or roti bread with their families. They all want a proper Indian meal."

It took McDonald's decades to break into the Indian market. When it finally succeeded, it was by Indianizing its brand. McDonald's adopted the slogan "As Indian as you and me" and catered its menu to Indian tastes—no beef burgers, and a long list of spicy vegetarian items. Now every Delhi McDonald's is crammed with teenagers celebrating a very Indian version of globalization. Parvati, predictably, found it disgusting.

"All this makes me feel like I belong to the old India. Do you know that before I went to college I'd never tasted any kind of food except Indian? When I landed up in a bigger town, to start college, one of the first things I did was try out the Chinese fast-food place. I'll never forget the taste of those greasy noodles—so different from anything I'd had before."

When Parvati and I were alone, the conversation almost always turned to her childhood, a subject we both loved. In spite of her unconventional lifestyle, Parvati believed much was right about her traditional village upbringing and liked to talk about it, as though to come to terms with how much she'd changed and the person she'd become.

"We lived in a big joint family, so my mother and aunts had to cook enormous quantities of food. Hot meals a few times a day and every-thing from scratch—that was the only way. I loved it when my mother made green mango chutney: She'd lay out salted slices of unripe mango in the courtyard so they would dry in the sun. My brothers and I grabbed it when she wasn't looking."

I tried to picture Parvati as a village girl in a government-issued school uniform.

"My mother never once cut my hair. Every day she braided it down my back. By the time I got to be a teenager, it was below my waist. That was how all the girls in the village had their hair, so naturally I hated it. One day, I hopped on a bus to the next town and got it all chopped off. Just like that." Her mother didn't speak to her for days, she said, beam-ing with satisfaction at the memory.

It struck me that Parvati had reverted to the village-girl hairstyle in her adult life; she almost always wore it in a long braid down her back now.

I could understand wanting to stand out from the family; as a teenager, I'd done my best to resist my parents' view of life, too—but, to my constant annoyance, my aesthetic and political choices had hewed pretty closely to theirs. They'd scarcely blinked when I dyed my hair red, pierced my ears multiple times using a needle, an ice cube, and a potato, and spent my high school weekends slam-dancing at punk rock shows. I'd had to work hard to come up with ways to piss them off, like cutting school and dating an alcoholic high school dropout. Of course, none of that was anything serious, whereas Parvati's rebellions had ac-tually shaken the foundations of her family traditions.

She tossed the diced onion into a pan already fragrant with mustard and cumin seeds and said that as a teenager, she'd once confronted her grandfather, the grand patriarch of her Brahmin clan. He was showing them a diagram of their family tree. When she saw that her two broth-ers were listed under her father's name, she asked her grandfather why her own name was missing.

"He told me, 'Well, *betee,* that's how it is with women. When you marry, you will go to another family, and you will no longer have this name.' So I just said very respectfully, 'Dada, I am not going anywhere.

This is my family. Please put my name in.' And he did. He wrote it in under my father's."

After that, Parvati declared that she wouldn't take her husband's name even if she did get married. She also informed her family that she did not want them to arrange her into marriage, the only acceptable destiny for a village girl.

"My father convinced the rest of the family to let me be. He was the one who understood that I am different. Now I guess the family just considers me a lost cause. My dad was the only one who would have dared to ask me about Vijay. The rest of them are afraid of me."

The dark lines of kohl under Parvati's eyes had smudged where she'd rubbed them, giving her a haunted aspect. She had rarely mentioned her father, other than to say that she'd adored him and she wished I could have met him before he died a couple of years before. I wondered whether his death had somehow made it easier for her to refuse to meet the family's expectations.

She and Vijay had been together for four years, but I'd never seen them hold hands or nestle up to each other. Their Press Club friends must have assumed they were a couple, but I don't think Parvati talked about him to anyone. In India, I was discovering, liaisons are given the "don't ask, don't tell" treatment, and even close girlfriends don't confide in each other about their romantic lives. Sometimes, Parvati would call Vijay by a Hindi endearment, but he seemed ill at ease with her displays of affection. At the end of an evening in his apartment, she'd occasionally slide over to Vijay, but he'd remain rigid in his seat. It made me wonder why they didn't just get married for the sake of practicality, if nothing else.

The earthy smell of cauliflower curry filled the kitchen. Parvati left it simmering and poured ghee, clarified butter, into another pan to start on the next dish. I worked up my nerve.

"Have you guys ever considered doing a live-in?"

Parvati tossed a handful of cumin seeds into the mortar and leaned hard on the pestle, grinding them into powder.

"You know what?" she said, her voice live with anger. "Forget call centers and fast food, okay? This country is stuck in medieval times in so many ways. The trouble you had here, trying to get an apartment—it's typical. If I was to live with Vijay, I would have to say we were married. Otherwise it would just be so much worse."

Although she'd been living in her building for several years, Parvati said, her landlord still asked when her family was going to find a husband for her. Her neighbors were a little scandalized by the unmarried lady who worked in an office, drove her own car, and regularly entertained a male visitor. She said they would wait to hear her footsteps on the stairs, and then swing open their doors and invite her in for *chai.*

"Believe me, I always tell them I'm too busy."

"That doesn't sound so bad to me," I said. "I like that sense of community you have in Delhi."

Parvati had a habit of swiping her loose strands of hair back with her fingers when she was annoyed.

"You have to realize what it is they *want* from me, Miranda. It's not just nice neighborly stuff. I know they will find a way to ask why I am alone. The moment they have a scrap of information, the rumors will start flying. Next thing you know, they'll be calling me a slut behind my back."

I thought about it.

"It must mean you have to put up a lot of walls."

Parvati came from a village where everyone knew everything; having escaped to Delhi, she had no intention of explaining herself to the people around her. But my own break had been from a life of not especially belonging anywhere. In Brooklyn, my only reason to talk to my neighbors had been to complain if they left their trash in the hall. It was already different in Nizamuddin, and even though I knew I wouldn't ever really fit in, I wasn't about to let go of the hope of familiarity.

Parvati poured herself a whiskey from the bottle on the kitchen counter and gave me a sour smile.

"Just you wait. You'll see. Delhi is an aggressive, conservative place. To survive on your own, you have to be a bitch."

· · ·

Diwali was coming, the biggest Hindu celebration of the year. Geeta cautioned that although it's traditionally known as the festival of lights, in Delhi, Diwali is all about noise.

"In the old times," she said, referring, as she often did, to a simpler India of the unspecified past, "it was supposed to be a celebration of good prevailing over evil. Now people have too much of money. They aren't satisfied with candles—they go crazy bursting firecrackers."

A week before the festival began, I started to wish I'd gone with her to Patiala for the holiday after all. Delhi became an explosives free-for-all, the noise intensifying each night, so that by the time the festival arrived, it felt like a full-scale insurgency. There was no city-sponsored fireworks display, just black vapors spreading out over the dusty flat plain of the city. In fact, the pollution and noise got so bad that in subsequent years, the city initiated a public campaign against firecrackers and limited their availability.

My cats retreated to a far corner of the apartment. I felt like huddling with them under a sheet until morning, but Parvati's mother was visiting, and they'd cooked a special meal of festival foods. I forced myself out of the apartment when I heard K.K. pull up with a squeal. He had his own stockpile of firecrackers on the passenger seat and was eager to get back to the taxi stand to set them off.

"Top-class crackers, Miss Mirindaah! Pukka quality, making many bangs all in one go." K.K. sped us through the smoky streets, only adding to the sensation that we were trying to escape to safety through a war zone.

Parvati's place was a white sanctuary, lit only by small oil lamps and flashes of color from the firecrackers outside. She and her mother were on the bed, which served as a sort of family den, much like Joginder and Maniya's charpoy. Parvati's mother was a tiny, elegant woman in a crisp white sari, her hair neatly combed back from her face. I folded my hands into a respectful gesture of greeting: "*Namaste*, Auntie."

"*Namaste,*" she replied, and then corrected herself with an English hello. I sat down and practiced my Hindi sentence structures on her until Parvati rescued us both by reverting to English. Her mother picked up a Hindi-language magazine.

Although Parvati's father had learned English in high school, her mother's education had ended in the fifth grade, when she was expected to prepare for marriage by mastering domestic skills. You wouldn't know it from educated middle-class circles in Delhi and Mumbai, but fewer than a third of Indians speak English. There are twenty-one other official languages in India, not to mention 844 officially recognized dialects and thousands of other unofficial ones.

English was, of course, the language of the British colonialists, but Indians used English words to communicate with foreign traders as far back as the seventeenth century. They spoke a pidgin dialect known as *Firangi,* which has the same root as *feringhee.* During the independence movement, Mahatma Gandhi called the English language a symbol of colonialism, even going so far as to say, "To give millions a knowledge of English is to enslave them." But when India's leaders proposed Hindi as an alternative, South Indian politicians denounced that, too, as "language imperialism." Because Hindi has never been spoken in South India, choosing India's official language was the single greatest controversy in the writing of the Indian constitution. Since no single tongue could satisfy India's heterogeneity, Hindi was named the "official language of the union," with English to be used for "official purposes of the union."

Today, English is spoken in the courts and financial markets. It is much more than bureaucratic babu-speak, though; it is the language of those who aspire to a better life. Like many lower-middle-class Indians, Parvati had spoken her local dialect at home and learned Hindi at school. English was her third language, and it was only with persistence that she became fluent. For many Indians, the effect of the fractured language policy is that they end up speaking multiple dialects badly.

Judging people's speech is a quick way to take a measure of their class and caste in India. If you can't tell their upbringing from their clothes or occupation, you can tell from how strongly accented their Hindi or English is. Both Radha and Maneesh spoke vernacular Hindi speckled with only the occasional word of English, though they both longed to be familiar with the tongue that they associated with well-paid jobs in the private sector. Of course, neither of my maids could afford to send their children to private schools, so they had resigned their children to the limits of the Hindi language.

The Hindi speaker's world may be one of smaller job horizons, but it is far from restrictive when it comes to culture: It's the tongue of politics, Bollywood, cricket, and religion. Parvati's mother lived a full life inside the language, avidly consuming Hindi news shows, magazines, and books. She was closed off from fully half of her daughter's experience, though, because Parvati worked for an English-language paper and spoke the sassy urban patois of Hinglish—delivering most of the information in English and the punch lines and curses in Hindi.

Sitting on the bed with the two of them, I had the thought that Parvati might actually prefer to keep her English-speaking life separate from her mother; it probably made it easier to dodge uncomfortable topics. I noticed that the bottles of Blenders Pride and packs of Gold Flake cigarettes were gone from her kitchen and that Vijay's jacket was no longer hanging on a hook in the entranceway. It reminded me of how I used to hide my journal and beer bottles from my parents in high school.

I followed Parvati into the kitchen so she could warm up the dinner. Cleansed of signs of her unconventional lifestyle, it looked much like those in other cramped Delhi homes. The cooking space was now dominated by a shrine. Alongside the jars of lentils and spices on the newspaper-lined shelves were a couple of sandstone statues of gods. I noticed that the long trunk of the elephant god, Ganesh, had been rubbed to a shine. A sketch of the goddess Lakshmi hung on the wall above the two-burner stove.

"My mother did that sketch for Diwali. She really would like a separate room to do *puja,* but I don't have the space."

Luckily, it's acceptable, in Hinduism, to stick a shrine just about anywhere, and Parvati didn't seem to mind it encroaching on her kitchen. Unlike Vijay, who was a staunch atheist of the Marxist variety, Parvati liked to be reminded of the good things about her religion—its openness, its mythological tales. Sometimes she even told me funny stories about the gods, as though she were talking about her friends, always sounding more irreverent than earnest about Hinduism.

In the week leading up to Diwali, Parvati said, Hindus clean their houses and leave the front door ajar so that Lakshmi, the goddess of wealth and good fortune, will come in and bless the place. She chooses the cleanest house first. Parvati smiled a little as she said her mother had spent the day getting the apartment ready, even painting a path of tiny red and white footprints to represent the delicate feet of Lakshmi.

We sat cross-legged on Parvati's bed for the festival meal: fried golden puffs of *poori* bread with spicy potato curry and grilled cubes of *paneer,* a ricottalike cheese. I watched Parvati tear off pieces of *poori,* scoop up the curry, and wipe the plate clean with the bread, and wondered at how graceful she made it look. I tried to mimic her rhythm of scooping and wiping, but I longed for a fork. Watching me eat without silverware was a regular source of amusement for Radha; luckily, Parvati was too focused on the food to notice.

When we'd finished, Parvati handed us a plate of her mother's homemade sweets, or *mithai:* ground cashew-nut cakes coated in edible silver foil, big round *laddoos,* and *halwa* made from red carrots. I fell back on a pillow, dizzy from overeating. Parvati looked at her watch. It was a little after ten.

"*Chelliye.* Let's go."

When I didn't stir, she shot me a look that made me feel like a teenager and told me to take a handful of fennel seeds to help digest the meal.

The air outside was still thick with the smoke of explosives as we walked to her car.

"Even though Vijay's house is just around the block, it's not safe to walk there at night. Everyone will be out carousing on Diwali night," Parvati said, as though driving there was the only surprising element of our outing.

"Wait, doesn't your mom wonder where we're going so late at night?"

"Oh, she knows." She started the car, deliberately ignoring my confusion. Then she shot me a sideways glance and softened.

"Look, I just assume my mother has figured out that Vijay is my boyfriend. But we don't talk about such things. I certainly can't even use the word 'boyfriend.'"

I thought of my own misadventures with the word in India.

"Yeah, I can understand why you'd avoid it."

"I don't want to lie to my mother, so I can't bring it up at all."

"Has she met Vijay?" I ventured.

"There's no way she couldn't. She lives in my apartment for months at a time. That's one of the reasons I could never have a live-in with Vijay. Well, there's lots of reasons why, actually." She laughed sardonically, more to herself than me. "But sometimes Vijay comes over for dinner with us, and then I'll go with him to his place afterwards, so we can have a couple pegs of whiskey."

"Do you ever stay over at Vijay's when she's here?"

Parvati pursed her lips.

"No. I can't do that to her. When I say I'm a bitch, that doesn't include how I act with my family. It means a lot to me to have my mother in my life, to have her accept me mostly as I am. If I can't be one hundred percent truthful with her, that's a small price to pay."

I knew I should drop it, but I couldn't restrain myself.

"How do you refer to Vijay when you are talking to her?"

Parvati sighed. Her eyes glowed yellowish in the dark of the car.

"I just call him 'my friend.' In India, everyone knows what you mean by that—even your sweet mother who doesn't want to know."

CHAPTER 6

Ladies Only

It was too hot to stomach one of Radha's Bihari curries, so I was fixing a light Saturday lunch for myself and Geeta, who'd stopped by that afternoon. I switched on both overhead fans in the long kitchen in a mostly unsuccessful effort to counteract the muggy monsoon air. Outside, the chaos of midday Delhi: old movie tunes blasting from a neighbor's window, a servant clattering the pots in the sink of the apartment below, the vegetable sellers competing with one another's cries. I dug through the minifridge for a handful of hard Indian lemons and handed them to Geeta with a hopeful smile. I loved it when she made *nimbo panne,* a summery lemon drink that she flavored with both sugar and salt. Then I pulled out the ingredients for the Indian railway sandwiches she'd taught me to make—thinly sliced tomato and cucumber dashed with pepper and salt, laid on white bread, and coated with a layer of Maggi Hot & Sweet, a spicy Indian tomato ketchup. Geeta liked to say that the Indian railway network and the sandwiches it had inspired were the best legacies the British left India.

"What an improvement over Afghan rice and mutton stew."

Geeta made a face. Like Radha, she was disgusted by my occasional lapses into meat eating for the sake of convenience while traveling in the meat-centric Muslim world. To them, even eating eggs was a violation of upper-caste Hindu vegetarianism, and it seemed heretical to undermine the Brahmin-friendly vegetarian diet of my upbringing. This was just one of the many aspects of my life as a reporter that Geeta didn't get. I'd started working full-time for a public radio show and traveled about eight months of the year, much of it outside of India—especially Afghanistan and Pakistan, because that was where the news was. Geeta thought my new life sounded uncomfortable and frightening; what she didn't see was that this was probably the proudest achievement of my career.

I'd moved to India without real cause to believe that I'd succeed in getting my stories on the air in any regular way; and after a couple of years of unheeded story pitches, living off my savings and less than regular assignments, I'd scored a contract with one of my favorite radio shows. Now I was expected to cover major stories for them. The thrill of that pretty much eclipsed the difficult parts—my thoroughly unpredictable schedule, the regular travel to dangerous places, and the inevitable loss of friendships.

"Why don't you just tell your boss that you won't go?" Geeta would say. "Isn't there plenty for you to report on here in our India? At least you won't be killed here. You won't be forced to eat meat, either!"

Geeta had left India only once, to visit an uncle in Texas. Although she dreamed of seeing Thailand's beaches, she had no interest in India's Muslim neighbors—or in hearing about them, for that matter. Geeta had learned about Pakistan from her grandparents, who were born there before India was divided. Like most Hindus who fled to India during the 1947 partition, they'd never returned. India and Pakistan have fought three wars since the latter was formed, and the enmity between the countries is still so great that Geeta's grandparents would have been unlikely to be granted Pakistani visas even if they'd wanted to return, which Geeta made clear wasn't the case. The two governments have been in a diplomatic standoff for decades, which means it is virtually impossible for Indians to visit Pakistan and vice versa. In 2004, the countries began a slow and inconsistent process of détente, but it started to collapse after Pakistani president Pervez Musharraf was removed from office. Everything worsened again after Pakistani militants attacked Mumbai in 2008—two years later, relations were still toxic.

In school, Geeta had learned that Pakistan distinguished itself from secular India by calling itself "the land of the pure," a homeland for Muslims. Her grandmother told her that Pakistan had become a fundamentalist state and that women weren't allowed out—even in Islamabad, the capital—unless they were wearing a burka. This kind of stereotyping was pretty common. In the Indian media and Bollywood films, Indian Muslims are more often portrayed as criminals and terrorists than anything else, and Pakistani Muslims as long-bearded militants who fantasize about murdering Indians. Geeta, like many middle-class Hindus, didn't have many opportunities to develop a more nuanced idea, or to know when to separate fact from overwrought fiction. Not that she seemed especially interested in doing so. She'd never followed politics or foreign policy very closely.

Still, I couldn't think about much else that day other than my recent trip to Afghanistan. I professed not to want to live in the foreign correspondent bubble, the state of mind that means you are always thinking about a different country than the one you're in, but it took me a while to digest and download my experiences before I could feel normal in my Delhi life again after being somewhere intense, such as Afghanistan. Still, I knew that if I started talking about the spread of the insurgency or of the poppy industry, Geeta would gulp down her sandwich and take off, back to Nanima's. So as I poured us each a glass of her *nimbo panne*, I tried to come up with anecdotes that would hold her attention—the stuff that hadn't made it into my radio pieces.

I told her about driving out to Bamiyan, a lush valley of the Hindu Kush, in the central part of the country, whose ancient Buddha statues carved into sandstone cliffs had drawn tourists and religious pilgrims for centuries. During the years of Taliban rule, from 1996 to 2001, pilgrims of a different sort traveled to the Bamiyan Valley. Taliban soldiers would climb up into the caves and shout "God is great!" as they shot at the wall paintings to disfigure them. Images of humans and animals were banned under the Taliban regime. A few months before the 9/11 attacks, the Taliban stuffed the statues with explosives and dynamited them into a pile of rubble at the bottom of the cliff face.

I wanted to see the United Nations' effort to restore the statues, and to get a sense of what had happened there under the Taliban. It was only a couple of years after the 2001 U.S. invasion, and it wasn't yet too dangerous to make this kind of reporting trip. The insurgency was only starting to spread around the country. Western journalists traveled without the military or armored cars, relying solely on "fixers," basically Afghan translators with extra responsibilities. My fixer, Najib, was a young medical student who'd figured out that putting foreign journalists at ease could make him a great deal of money. We paid guys such as him a hundred dollars a day, sometimes more, for their skills: smooth-talking in both of Afghanistan's national languages, scoring meetings with warlords, informing us about the country's complicated tribal history, and checking out whether it was safe to meet with a former Taliban official or take a certain route out of Kabul.

Najib was worldly by Afghan standards, though his experiences were limited—he'd grown up in one war after another and had never left Kabul during his childhood. He'd honed a distinctive look during those years, modeled on the singer Ahmad Zahir, or the Afghan Elvis, who lived on through Najib's pompadour and his close-fitted shirts with the top three buttons left undone. Najib's cell-phone ringtone, when I first met him, was a song from the Bollywood hit *Kal Ho Naa Ho*. Shah Rukh Khan played an important role in Najib's life during the Taliban regime, when TV and radio were forbidden. He and his teenage friends had managed to acquire a stockpile of Bollywood DVDs, smuggled across the border from Pakistan.

The Taliban also considered fashionable hairdos degenerate. Najib's vanity more than once got him in trouble with the Taliban's moral police, the infamous Vice and Virtue brigade. For a while he'd styled his look after Leonardo DiCaprio's character in the 1997 movie *Titanic*, with one long piece of hair flopping over the forehead. He assured me he was not alone in mimicking the Leonardo flop: black-market videos of *Titanic* made the movie so popular in Afghanistan that there's an outdoor shopping area in Kabul named after it—the Titanic Market. Vice and Virtue used to patrol the streets searching for Leonardo mimics, with hair too long or beards too short.

It struck me that Najib's current hairstyle wouldn't be popular with today's incarnation of the Taliban, either, if we were unlucky enough to meet them on our journey to Bamiyan. He assured me that central Afghanistan was relatively free of insurgents, and he was right. Our trials were of a different nature. I'd told Najib to rent a battered van rather than one of the more expensive Toyota Land Cruisers used by the UN and the military, a frugality I soon regretted. It took us ten bone-rattling hours to drive only ninety miles from Kabul, along shattered, pockmarked roads ruined by decades of shelling.

Not being able to relieve myself made the ride seem even longer than it was. Ladies in Afghanistan certainly do not crouch behind trees to urinate. Of course, in rural areas, ladies rarely leave their compounds. The few times we passed women walking on the road, they turned their burka-clad backs to the car, to further conceal themselves from the eyes of strangers. When I traveled with the military, the soldiers would hold up a blue plastic tarp as a shield for me to pee behind, but Najib thought this was dangerous since it only drew attention to the foreigner humiliating herself on the hillside. Several hours into the drive, though, my discomfort started to outweigh my sense of propriety. Najib took pity on me and walked me out to a remote dirt pathway away from the road, checking for signs of uncleared land mines. Just as I was about to crouch down behind a stone wall, we saw an old man leading his donkey up the path and dashed back to the van.

Later we stopped at a teahouse in a bustling town. As Najib had predicted, there was no ladies' toilet to be found, because there were no ladies—not a single billowing blue burka to be seen. Najib convinced the owner to let me use the stinking men's outhouse—two planks of wood erected around a maggot-festering pile of feces in a shallow pit. It was no worse than dozens of Indian toilets I'd used, though I never got accustomed enough to such outhouses not to gag. When I returned,

Najib was making small talk with the men at the next table, large-framed Pashtuns from southern Afghanistan wearing rolled woolen hats, or *pakols*. They split open fresh apricots to share with us, glowing little suns. I asked Najib to find out whether their wives ever came into town. The men looked surprised at the question.

"Of course not. Our women stay home."

Najib asked something else, and then translated the answer: "If they don't need to leave the house, then why should they? We do the shopping and bring their relatives to visit them. They have an easy life."

The idea of women being completely forbidden from entering public life was less surprising to me after my exposure to Indian villages. Still, rural Afghanistan makes even the most impoverished corners of India seem liberated. After thirty years of war, more than 80 percent of Afghan women are illiterate.

I continued asking questions, and the men's voices escalated; eventually Najib stopped translating. The men were gesticulating and talking over one another, and Najib's expression made my heart beat fast. I'd come to know him pretty well during our long days together, and he usually seemed as cool as the Afghan Elvis he idolized. I could tell from the strain under his eyes that all was not well now. I lowered my eyes, trying not to make things any worse. Eventually, one of the men smiled. Najib pushed his chair back, and they bade each other elaborate goodbyes, wishing each others' families well, as is polite in Afghanistan.

When we got back to the van, Najib told me that the men had turned his questions around on him. They'd asked whether he was aware he was breaking the moral code of Islam by bringing a Western woman into a teahouse in their town. Female visitors weren't welcome, they said, especially if they were "naked," meaning not wearing a burka.

"It wasn't that we were in danger. It was just . . . better to leave."

"I'm surprised they took offense at me. I'm dressed so carefully today."

I rarely wore a burka, but Najib gave me an outfit check each morning to make sure I was sufficiently covered. That day my head scarf was tied tightly around my head so that no tendrils of hair could escape, and my wrists and ankles were covered by a long, loose *salwar kameez*.

"I know. But they didn't like your face—seeing it exposed, I mean."

I laughed, but I stayed in the van the rest of the ride.

"Were you worried?"

Geeta looked interested for the first time since I'd started talking about Afghanistan. It wasn't actually the most dangerous situation I'd been in there, I said, but it stood out to me because the men seemed so certain about women's place. It was always a relief to return to Delhi, where at least it felt like the twenty-first century. Driving back to Nizamuddin from the airport, I'd seen a college-age guy with a girl on the back of his scooter. She was wearing jeans and a tight T-shirt, and she wasn't tilting sideways on the scooter, like women so often were. She was straddling the seat, her arms wrapped around the guy's waist as they threaded through the traffic. She might have been his sister or his girlfriend, but either way it was an unthinkable sight in Kabul—or, for that matter, in many parts of the world.

Geeta's cheeks dimpled at this compliment to her India.

"Yes. India is coming into a modern life pretty fast, isn't it? Just think. In Nanima's time, I would have been a scandal—an unmarried girl, at my age." She paused. "Still, India hasn't changed *that* much. Society pressure is tremendous on my parents even now. In Patiala, our relatives ask my parents, 'What happened? Why isn't your daughter married yet?' Even shopkeepers sometimes ask them."

Geeta puckered her mouth at the sourness of her lemon drink and stirred in another spoonful of sugar. Something about the curl of her mouth made her look quite young and vulnerable.

People found it baffling that she hadn't been married off yet, she said, because she didn't have any obvious defects that would limit her appeal: She wasn't fat, bad natured, or dark skinned. A good-looking spinster raises suspicions. Underneath her relatives' questions were other, unspeakable, ones: Was there a money problem, so they couldn't afford a decent dowry? Did the girl have past relationships she was hiding? Was she unchaste or infertile?

Her relatives wouldn't ask these questions outright, but they felt they had a right to know. An unmarried girl can cast a pall on her sisters' and cousins' chances of finding a match. Knowing that her decisions had consequences for others upped the stakes for Geeta.

"My parents keep telling me this is unsustainable. I need to find a match. I can't stay unmarried forever; I mean, who wants that?"

I sipped my *nimbo panne,* pondering the question. Geeta and I had developed an unlikely, almost sisterly, relationship over the last couple of years, and we'd both learned to avoid talking about issues we didn't agree on. Although she claimed not to find it offensive that I'd "do a live-in" with Benjamin, she'd started making joking remarks about planning my "real wedding." And yet I'd started to realize just how much Geeta and I had in common: Both of us were straining to choose between convention and rebellion, between our independent identities and our relationship-oriented selves.

My stint in Afghanistan had made me feel more exposed than I liked to admit. Sometimes, at night on some military base, surrounded by the army corps reservists I was embedded with, I'd remind myself of a line in a book I'd read as a child: "Aloneness is not loneliness." I had no problem being alone if I wasn't also scared and sad, but in Afghanistan, I was lonely for Benjamin and wished he could be a steady presence in my life—though I wasn't going to tell him that.

I joked to my friends that Benjamin probably missed his Enfield motorcycle, sitting unused in a rented Delhi garage, more than me. Sometimes I'd catch myself talking about him in the past tense. I wasn't sure what either of us wanted from the relationship anymore, or whether we even knew the current version of each other. The time we'd spent together, in New York and Delhi, had been intense and short. Had India changed me as much as it felt like it had? Perhaps he'd changed, too, and I was just clinging to a fantasy version of my boyfriend—running toward me, arms spread wide, through Bollywood fields of swaying wheat.

. . .

Geeta picked distractedly at her Indian railway sandwich. I could tell she had something she wanted to talk about, so I kept my thoughts to myself.

"I've never told you about college, Miranda."

I shook my head.

"It's a little hard to talk about because now it is all mixed up with the most depressing event of my life. Recently I've been thinking I should try to remember the good parts about it."

Geeta lived at home through college, and her social revolution came not from dorm life but from the cafeteria. That was enough: For the first time, she was hanging out, unchaperoned, with a circle of friends that included boys. She bought her first pair of jeans and started listening to what she called "American tapes," cassettes of top-forty singers such as Bryan Adams. Geeta had always considered herself shy, but in college, she surprised herself by making a lot of friends.

"Especially one boy. He was the one who everyone called my friend—you know what I mean?"

I didn't exactly know, but the way she said it made my mind spin through the most melodramatic Bollywood possibilities. I swallowed a mouthful too quickly and felt the crust cut against my throat. Had she broken the vow of chastity of an unmarried Indian girl? Been betrothed to a crooked character? Ended up the vamp in a sad triangle of deceit?

When Geeta said, "I first saw Mohan in the cafeteria," I felt a flutter of impatience. It was going to take a while to get to the climactic love scene, if there was one. Then I considered those words in context. If Geeta had been one of those college girls who'd had a close male friend—even a purely platonic one—it would help explain who she was now.

Mohan attracted her attention the first time she saw him. He was popular and always told the loudest jokes, "and he was always looking straight at me when he said the punch line," she said. That, in small-city India, was enough to qualify them as marriage material. Soon, her girlfriends started referring to him as "Geeta's friend." Everyone assumed they would marry, including their parents. The only really acceptable form of love is still that which follows marriage, even in today's India. But love matches—relationships that spring up without family intervention—are no longer unheard of among the urban middle class. If these relationships do not cross religion or caste lines, families may accept them—as Simran's family finally did in *DDLJ*.

There was none of the *DDLJ* trauma in her own match, Geeta said, at least not at first; she'd been certain from the start that it was fate.

"It seemed like the most lucky thing that could have happened. Mohan was a good-looking boy—tall and well built. He was a Patiala Brahmin from a good family. He shared all the important things— religion and caste—and on top of that he was in med school."

Geeta had conveniently fallen into a relationship with one of the most desirable bachelors in her Patiala community: Every Indian family wants to marry its daughter off to a doctor or an engineer, professions that offer status and security. When she told her parents about him, they agreed that they couldn't have chosen a better match themselves. Even so, Geeta's mother reminded her that "until and unless the boy proposed, nothing is fixed." She continued to set Geeta up on arranged marriage meetings with other potential matches throughout college, just in case; after all, Geeta was her only child. She wanted to see her satisfactorily married off, and soon.

When Geeta told her parents she wanted to move to Delhi after she graduated, her mother knew it was because Mohan had been offered a residency in a Delhi hospital. She told her the risk was too great without a proposal from the boy. Geeta assured her that times had changed, that it was perfectly normal these days.

"I should have known better. Nothing was official yet, so it was a bad idea. Still, I wasn't the only one. Lots of other girls in college had boyfriends. I was insistent on coming to Delhi. Only now . . . I do kind of wish my mother had stopped me."

"So you expected you'd get engaged once you moved here?"

Geeta looked at me in horror. "Of course! No girl would keep up a relationship unless marriage was part of it. And anyway, why wouldn't

I marry him? He's from my community. He was working in a top hospital in Delhi. There were no negatives."

But in fact there were. As leakproof as the situation seemed, a boyfriend is always an unknown quantity in India. Her mother's concern about Mohan was based on a timeworn stereotype—that boys do not believe that good girlfriends make good wives. Love matches may be more acceptable in globalized India than ever before, but the Victorian notion of morality—virgin versus seductress-vamp—still holds sway in the India where miniskirts are only sometimes acceptable and chastity is always extolled.

"My mother kept reminding me not to get . . . involved with Mohan. I thought that was an old-fashioned idea. I thought things had changed." She looked at me and corrected herself. "Things *have* changed. Just . . . not totally."

"Okay, so *were* you 'involved' with Mohan?" I asked, trying to stick with her oblique terminology. I was pretty sure that Geeta hadn't talked about this to anyone before.

Her eyes returned to her plate. She and Mohan, she said, were more friends than a couple, even in Delhi. They obviously lived in separate apartments—she with girlfriends from college, he with fellow medical residents. When they hung out, it was usually in a group.

"But we did sometimes spend time alone. He kissed me, but never anything more—never really involved. At least that much sense I had. That's why when we split up, his lie made me so angry."

I forced myself to wait for her to explain. Geeta got up to make a new batch of *nimbo panne,* without my asking. From where I sat at the table, I could see her in the kitchen. She squeezed the lemons into the jug fiercely, as though she was trying not to cry. I was glad that Priya was out of town, spending the weekend with her family as she usually did.

Geeta had collected herself by the time she sat back down again. After she'd been in Delhi a year, her parents gave her the "marriage ultimatum": They had been patient enough with her love match. If he didn't propose, they'd resume their own husband hunt. Mohan's parents were saying the same thing, so he gave in. Only once Geeta and Mohan started discussing the marriage they'd long assumed would happen did she realize that he had very different expectations for his wife than he did for his girlfriend. In Delhi, he liked her to don jeans and come out with him to nightclubs. After they married, he told her, all that would end. They would move into his family home in Patiala, where he would get a new job and she would not. She'd be expected to exchange her city clothes for saris to show respect to his family.

"I wouldn't have minded to live with his parents. That's the normal Indian way. But he couldn't just *forbid* me from wearing Westerns and working. Well, I guess that's normal, too, but not for me."

Geeta stewed over their differences for several weeks until, she said, "My Punjabi temper just came out." She accused Mohan of wanting to marry a backward village girl he could order around. He was shocked. He'd never heard her raise her voice before. He declared that he didn't want to marry an angry feminist type, adding that a boy should never trust a girl who'd had a boyfriend anyway.

"*He* was my boyfriend all that time." Geeta's face was twisted with anger. "*He* was the one who knew my secrets. Now he was making it sound like this was proof that I wouldn't make a good wife."

When he sent her flowers two days later, Geeta did as a stubborn Punjabi princess should and threw them away. She refused his calls. Eventually, she told her parents that the wedding was off. Word spread rapidly around Patiala. Marriage isn't personal in India. From the out-side, it looked as though Geeta's family had rejected Mohan's. Mohan knew that Geeta's family was devastated that she'd wasted the four most marriageable years of her life with a perfectly marriageable guy and that they would be doing all they could to limit the damage to her repu-tation.

"He called my father and insinuated the worst thing."

Geeta raised her eyes from the table and looked at me expectantly. The motion of the fans had picked up several loose strands of her high-lighted hair, and they drifted strangely above her head. I could hear the pained yowl of a sick cow that had taken up residence in the alleyway. I'd been wishing for days that someone would put the sacred beast out of its misery, though I knew no one would.

"You know, Miranda, he said that we had s-s-sex—to my father," she said, stuttering on the word *sex*. I wasn't making it easy for her; I was having trouble coming to terms with the realization that Mohan was, after all, a crooked character.

"What? Why would he do that?"

"I don't know. He didn't have a good nature! I guess he thought I would have to marry him if he told my father I had gotten involved with him. Or maybe he just wanted revenge."

I still found it hard to believe that in today's urban India, the suggestion that a girl is unchaste can wreck her chance of marriage.

"Did your father believe him?"

"I think he did at first. Then he gave it some thought. I am his only child, Miranda, the only daughter he can see married. So he called me and asked whether it was true."

"God, that must have been an uncomfortable conversation," I said.

"It was awful. But at the end, he decided he believed me. He said, 'That boy is trying to ruin your life, and I won't let him. I'm not going to tell your mother what he said.' That's when I knew my father really loves me. And that's why I say thank God I never got involved with Mohan. Because I couldn't have lied to my father about it if I had."

We sat listening to the cow making its pained plea to the dark street.

"Did you manage to keep that rumor quiet in Patiala?"

Geeta looked the vision of a crushed Bollywood heroine, much of her hair now swirling above her head in the breeze from the fan, her eyes in shadow.

"I don't think Mohan dared to tell many people after my father dismissed him. Still, some families in Patiala have heard. Even if all they know is that I had a boyfriend and then something happened, that's bad enough. Believe me. No family wants to align their son with a girl with a past."

Saturday afternoons were reserved for Madame X. I'd seen the hand-written signs when I first moved to the neighborhood—"Madame X Beauty Saloon"—and I'd been confused by the double *o* into thinking it was some kind of middle-class bordello or ladies' drinking venue. In fact, Madame X was nothing more than a dinky neighborhood beauty salon with a misspelled name. It was two dank rooms that smelled of nail polish and hair dye, decorated with peeling 1980s posters of Bollywood stars. Actually, the stars were the same as those today—just with big eighties hair.

Geeta would spend whole Saturdays there, gossiping with the owner, Sameena, her hands and feet proffered for a ten-rupee manicure and pedicure. I was amazed to discover that there was anywhere in the world where you could get your nails done for a quarter, even if the arm massage was listless and the polish chipped off the next day. For Geeta, being pampered badly was better than not being pampered at all. Like many middle-class Indian women, she'd grown up relying on "beauty saloons" for personal rituals such as body waxing and facial hair threading, a way to remove hairs with two cotton threads.

The latest tidbit from the Madame X proprietress was that a women-only gym had opened up in Nizamuddin. The Fitness Circle was "completely American style," apparently, with machines and trainers imported from the United States. I was skeptical: The health craze had been much slower to catch on in India than had other influences of globalization. Delhi could boast a couple of dozen European restaurants, lounge bars, and nightclubs, but its fitness facilities were limited to men's boxing clubs and prohibitively expensive hotel gyms. If a state-of-the-art facility had sprung up in Nizamuddin, it definitely warranted checking out.

LADIES ONLY warned a sign outside the gym. Several black burkas hung on the wall like so many molted snake skins. The gym probably catered primarily to Muslim ladies from the *bustee,* I thought as we entered, since many are forbidden to interact with members of the opposite sex. I thought I saw Geeta stiffen as she had the same realization.

Growing up in a close-knit Brahmin community had shielded her from much of India's diversity. Although we lived only a few minutes' walk from one of the biggest Muslim enclaves in Delhi, Geeta never ventured back there. When I tried to get her to visit the Sufi Muslim shrine with me, she'd plead, "I can't help it. I was brought up to be afraid of those people." Islam is India's biggest minority religion, but she'd never even spoken to a Muslim until she met Sameena, and the experience astounded her.

"Sameena is a Muslim, but you know what? We eat the same vegetarian breakfast," she pronounced in a voice of amazement.

Geeta had more than once recited the clichéd anecdote that when India and Pakistan play a cricket match, Indian Muslims root for Pakistan's team. She'd long heard this rumor cited as evidence that Indian Muslims are more loyal to their religion than to their country. It's a fear that has plagued Hindu-Muslim relations since partition: that Muslims are less patriotic than Hindus. In fact, in 2010, when Shah Rukh Khan—who owns an Indian cricket league team—suggested that Pakistani players should be included in the Indian Premier League cricket tournament, there were protests on the streets. One parliamentarian declared that Khan "could go play his matches in Lahore, not in India," insinuating that SRK took this position because he was a Muslim.

The Fitness Circle was a small, fluorescent-lit basement room with water stains creeping along the baby-pink walls. It was crowded with weight and cardio machines, none of which looked as if it was intended for commercial use. I noticed immediately that the gym had neither a generator nor an inverter; living in Delhi had given me a keen eye for such details. Clearly all activity would grind to a halt during the routine midmorning power cuts. Red FM, the Hindi pop radio station, was blasting out of a cheap boom box in the corner.

Having shed their burka skins, the gym members were clad in unlikely outfits—sweatpants over close-fitting silk tunics, for instance—not clothing that seemed conducive to hard workouts. These women seemed unenthusiastic about their fitness regimes in general, which was a disappointment for Geeta.

The owner came over to show us around. Leslie was American—that much of Sameena's description was true—but she was hardly a top trainer; she had no experience teaching classes or anything.

"I got the idea to open a gym from my neighbor. She was one of the first people I met after I moved to Delhi, and I felt really sorry for her. She was cooped up at home all day, not even allowed to walk around the local park unless a male relative came with her."

After the birth of her son, Leslie said, she'd felt trapped indoors, which made her want to open a place where it would be acceptable for neighborhood women to get out and about. She started learning Hindi and Urdu, the language spoken by many Indian Muslims; she invested in treadmills and a hydraulic resistance weight-training set and rented a basement space in Nizamuddin. The husbands and fathers considered the windowless room an advantage since their wives and daughters would be safe from prying male eyes.

Leslie decided to charge just seventeen dollars a month for membership, and partly because it was so cheap, the Fitness Circle had turned into more community center than gym.

"In the States, everyone shows up determined to burn calories, sticks their iPods in their ears, and runs hard on the treadmill. No one talks to each other. It's the opposite here—I can't convince the ladies to stop chatting! I figure that even if they barely break a sweat, at least they're telling stories and getting advice."

The gym ladies spent most of their time lounging on the gym mats, complaining about their husbands and exchanging tips about physical ailments. For most of them, it was the first time they'd done so out of earshot of their husbands and in-laws. Leslie was taken aback at the intimate stories that poured out onto the gym mats. They wanted advice on everything from how to lance an unsightly boil and how to shed twenty-five pounds to how to end bad dreams. The gym members assumed that because Leslie was a health-conscious American, she was also qualified to dispense advice on all matters nutritional and medical. After a couple of months of insisting she was neither a neighborhood health consultant nor a nurse, Leslie gave in. She'd look up stuff online and come back the next morning with suggestions for how to ease back strain or cook low-fat curry recipes.

By far the most popular class at the Fitness Circle was a yoga stretch session led by a timid slip of a woman, Usha Gotham, who Leslie had hired after a fruitless search for an experienced female trainer. Usha's classes were not what I expected in the land that gave birth to yoga. There was an emphasis on breathing but no sun salutations or *vinyasas*. The gym ladies loved it because they could intimidate Usha into conducting the class they wanted. When they thought a move was too tough, crows of protest would rise from the back of the room, and Usha, whom everyone knew was a pushover, would modify it.

One of the loudest voices in the back was that of Azmat, a young Muslim girl who cleaned the gym each morning. Leslie had not hired Azmat for her meticulous cleaning abilities—there were always dust bunnies floating in the corners—but because she wanted to help her family out. The boy at the door was Azmat's brother. The parents had died before Azmat or either of her two sisters had married, so Azmat's forty-dollar monthly salary was being saved toward her dowry.

Since she didn't have to pay for membership, Azmat was unconcerned about getting her money's worth from the classes or machines. After she finished her mopping duties, she would clamber onto an elliptical trainer and do a few turns before pausing to inform the room of her most recent scrap of news: "Nasmeen won't be coming to the gym for the next week because she has relatives in town" or "Leslie-*deedee* told me she stayed up late watching a movie, so she already had three cups of *chai* this morning." If she got any response at all, she'd eagerly fill in other details for the room to hear. After a while, she'd remember she was supposed to be working out and absentmindedly move her legs again.

The only time Azmat moved energetically was during the ladies' impromptu dance circles. One of the women would lumber over to the boom box and raise the volume. Azmat didn't need to be persuaded off her machine. Soon the bass was distorting and the mirrors were trembling on the basement walls, and all the ladies were making their way out to the "dance floor." Once there, the ladies would break out grinding and shaking in their uncoordinated workout clothes. I preferred to watch from the machines, but I was rarely spared.

"Come on, *deedee,* show us your stuff!" the ladies would shriek as Azmat dragged me into their midst.

Azmat was the Fitness Circle's self-appointed social secretary. She organized gym parties any time a lady shed ten pounds and for Muslim, Hindu, and Christian holidays. One Saturday my first year at the gym, the ladies showed up in especially jazzy outfits for Leslie's birthday celebration, carrying plates covered in aluminum foil. Class was particularly short that day. As soon as it was over, Azmat laid out the spread the ladies had brought, of homemade *mithai* and fried snacks. Leslie jokingly despaired at the caloric feast—"What about all my suggestions? What about fruit?"—and Usha laughed as she handed around plastic cups of *chai.* "It's just one day, *deedee!* Let the ladies enjoy," she said. They'd clubbed together to get Leslie a peacock-blue *salwar kameez* suit. When Azmat presented it, with a little speech about how Leslie had inspired them to be healthy, the unsentimental Leslie had tears in her eyes.

Afterward, Azmat sidled up to me.

"More *chai?*" she shouted above the music.

I nodded, and she sweetly poured half of her cup into mine. We leaned against Leslie's desk. Azmat was wearing her most prized workout T-shirt, a gift from one of the other ladies. "Only One Angel" it said, in pink cursive letters. Her English was as bad as my Hindi, but she must have been practicing, because she managed to ask, "Have you done your marriage yet?"

It was a direct translation from Hindi, in which you say that a marriage "has happened" or "is over," which seems appropriate since it is, after all, a foregone conclusion in India.

"Um, yes," I said uncomfortably. "My husband is in New York now."

I switched to Hindi and to Azmat's own marriage plans. Her older brother, Mehboob, was overwhelmed by the responsibility their parents had left him with—of finding matches for her and her two sisters and funding three weddings. Even though siblings are supposed to be married off in chronological order, he'd decided to look for husbands for Azmat and her twenty-four-year-old sister, Rhemet, simultaneously, to minimize time and cost. If it depressed Azmat to be half cheated out of the most important event in an Indian woman's life, she didn't show it.

"This is the simplest way. And he'll easily find a match for Rhemet. Even though she's two years older than me, she's slim, and she makes the best *biryani* in the neighborhood. Her only problem is the mole on her face. Still, I don't think it will be long before we're both married."

The more Azmat talked, the less I believed that. I was hardly an expert in arranged marriage, but the odds didn't seem to be in her favor.
She and her sister were uneducated, they had next to no dowry to offer,
and they wouldn't marry anyone who didn't meet their religious and
caste criteria. Azmat informed me that as a member of the rarefied
Syed caste—"the top rank of Muslims"—she would never consider marrying a boy from the butcher or barber caste; such boys fought constantly inside their families, she told me with authority.

For centuries, marriage brokers took care of such concerns, pairing off couples based on their caste and horoscope. Each community
in India had its own version of the matchmaker: In some villages, it
was the barber's wife, in others, the Hindu priest, or *pujari.* Then, a
couple of decades ago, the classified pages of the Sunday newspapers
broke the matchmaker's monopoly, widening the pool of potential
partners. With access to the classifieds, families could choose from
hundreds of listings for girls and boys from across the country. In theory they could pick a match from a different religion or caste, but they
rarely did.

Mehboob had first put the word out in his mosque and then around
the rest of the neighborhood. When no boys appeared, he tried to hire
a local matchmaker, a Muslim woman who had a reputation for making
quick, caste-specific alliances via cell-phone calls to the families. She
demanded more than a hundred dollars per girl, though, and wouldn't
give a discount for sisters—which Azmat thought was terribly cheap of
her. Mehboob seemed at a loss.

I came into the gym one morning to find Azmat holding court. Her
face was flushed with excitement. She'd stumbled on a juicy piece of
neighborhood gossip, and she'd clearly been milking it for all it was
worth. It was an update on a story we all knew: A Muslim boy had
eloped with a Hindu girl the previous year, and it had been the talk of
the neighborhood. The girl's family had promptly disowned her, and
the couple had disappeared from Nizamuddin. Now Azmat had found
out that the girl had resurfaced, eight months pregnant. The gym ladies
were all abuzz. The boy's family had agreed to take the couple in, but
the girl's family continued to refuse to acknowledge the marriage. This

was only natural, according to the gym ladies, who spoke up from their various exercise-machine perches.

"The girl must have got herself pregnant to try to get sympathy from her family."

"It's much harder for the girl's family to accept such a match, because she's the one who converts to his religion. A Hindu girl raising her child a Muslim—no one wants that in their family," another said.

Azmat nodded knowledgeably from her cross-legged position on the gym floor.

"It's very difficult for the girl's side. If I ran off with a Hindu boy, my family would have to leave our mosque. The boy's family gets a new wife and child, but the girl's family gets nothing from an interreligious match—nothing but shame."

CHAPTER 7

A Million Matches

The home page of Shaadi.com exhorts the unmarried to have faith: "20 million miracles and counting: Register free." Shaadi, named after the Hindi word for "marriage," styles itself as an online wedding clearinghouse: Members can search among 450 castes, sixty-seven regional languages, and every possible Indian religion for a match. It provides much the same service as the village barber's wife—aligning couples based on community and background—just online.

Despite India's renown—or notoriety—as the world's IT helpdesk, only about a third of Indians have Internet access. The percentage is growing exponentially every year, though, and more than a hundred websites have popped up to cater to the Indian matrimonial market. Although Azmat liked to drop the English word *computer* into her sentences—she pronounced it robotically, in three distinct syllables, "com-*pooh*-ter"—neither she nor her sisters had ever used one. The relatively savvy Mehboob spoke English and had learned to type in college, but he didn't own a PC. So when a friend convinced him to fill out the online form seeking husbands for his sisters, he did so from an Internet café.

Even while matrimonial sites such as Shaadi retain the most traditional aspects of Indian marriage, they are revolutionizing the institution. They are the portal for the new generation of arranged alliances, striking a compromise between love matches and pure arranged marriages. Ungracefully called "love-cum-arranged marriages" in Indian English, these are Indian marriages with Western influences, like Pakistani-style democracy or capitalism with Chinese characteristics. Theoretically, at least, the couple can have as much input into the process as their parents do. Traditionally, the boy's parents would send an inquiry to the girl's parents, but now the boy can now do it himself by clicking the "express interest" button on Shaadi—the less playful equivalent of a sending a "wink" or a "poke" on Match.com or Facebook. Like many American dating sites, Shaadi also features its own instant messaging feature, a socially acceptable form of direct, live communication. It's virtuous virtual dating.

In *Kal Ho Naa Ho* (Tomorrow May Never Come), which is best abbreviated to *KHNH*, Shah Rukh Khan shows us that this, the compromise method, is the way to be modern. Until recently, the only acceptable expression of love in Bollywood was karmic, family-approved marriage—but in this film, the heroine meets SRK's character without family intervention and falls for him on her own. Standing in front of an elaborate Hindu shrine, her grandmother chastises her. "There is no such thing as love. If there is marriage, it is always arranged!" she says, and in the film's progressive eye, she becomes a caricature of the old, slightly embarrassing India.

Later in the film, the heroine describes the sensation of love to a girlfriend.

"Before, I used to get annoyed with all the little things he did . . . and now I love those same things!"

"This is what love is! Oh my God, I'm so excited!" her girlfriend shrieks.

Geeta had said unequivocally that she'd never again "spend time with any boy without a proposal." Being burned by Mohan made her feel she should seek the safety net of a marriage with parental sanction, but she was also struggling with the idea of spending her life with someone her mother selected for her. I thought Shaadi seemed like a promising alternative to her mother's endless stream of chaperoned arranged marriage meetings, and the day Azmat told me about it, I went straight from the gym to Nanima's apartment.

Her maid let me in, and I tiptoed past the old woman sleeping on the sofa. Geeta was on the floor of her bedroom amid stacks of clothes, looking overwhelmed as she tried to clean out her overstuffed closet. I leaned into the doorway and asked, rather breathlessly, whether she'd heard about the site.

Geeta eyed me suspiciously over the piles of clothes. I felt suddenly silly for rushing over before I'd even changed out of my gym clothes.

"Of course I have. I already have a profile up on the site." She returned to her folding, but I came in and sat down on her bed anyway. After a moment of trying to ignore me, she sighed and spoke up again. "My dad thinks Shaadi is great. But that's because he likes anything to do with technology. You know how we were the first family in our neighborhood to have a vacuum cleaner or a TV? It's the same with this. He thinks that because it is modern and up to date, I'm going to find my husband this way. But I'm not so sure."

"It seems like if you do it online, you get a lot more freedom and control of the whole process, right?"

Geeta shifted impatiently. "Maybe, but you know what? I'm not sure having more freedom is a good idea. It might work on American dating sites, but I've had some bad experiences. Some boys on Shaadi confuse the arranged marriage thing with dating. They act like we're in America, just dating on and on, with no wedding in sight."

She looked down at the unfolded clothes scattered across the floor. Geeta had seemed sad in recent weeks. She'd told me her mother had been calling a lot, nagging her to choose a match. I told her we could talk about it another time, and walked home through the dusk. It wasn't easy to be a friend to Geeta these days. I don't think she put much stock in my advice because she didn't take my own relationship issues seriously. She thought I had it easy, and she was right, in a way: As muddled as my Benjamin situation was, at least it didn't involve our families, and neither of us was being pressured into marriage. My mother would occasionally make wistful comments about how happy children would make me and that kind of thing, but if she didn't consider Benjamin husband material, she didn't say so. I took it for granted that my parents would accept whomever I chose to marry, and that if I decided not to get married at all, they would accept that, too. In India, though, it is not just the parents' right to marry off their children—it's their duty.

Geeta called a few days later to ask if she could stop by. She sounded a little sheepish.

"I promised my father I would look at some Shaadi profiles this evening. He has sent me all their bio-data," she said, using the Indian English word for résumés used in personal ads. She paused. "Would you mind going through them with me?"

I wanted to encourage her efforts, but my "Of course!" probably sounded a little too perky. I wondered briefly whether I was trying to live vicariously through her dating life, a possibility that seemed especially pathetic, since Geeta's dating life consisted of reviewing the résumés of boys her father had chosen for her. My enthusiasm was not, in any case, contagious. I could tell that Geeta was trying to look cheery when I let her in, but when I pulled up a chair to my desk for her, she slumped into it as though she dreaded the task ahead.

"I try to tell my parents that the emphasis should be on getting married to the right boy. Not just anybody. But my mother doesn't hear it— she just keeps telling me my time is running out." She pushed her hair back from her face and sat up straight, as though to resolve herself to tackle the task ahead. "She's probably right. I need to get serious. I have decided I should start spending at least a couple hours a week looking for a boy."

She pulled up a browser window on my laptop.

GEETA SHOURIE

TRAITS
She is gregarious and responsible.
Also she is well-mannered, confident & helpful.
She is a good cook.

APPEARANCE
She looks quite young than her age. And she is slim.

HEIGHT
5'1"

COMPLEXION
Very fair

FEATURES
Soft

FATHER
Retired Head Doctor in top Government Hospital in Patiala.
Having his own flat in Patiala.

MOTHER
She is sweet natured, friendly, helpful and understanding
and God fearing lady. She has been a house-wife and
schoolteacher.

PATERNAL UNCLE
Manager in company in Texas, USA. He has been an
American Citizen since long.

MATERNAL UNCLE
Recently retired as Senior Engineer from Government
Organization.

FAMILY BACKGROUND
We are Brahmins & will supply our gotras [the patrilineal
lineage or clan] on request.

The photo on her profile page showed a younger and happier Geeta than the one I knew. She grimaced, as though she already regretted sharing this intimate view of herself with me.

"That picture was taken some time back. My mother says I need to keep it up to counteract my age, since they make you list it. Even one year over thirty puts me out of range for marriage, according to the way most Indians think."

"Do your parents go into your Shaadi profile?" I asked.

"Actually, my parents pretty much created it. They said it would help me look more serious about marriage if they took charge of it."

She scrolled through, and I realized how little the site shared with American dating sites. Profiles on Shaadi are formal, not flirty; the focus is on practicality rather than individuality and romance. Most of the information seems boilerplate, intended to put families at ease. There are no questions about the worst lie you've ever told or your favorite on-screen sex scene.

At Shaadi, they told me that their member surveys show that new priorities, such as "compatibility and geographic proximity," are consistently outweighed by age-old Indian marital concerns, such as caste and astrology. Few Hindus will agree to a marriage unless a *pujari* or astrologer verifies that the couple's birth charts are aligned. At Shaadi, they streamline the process with a function called "AstroSoulMate Search," which allows members to search the database using over forty criteria from their horoscopes.

For women in search of a husband, the most important categories are education, profession, and height. According to Shaadi's research, the biggest priorities for men in search of a wife are "innocence and fairness." It took me a moment to realize that "fairness" referred to India's centuries-old preference for light skin, and "innocence" to virginity, which is a particularly difficult trait to measure. Even in India, matrimonial sites can hardly ask female members to provide a list of boyfriends and activities performed together.

But Geeta told me that families have their own ways to figure it out: The parents of a potential groom will often ask about "a girl's past" and "whether she has had experiences." These phrases, so opaque to me, could not be clearer to marriage-age Indian girls such as Geeta. The line of questioning is harsher if a girl has lived alone, she said, because that increases the chance she's been boyfriended.

It's rather easier for a girl to offer positive evidence of her fairness than of her chastity. Shaadi members are given half a dozen word choices to help them get specific about their skin type in their profile, ranging from *very fair* to *wheatish* to *dark*. I found it hard to imagine any family actually choosing the last term to describe their daughter or son. Darker skin is associated with lower status in India, partly because the poorest are exposed to the sun as they toil as manual laborers. A pallid hue, on the other hand, evokes the more comfortable lifestyle of the higher castes.

Today, India has a multimillion-dollar fairness industry. The leading brand of skin-lightening cream, Fair & Lovely, is so popular that it now manufactures a "Menz Active" version. In the ads, a fair-skinned hero revs his motorcycle, in an effort to prove that it is possible to be manly while investing in a product to smooth your skin tone.

In a Fair & Lovely ad aimed at women, a father sits in his modest village shack, brooding over how unlucky he is to have a daughter because he'll have to save money for her dowry. The dark-skinned daughter cowers in an ill-lit corner of the hut. In the next frame, she discovers Fair & Lovely cream, and she's shown accepting an office job, clad in a Western business suit, her skin washed out from its original brown. The glamorous globalized lifestyle calls to India's village girls, the ad tells us, but it's open only to those who meet the traditional vision of Indian beauty.

Geeta clicked disconsolately through her profile.

"It seems like this should be a good method, but you'd be amazed at how many guys on Shaadi are confused about what they want. I have a theory of why. India is in a transition phase now. It's difficult for modern boys to know whether they want a love type or an arranged type. I keep meeting boys who think that if I am willing to chat online, I'll be willing to date them, too."

"Even on this site? It seems pretty obvious that the whole point is marriage."

Geeta flopped back in the chair. A couple of years ago, she said, she'd started instant messaging with one boy, Aditya, who'd expressed interest by planting a Shaadi smiley-face emoticon beside her name. He was a Punjabi Brahmin with a professional career, over thirty, and never married—but even though he fulfilled all her criteria, Geeta didn't tell her father about him, because she'd agreed to meet him alone, in person.

The first arranged marriage meeting is supposed to be escorted. In some communities, being seen alone with a boy can destroy a girl's reputation. Geeta was trying to loosen up and play it cool, though. She agreed to meet Aditya in a Barista coffee shop, an Indian-owned chain that helped spread what the Indian media like to call the "urban coffee craze" to the land of *chai.* Barista coffee shops feature Starbucks-style merchandise, sayings about coffee on the walls, comfortable chairs, and a variety of blended coffee drinks, none of which Geeta would drink.

Aditya bought her a smoothie and sat opposite her on a high stool. Their conversation skipped between the appropriate topics for an arranged marriage date—families, plans for the future. Geeta was well accustomed to the protocol of such meetings. In the absence of the boy's parents, who usually take the lead, she let Aditya ask the questions and revealed little. Coyness is essential to the initial presentation.

Eventually Aditya turned to the meat of the matter.

"What about your past—any prior relationship?"

Against her better instincts, Geeta lowered her eyes and acknowledged that she'd had "a friend" in college and afterward.

"I already knew I didn't like him enough to marry him, so I didn't care that much, but I still don't know why I said it. There's nothing to be gained from admitting such things to a boy."

Things got awkward then. Aditya wanted to stay for another coffee, but Geeta told him she had to go—it was already getting dark outside. As he walked her through the parking lot to her car, he tried to take her hand.

"I already have strong feelings for you, Geeta. You are so pretty. Please, can I hold your hand?"

Absolutely not, was the outraged response. Geeta tugged her hand away and leaped into her car, terrified both about what could happen and about what the people in the parking lot might think had happened. Aditya stood there as she pulled out, text messaging her not to leave. Tears sparked to her eyes even now, as she recalled it.

"This is what I get for telling him I had a friend before. Immediately he thought I am the kind of girl who he can just take advantage of. As though this automatically makes me the kind of girl who has boyfriends, and who will just keep meeting him—maybe five times, maybe ten times—who knows how long it would go on like that, getting nowhere toward marriage."

To me, the incident sounded more like a routine high school fumble than the kind of thing that would bring a thirty-something woman to tears. But I reminded myself that I had to apply a different standard to Geeta. She couldn't help but think that by meeting Aditya alone, she'd been asking for it. That, combined with the mention of another man in her past, had sent a message that she was a boyfriended girl, she thought; or, at the very least, that she was looking for something other than a traditional marriage.

Sobered by the memory, Geeta returned to her profile.

"I need a boy who seems serious about marriage. It's hard to tell, though. How do I know whether he'll be the kind who wants to grab my hand? The only way is to have an escort and limit the meetings."

When I asked how many meetings she thought appropriate, she had the answer at the ready.

"I can tell in half an hour whether I want to marry a guy or not."

This seemed ill-advised, since Geeta hoped to establish an emotional connection with her prospective husband. I wondered how she rendered such a quick judgment, and how often it was right. My own first impressions of men were consistently off the mark: overenthusiastic at first, followed by precipitous disappointment. Apparently it was not so with Geeta.

"By the time I meet a boy, I've already seen his photo. I already know his family background and his job. The only thing left is to see whether there is some attraction and whether he is pleasant and down to earth. How much time can it take?"

She clicked on her name to see how many Shaadi members had expressed interest in her in recent weeks. There were just two emoticons beside her name, from the profile names "Rohit2555" and "InnocentinLove." Geeta sank a little lower in her chair, as though imagining that "InnocentinLove" would not consider her innocent enough.

"I don't think I can do this," she said abruptly, her hands on her thighs as she pushed the chair back from my desk. "There's a reason why pure arranged marriage worked for so many years. Girls shouldn't have to do it by themselves. I'm going home to watch TV with Nanima."

My friend Kalpana, a newspaper columnist in Mumbai, told me once about a speech she had given to a group of students at a women's college. She'd been asked to talk to them about the ways women's lives were changing in India and instead found herself talking about all the things that have stayed the same. Kalpana asked the students to name the biggest issue in their lives; they all said marriage. Then she asked for a show of hands from those who would be responsible for deciding who they would marry, and none of the women stirred. When she asked how many wanted to be able to make that decision, all the hands flew into the air. The experience stuck with her.

"It's a terribly frustrating time for young women," she said. "They're allowed to make all kinds of choices that previous generations of women couldn't make in India—what they will study, where they will work, where they will live. And yet, when it comes to the most important decision of their lives, their parents don't trust them with it. It's like they're only partly allowed to enter the real world."

Geeta's parents taught her that the Hindu marriage is decided by fate and sanctioned by God, but her friends spoke about a very different idea of marriage, one born of love and ended when it is no longer satisfying. They were moving in their own circles in colleges and offices, where they were falling into relationships that had nothing to do with the family. Many women of Geeta's generation wanted to abandon the traditional extended Indian family, with its expectation of sharing and conformity, and live separately, instead, in nuclear families. It seemed that upward mobility and fewer children might eventually drive the multigenerational family out of fashion in India, which is exactly what happened to it in the United States and Europe.

English-language Indian magazines were raving about the new mind-set of young Indians. *India Today,* one of the country's most widely read publications, expanded its popularity with cover stories that claimed to capture "the new Indian woman" or "the new attitudes to sex in India." One article found that more than 40 percent of women favor intercaste marriage and that the vast majority want to work after their weddings. I didn't put much stock in the findings, though, because the survey was anonymous and the sample ignored rural and uneducated women—the vast majority of Indians.

India Today's annual "Sex Survey" issue was consistently awash with sensational statistics: Almost 40 percent of men in Delhi have had an extramarital affair, it declared one year, and 30 percent of Indian women approve of "kinky sex." Of course, the same survey found that only 16 percent of women nationwide had their first sex with boyfriends, rather than husbands, and that one out of every ten Indian women between the ages of thirty-five and forty was still a virgin. So much for the prosex Indian woman of today.

For help sorting out Indian attitudes to sex, I kept turning to Bollywood, which the acclaimed psychoanalyst and writer Sudhir Kakar calls "the primary vehicle for shared fantasies" of the subcontinent. "Hindi films may be unreal in a rational sense, but they are certainly not untrue," he writes. Bollywood has ample evidence of the same confusion and insecurity I saw in Geeta and Parvati.

The historical epic *Jodhaa Akbar,* for instance, is an unlikely canvas for female sexual liberation. It's a story about the purest form of Indian arranged marriage, a sixteenth-century political alliance between a Hindu princess and a Muslim Mogul emperor. Jodhaa, the princess character, sings the film's first love song not to her lover but to the deity Krishna. Jodhaa only begins to love her Muslim husband after he shows that he will allow her to worship her own gods, rather than taking on his religion. This is to be expected from a good pious virgin, but what is not to be expected is her obvious sexual attraction to her new husband. In one scene, the camera pans the length of the emperor's muscular body as he practices sword fighting alone in a verdant courtyard. The demure Jodhaa eyes him longingly through a gauzy curtain, her eyes following the streaks of sweat pooling on the small of his back.

Girlfriend (named for the English word, because there is no comparable Hindi word) goes even further: It gives Bollywood its first—and some of its only—gratuitous scenes of lesbian lust. Depicting a female character expressing desire for another woman is still considered shocking—after all, homosexuality is a criminal act in India, where an 1861 British-era law prohibiting "carnal intercourse against the order of nature with any man, woman or animal" remains on the books. At the end of *Girlfriend,* sexy scenes or no, the lesbian character is pushed out of a window to her death by a rescuing hero. The highest-profile Bollywood film dealing with homosexuality to date, the 2008 *Dostana* (Friendship), is about two straight guys *pretending* to be gay.

Bollywood is only very slowly inching out of its conservative comfort zone. In today's mainline films, characters occasionally fall in love with someone from the "wrong" caste or religion, but they almost always come back around to family and tradition, as in Shah Rukh Khan's 2008 blockbuster *Rab Ne Bana Di Jodi* (A Match Made by God). When the film's heroine, Taani, starts taking dance lessons in a bid to spice up her dull housewifely existence, she falls for a flirtatious dancer in ripped jeans. He's the opposite of her bureaucrat husband, Surinder, who wears a bad mustache and high-waisted slacks.

Like many modern girls, Taani is tempted by the idea of love. She considers rejecting her parents and her marriage and running away with the dancer. Then she realizes that her marriage is sacred, and her sense of duty to her husband begins to transform into other emotions: "I see God in him," she says. She experiences not a heady Bollywood romance but a gradual warming toward the man she married, a warming that is, in the lyrics of the film's first love song, "soft, sweet, and slow."

When Geeta threw up her hands in frustration over her husband hunt, Nitin Shourie was happy to pick up the reins.

"Who could know better than her father the right boy for her?" he'd say to his family. Geeta's father sometimes joked that it was his own fault the girl wasn't yet married: He'd spoiled her, and now she couldn't leave him for a husband. This was a conceit they both liked, because it reinforced their special closeness.

Nitin was a compact, solid man who believed firmly in his own achievements. When members of the Patiala community referred to him by the respectful term Nitin-*ji*, it gave him great pleasure. As a young man, he'd passed competitive exams to secure a lifelong position in one of India's highest-status, if lowest-paid, professions—a doctor in a government hospital. Nitin-*ji* was not too shy to remind his neighbors and family, if they seemed to forget, that he'd dedicated thirty-eight years of service to the best hospital in Punjab state. He noticed that he had to remind them more often since he'd retired.

Nitin also liked to tell anyone who would listen that he'd had his pick of Patiala girls in his time—or, more precisely, that his father had the pick on his behalf. It wasn't until his engagement ceremony that Nitin met the girl who had been chosen for him. But his father had done his due diligence—ensuring that the girl was pleasant looking, that she shared their Punjabi culture, and that she "had a good nature," meaning she was quiet, amenable, and family oriented. It had turned out well, Nitin thought. Even though his wife had been a schoolteacher—in an era when Indian women rarely worked outside the home—she'd never neglected her wifely duties. Each morning, Pooja offered a quick prayer at her bedroom shrine for the family's health and happiness, before overseeing the cook's duties around the house. She had never once called Geeta's father by his name, instead addressing him as *aap*, the respectful form of *you*.

"Sometimes I wish I lived in my mother's time—or even my grandmother's. Things were so much simpler then."

It was a rather random thing to say. Geeta and I were sitting in the stultifying heat, the fans whirring overhead as we waited for our sandwiches to be delivered. On Sunday nights, she often joined Priya and me at my apartment, and we'd order in from Subway. On weeknights, Geeta wanted to eat Punjabi home cooking and would occasionally compromise by agreeing to Radha's Bihari meals, but on Sundays, what she craved was an Indian version of the classic sub. Geeta always ordered the same thing: the slightly spicy Veggie Patty sandwich from Subway, one of her favorite indulgences of the newly globalized India. The choice sang to her of Americanized cool, though it tasted more Indian than American to me.

"Back in those days," she continued, not noticing that I was still trying to catch on to what she was talking about, "everyone still believed that love *follows* marriage. Now we've all been influenced by the American idea that love comes first. I'm·not sure this is a good thing."

Geeta had reason to be skeptical about adopting the Western relationship model: At least on paper, arranged marriages have a much better track record than love matches. Couples rarely separate or divorce in India; 30 percent of American relationships collapse within ten years of marriage. India has never been accepting of separation of couples. When the country's first prime minister, Jawaharlal Nehru, began trying to legalize divorce in India, it caused a fury. In 1954, one minister spoke up in parliament with this view: "The bill is inspired by the Western view of life which attaches more value to the romance of marital relations and married life than to parenthood in which marriage attains its function. The Hindu system conceives of parenthood as something which is permanent, unchangeable, and inviolable."

Divorce was made legal a year later, and yet you still hear a similar sentiment in the India of today, a time of almost equal social turbulence as the postindependence years. The highest estimates peg India's current divorce rate at a mere 6 percent nationwide. Because the courts in India move at a glacial pace, it often takes fifteen years for a divorce to go through; more to the point, though, most couples are unwilling to break the cultural taboo against it.

How do you tell the difference between a good Indian marriage and a bad one? The cynical punch line to that joke is that you can't: Both are grim tests of endurance. Women at domestic violence shelters almost always say they are simply resigned to returning to their abusive homes. Urged by both sides of the family not to bring shame on them by leaving their husbands, unable to survive financially on their own, and unwilling to deal with the humiliation of ending the marriage, most see it as their fate to stick it out in a bad home.

The Indian government doesn't track the national divorce rate—which is a telling fact in and of itself—but independent research shows that its incidence is rising. According to some studies, divorces actually doubled in Delhi and Mumbai in the two decades after 1990. Sociologists attribute it to the growing number of financially independent women, and to the new cultural emphasis on romance and happiness in marriage—which is exactly what Geeta was always saying.

"My girlfriends joke that if divorce was socially acceptable in India, 95 percent of marriages would end up that way," she said. "But I don't agree. I see my parents, and they don't talk all romantic like on American TV shows. Still, they are perfectly happy. That's the difference: With the arranged kind of marriage, you don't have such high expectations."

Her voice was somber when she spoke again. "Actually, I have been feeling very upset the last few days. A girl I know from college is getting a divorce. And, of course, it was a love match."

This was probably the first time Geeta had ever had a personal link to a divorce, and she seemed to find it deeply destabilizing. To her, marriage had always been a refuge from the conflicts of modern-day singledom. I'd never had such high hopes for the institution, myself. Even though my parents are still married, they seem the exception, not the norm. I'd never really considered marriage to be the goal in itself: more like the protective bubble wrap around a delicate china jug. You couldn't assume that the wrapping would protect the jug in a hurricane; you still had to hold it close. But in India, the wrapping itself is considered as precious as the china inside.

I didn't succeed in keeping my views to myself.

"Even if your family helps you choose a guy with a good reputation, how can they predict what will happen between two people?"

"They can't tell everything, it's true," Geeta said. "But it's something. Your family looks into the background and personality. At least they provide some kind of network to help you know whether the boy is good or not. After that, it's up to you only."

"Do you think that's why the girl from your college is getting a divorce—because the guy wasn't tested out by the family?"

"It must be the reason. Why else? He was a perfectly nice boy."

The glibness of this remark made me wince, but I said nothing.

"My mother always said that getting into a relationship is like heating water: First simmer, then boil. The only way to be sure is to marry first and wait for love to come later. Americans have it backward—you expect the water to come to a boil first. When the relationship cools down, you're disappointed, and you break it off."

This bit of metaphorical wisdom gave me pause. I was relieved when the Subway delivery boy arrived with our sandwiches. We sank onto cushions on the living room floor to eat, and I was silent for a while, thinking over what she'd said. When I first moved to India, I'd felt a classic American revulsion for arranged marriage. The lack of choice made it seem loveless; the emphasis on caste and dowry seemed crass and monetary; the classified marriage ads in the Sunday papers read like a spooky, parent-sanctioned meat market. I couldn't fathom the idea of my mother picking my mate for me, and it seemed fundamentally unfair that the girl had to abandon her independence and her past in order to enter the next stage of life.

A couple of years in India had softened my views. For one thing, I'd realized that India is scarcely alone in its interest in aligning the backgrounds of married couples. Statistics about U.S. marriage show that the vast majority of people choose a mate whose income group, race, and education match their own. When I thought about it, most of my boyfriends had mirrored my race and socioeconomic status. I'd been raised to think I should find a partner whose experiences and tastes matched my own, so that I wouldn't have to compromise my essential self.

"What will you do if he wants to watch sports all the time and you want to listen to jazz?" I remember my mother saying. "You'll have to spend your life in different rooms. How awful."

I'd focused my efforts on searching for someone whose beliefs lined up with my own, and I'd chosen men who were, in fact, too much like me. If Benjamin was emotionally distant and independent to an extreme, he was no more so than I. We were a perfect example of the "boil first and simmer later" model. I think I must have read too much of John Keats's poetry as a teenager, because I seriously believed that a romanticized idea of love was the highest pinnacle of human relationships. Issues such as timing, life goals, and even monogamy all seemed pedestrian.

Talking to Geeta made me wonder whether I might have something to learn from Indian marriage after all. She'd grown up believing that it wouldn't matter if she and her husband had different likes and dislikes; it was in any case a wife's duty to adjust to her husband's preferences and fit in with his family. Although that sounded a bit much, I had to acknowledge that there was something to be said for compromise. If my boyfriend was openhearted and caring, it might not matter whether his political views or taste in clothing perfectly matched my own. Maybe a little simmering wasn't such a bad idea after all.

CHAPTER 8

The Brahmin Versus the Untouchable

Marriage, for Radha, was a matter of pure practicality. When I would ask her to describe her wedding or her husband, she'd shrug me off with "What is there to say?"

Hers was a traditional village event, planned and executed by her relatives, and she had been too young to remember much about it. She doesn't know her age at the time, because like most people in rural India, her parents didn't keep track of birthdays. She did tell me that her family had had to compromise on the match. They didn't have the means to offer a substantial dowry, which most families require if they are to bring a bride into their fold. To try to get the price down, Radha's parents opted for "a boy with faults." This narrowed the field of potential grooms to lower-caste boys, the disabled or mentally slow, widowers, and much older men. Of these unappealing options, Radha's family chose the last: a poor Brahmin, never married, named Bhaneshwar Jha, who was twenty years her senior.

Radha's parents considered it "watering somebody else's garden" to send their daughters to school, since they would inevitably leave the natal home to join another family. Although the government school in Radha's village was free, books and uniforms were not, and her parents didn't see that it was worth the investment. Already, they had to send Radha's brothers out to the fields to earn something toward their sisters' dowries. At home, the girls were sent into purdah, or seclusion, when they reached puberty, as was the custom among Brahmins in their area—the Madhubani district of Bihar. Radha always identified herself as a Madhubani Brahmin, as though it was important to distinguish herself from other Bihari Brahmins.

Purdah in this region meant she covered her face with her scarf, or *dupatta,* in front of her elders. The only occasions when she and her sisters were allowed to leave the family home were for religious events. Before she moved to Delhi, Radha had never heard of a woman who worked outside the home. She'd spent her days learning the skills that would make her a more desirable wife: pounding dried chili into a fine powder and forming chapatis into perfect, slightly puffed circles.

During the marriage rites, both her and her husband's faces were covered by veils. Even after Radha's world opened up dramatically—after she moved to India's capital and was exposed to so much, including my rather untraditional household—it was as though she continued to live behind a veil. She was startlingly unsure about both her history and her present world. When I asked for her husband's name, she had to think a minute to come up with it since she had never used it, either to his face or behind his back. Radha didn't know the name of his village or how much schooling he'd had, either; her cousin-brother, Joginder, told me all that. In fact, Joginder seemed to know more about most of the events of Radha's life than she did. History was a fairly irrelevant blur to her. Most of her memories were sketchy, undated, and closely held.

One morning Radha was bringing the day's milk to a boil, which she did every day because it is sold unpasteurized and is unsafe to drink. I joined her in there and started cleaning out the stove-top espresso maker I'd imported from the States—one of the kitchen tools Radha considered high-tech and refused to touch. She seemed to be in a good mood, so I asked her about the tattoo on her arm. I'd wondered about it since she'd started working for me. The pale, inexpensive ink was faded like a prison tattoo; the Hindi script was blurred and illegible. Radha waved me off, but when I persisted, she leaned against the kitchen counter. Soon after she was married, she said, she'd seen the tattoo wallah outside the temple in her husband's village and had been tempted to make an unlikely romantic gesture. She'd asked him to inscribe their names on her arm.

"I was naïve and silly. I didn't know he was going to pierce the skin with those needles to make the picture come! It hurt!"

She'd hurried back to her husband's house to dunk her arm in cold water. Only later did Bhaneshwar look at it carefully and inform her that the tattoo wallah, who was probably as illiterate as Radha, had tattooed the wrong name on her skin. According to her arm, her husband was married to a woman named Devi.

In ancient times, Bihar was a great cultural empire. During Radha's lifetime, though, her home state was famous for the wrong reasons: endemic corruption and extreme political instability. Now the adjective most often used to describe the place is *backward*. Only 5 percent of households in Bihar have electricity, compared with 40 percent nationwide, which is a fairly miserable starting point. Education levels are lower in Bihar, infant mortality is higher, and more of Bihar's citizens live below the poverty line than in the rest of the country. Indian intellectuals joke that the government would happily hand off the long-disputed region of Kashmir to Pakistan—if Pakistan would only agree to adopt disastrous Bihar as well. One Bihari politician liked to quip that kidnappings were his state's sole industry.

Bihar remains as feudal as medieval Europe; land is the primary source of power. The landowning castes have never been Brahmins, though. According to the laws of Manu, members of the highest caste were supposed to live in poverty, collecting alms in return for priestly work. These days, there are other acceptable Brahmin occupations for the educated, such as accounting work and government jobs. But undereducated Brahmins such as Radha's late husband are pretty much relegated to joblessness in India's caste-based economy. He was as landless as the Dalits who toiled in the fields, and unlike the merchant and warrior castes who fell beneath him on the hierarchy, he had no traditional occupation except one that required an education. Bhaneshwar's last name guaranteed him nothing other than a sense of entitlement.

Like so many others who could not survive on the land, Bhaneshwar fled Bihar for Delhi in search of work. It took him more than three days to get to Delhi by the cheapest bus and train tickets. When he arrived, he tracked down Joginder, who found him work as a *chowkidar*—a neighborhood guard—with a monthly income of eleven dollars. This he supplemented by selling roasted corn from a stall on the side of the road: six rupees for two ears. It took Bhaneshwar many months to be able to afford to send for Radha, and when he did, they began their married life in a tiny bamboo shelter offered to him by his employer. Radha could cook only one meal a day—though this was an improvement, because even that much was not a certainty in the village.

When Bhaneshwar fell ill, he didn't want to take a day off work to see a doctor, so he ignored his fever. By the time Joginder took him to the hospital, he was unable to walk. He had some kind of infection that spread to his brain—Radha and Joginder called it "brain fever." He slipped into a coma and died a few days later.

Radha scarcely remembered anything of the days after that.

"When they told me he wouldn't survive, I went into a trance. I was three months pregnant with Sujla. *Ay, bhagwan.*"

Joginder remembered, though. He told me he escorted Radha and her two young children back to her husband's village. They performed the cremation rituals, and she sat through the mourning period. Six months later, she gave birth to her daughter Sujla.

Radha's parents-in-law granted her a few days to recover from the birth before they kicked her out. They'd done their duty while she was pregnant, they told her, but they couldn't be responsible for feeding her and her children anymore. Among strict high-caste Hindus, women who have lost their husbands are considered bad luck. Traditionally, Brahmin widows were forced to shave their heads, join an ashram, and give their children away to their relatives. But Bhaneshwar's parents didn't want the children, so Radha piled everyone onto a bus back to Delhi.

Joginder, the neighborhood advocate for Bihari immigrants, found Radha a job doing the only thing she knew how to do—housework. That took only a few days; she needed much longer to snap out of her self-pitying daze. The ignominy of her life as a working widow haunted her, and was made much worse by the kind of work that she did. Radha described her life after her husband's death as a series of humiliations.

"Brahmins are not supposed to clean other people's houses, *deedee*. But this is my fate."

One of the few facts of her life that she told me clearly and repeatedly was that she would not be working if her husband were alive. Even when Bhaneshwar's former employer took pity on her and rescued her from the bamboo shack, the alternative didn't amount to much of an improvement: He gave her enough money to buy a *jhuggi*, a rough shack with a tin roof in a slum. Radha's new home was on the banks of the Ya-muna River, a tributary of the holy Ganges. Although it is a sacred body of water, it is best known as Delhi's sewer, because it is filled with the toxic effluent of thousands of unregulated factories. For Radha, though, the worst part about the slums was not the polluted living conditions; it was being forced to live in close proximity to Muslims and Dalits.

"In the village, we Brahmins don't intermingle with these people. If an untouchable passed by my house in the village, he would never expect to be let inside." Her chin was lifted; she met my eye directly. "Now these people live all around. There is nowhere in the big city you can live alone peacefully among your own caste people, without these others crowding around you."

Radha showed up at the apartment one morning with her face tortured into an exaggerated expression of concern. My maid was undeniably *filmy*, the word Indians use to describe a propensity for melodrama. Even before she spoke, my thoughts flashed to a formula my mother had come up with when she was living in Karachi: one tragedy per servant per month. Her six servants came to her with terrible stories—the death of a four-year-old daughter, an attack of malaria, and one outlandish tale about a brother who'd had all his toes chopped off in a prisoner-of-war camp. They wanted money for funerals and hospital visits, and my mother accepted that her role as memsahib of the household was to hand it out. She settled on twenty dollars each per disaster.

Because Geeta and Parvati thought I was being ripped off all the time, I was constantly trying to work out whether there was a subtext in my interactions with my servants. It didn't seem as though Radha was after money this time, though; there was panic in her voice that I hadn't heard before.

"They're saying our *jhuggi* is going to be destroyed. Some big government babu showed up this morning and told us they're going to knock down the whole shantytown!"

She'd paid sixty dollars for her shanty. That was two months' wages, an unbearable sum to lose. The government routinely bulldozes homes in urban India, because they are illegal structures occupied by squatters. Maneesh told us that her previous home had been destroyed a few years before.

Some forty million Indians are illegal squatters in *bustee*s. They are the underside of the new India, the migrant workers who fuel the fast-expanding economy. The Indian government never built low-income housing for its rural migrants, as did the United States, Europe, and, more recently, China. Instead, immigrants from the hinterlands rely on city slumlords, who pay off local politicians to protect the slums. The politicians allow the shantytowns to stay standing because that guarantees them the votes of the inhabitants and protects their careers. It's a perfect circle of corruption, at least until the politician is voted out of power. Then the city comes in with bulldozers.

This time, the Supreme Court had ordered all "riverbed encroachments" to be cleared, in an effort to save the Yamuna from further pollution. Tens of thousands of people were expected to be moved out of their shanties on the Yamuna Pushta, the embankment of the river. Radha had a flicker of hope in a rumor she'd heard that the Delhi government was allotting alternate land, far outside the city, to *jhuggi* owners who could produce their paperwork. The idea of trying to negotiate India's opaque officialdom was deeply intimidating to Radha, though. With neither formal education nor street smarts, she found it a challenge just to get around the city on a normal day. Radha couldn't tell time, so she had to rely on the height of the sun in the sky, and it was often blocked by buildings or smog. She couldn't read numbers, so I made calls for her on my home phone. She always asked someone on the street which bus to board; she couldn't identify the bus routes from the signs.

Luckily, Radha had her teenage son, Babloo, to help her manage city life. With no other man around, he'd considered himself the head of her household since he could walk. Babloo had grown into a serious fifteen-year-old with his mother's black emotional eyes. He'd started working in a doctor's office two years before, answering phones after school a few days a week. He told me that even though he gave all his income to his mother, he wished he could earn more than he did, so that she could quit the job she considered so demeaning.

Radha wouldn't hear of it. For all her provincialism, she was a firm believer in the importance of education. She often said that she wanted to make sure her children weren't *moork*s, or "idiots," like her, unable to read or write. She wanted her daughters to finish high school before they married, and she had high Brahminical ambitions for her son. Because Babloo attended a Hindi-language high school, she'd asked me to tutor him in English, which I did for most of the years I lived in Delhi. She hoped he'd achieve what few from the slums manage to do: go to college and pull himself into the middle class.

It was with Babloo's future in her sights that Radha endured the daily unpleasantness of her life. At four each morning, she collected the family's allotment of water from the shared outdoor tap, and woke Babloo so he could take his cold bucket bath before dawn. He combed his hair back with palm oil so it would hold the pattern of the comb's teeth through the morning. He visited the Sai Baba temple every Thursday afternoon to pray for his family's health, and never neglected to collect two packets of milk from the local dairy on his way home. His mother's shame about their low status defined his life. Only occasionally did he act his age. Radha told me, laughing, that she once caught him in front of the cracked mirror in their shack, doing a dance step and smoothing his hair with his hand, imitating his favorite Bollywood hero.

Babloo had kept the ownership papers for their *jhuggi* carefully folded under the mattress. He made sure their name was added to the government list so they would be allotted new land, and was advised by neighbors that they could make a profit if they sold it and rented a place elsewhere. Other slum dwellers lost everything during the Yamuna Pushta demolitions, and an unnumbered, unnamed few were even buried under the rubble of their destroyed homes, according to some reports I read. But Radha made out pretty well from the ordeal. With the money they made off the land, they were able to rent a room in a tenement, in a pukka building made of cement.

When she told me how relieved she was to have moved out of her ramshackle shanty, I'd joke that I was going to follow her home one day and stay with her in her nice apartment. She'd look pleased for a moment, and then add quickly, "No, *deedee*, you wouldn't like it. It isn't in a nice place." Her reaction reminded me of the obsequious character Dr. Aziz in *A Passage to India,* the E. M. Forster novel set in colonial India. He's so embarrassed about his run-down bungalow that he comes up with a complicated and ill-fated scheme to prevent his British friends from seeing it. I didn't want to imagine that my uppity Brahmin maid harbored similar insecurities about her memsahib. I told myself she was just being modest and pestered her to take me home to meet her daughters until she gave in.

Radha's neighborhood was only a twenty-minute walk away, but it was literally on the other side of the Nizamuddin tracks from my middle-class enclave, and I'd never been there. The track crossing was closed when we got there, and the midmorning heat was beating down on the traffic that had accumulated on either side: vendors with wooden handcarts of hard oranges and tiny red onions; impatient families piled on scooters, the men with handkerchiefs tied across their mouths to protect against the dust; a group of boys stacked sweatily inside the cab of an industrial-size rickshaw, its cargo of burlap sacks of flour slowly leaking white dust onto the pavement. Since the rail crossing could be closed for two or three hours at a time, Radha told me that pedestrians rarely waited for it to lift; instead, they scanned the tracks and darted across. Of course, she added nonchalantly, a couple were killed by oncoming trains each day.

We tried to make our way across quickly without stumbling on the raised rails. I was eyeing the distance for an oncoming train, so at first I didn't notice the desiccated feces scattered on the tracks. Since Indian trains don't have flush toilets, the passengers' business falls straight down. Radha shot me an embarrassed glance.

"I hate having to come this way."

On the other side, the street shimmied into a crooked laneway. Stagnant gray pools of gutter sewage lay between the sidewalk and the small houses. A stream of dirty bathwater spewed out of a window into the alley below, and I looked up to see a woman swinging her long, wet hair inside the window. Kids squatted in the dirt over their games of sticks and pebbles, their brown hair bleached orange-red by malnourishment. We passed a whitewashed temple, where Radha said a "miracle *puja* doctor" worked. Through the windows, I could see a long line of patients snaking through the dark interior.

Her concrete apartment building loomed enormous in the tiny lane. The hallways echoed with the squalor of a refugee camp—the sounds of many families living in close proximity and great poverty. On each of the four floors were thirty apartments, in each of which were crammed as many as twelve people. Radha shared latrines and bathing rooms with sixty of her neighbors. At the entrance to her apartment, I kicked off my shoes and followed her in, but then I couldn't figure out what to do with myself. I'd visited dozens and dozens of shacks and slum dwellings on reporting assignments all across India, and had sometimes wondered whether the tight quarters explained the emotional closeness in Indian family relationships. But my own servant's home was smaller than most of them. It was shocking that Radha paid any rent at all for this place—a single room the size of my bathroom.

Her sixteen-year-old daughter, Pushpa, was cross-legged on a cot, squinting at a textbook in the dim light. She smiled shyly, like a much younger girl, and gestured for me to climb up beside her onto the bed, which was raised off the floor with bricks to create space beneath. From this perch, I looked around. Long ago, someone had painted the walls an eerie combination of baby-girl pink and putrid green; now the garish colors were muted by years of soot from the stove. The sole window in the place looked out into the hallway; a curtain was pulled across it for privacy. The only other light came from a fluorescent tube. A shelf shrine with plastic statues of Ganesh and Krishna took up most of the wall space. Stacked in one corner were the family's electrical appliances: a battered fan and an outdated TV whose enormous antenna was doing little to appease the static snowing across the screen.

I thought of how pleased Radha had looked when I'd bought my first TV in India. Even though it was no bigger than my laptop screen, it was nonetheless a brand-new television with a cable connection, which seemed to make her feel proud of the home she worked in. Her own set received only the government-run channels—that is, when there was electricity in the building. If Radha finished her day's duties at my apartment early, she'd crouch on her haunches directly in front of my TV, pushing the buttons on the set—she was intimidated by the remote—until she found a Hindu prayer channel. As the camera panned across tens of thousands of pilgrims trooping toward a sacred site, her features would relax into righteous pleasure. "With God's blessing, one day I'll also visit Somnath Temple," she'd say.

I recognized my old minifridge crowded into the electrical appliance corner of the room. The power surges had eventually killed it, and I'd thrown it away—or so I'd thought. My heart suddenly pounded. Why hadn't Radha just told me she wanted the broken refrigerator? She followed my eyes.

"*Deedee,* I took your old fridge because we didn't have one. I was embarrassed to ask you for it."

I'd never noticed the streaks of gray in her hair before. We sat in silence for a moment, listening to Pushpa scribbling in her notebook with a pencil stub.

"Well, if you got it working again, then I'm glad you took it."

Radha set her jaw.

"The electrician wallah was going to charge fifty rupees just to look at it. I told him, I got this for free, why would I spend that much on it? So I just use it for storing food. It keeps the bugs out of the chapati flour."

As if on cue, a big brown cockroach scuttled across the floor. Earlier that year, when I'd found roaches in my apartment, Radha and I had spent several mornings strategizing about how to eliminate them. She'd instructed me to buy a chalklike homeopathic remedy, and in my desperation I'd complied. She'd drawn circles with it around the apartment and sworn that roaches wouldn't dare enter inside the lines because they were afraid of the stuff.

I'd never have guessed that the woman who bent down on her swollen knees to mop my floors to a luminous sheen lived in filth and squalor herself. Maybe because Radha couldn't apply her Brahminical notions of purity and pollution to her own home, she applied them instead to mine. I looked away so she wouldn't see the tears that welled up in my eyes. I wished I hadn't made her bring me here. Perhaps I really was no different from my great-aunt Edith, the British missionary decked out in a long frock and a European sun helmet who spent her life imposing her religion on the pagans. In spite of all my efforts to tread carefully in India, I was living out my own *Passage to India* story.

Female foreign correspondents have a bad reputation in expat circles: For the most part, we're considered either hard-boiled and callous, or desperate and flirtatious. I couldn't help but notice that the women journalists in Delhi were disproportionately young and single. Our male counterparts were generally older and more successful, and most of them were accompanied in Delhi by wives and kids. I'd banded together with the few other women my age. We'd often get together for brunches or drinks at someone's apartment and compare notes. We traveled too much and were beholden more to news schedules than to our own plans; most of us had messy personal situations as a result, but all of us got a high from the overseas reporter's life.

My friends and I would talk sometimes about what a rush it was to be intimately involved in the goings-on of the world, not from a newsroom in New York or Washington but from the center of the story. I felt lucky to get to see the wild beauty of places that were difficult to visit as a tourist, such as rebel-occupied Sri Lanka. My job allowed me to feel as though I was seeing the world from the inside out: I got to talk to poppy farmers and politicians, police recruits and militants, people whose dreams and expectations were completely different from my own. Whether I was sitting cross-legged in a Mumbai slum or running toward a building under siege in Srinagar, I was living life intensely.

Like my friends, I'd become somewhat addicted to the thrills of unexpected travel and reporting under harrowing circumstances. I still believe that working as a foreign correspondent is the only job I will ever truly love—but that doesn't mean it was good for me.

One night, curled into comfortable chairs in my friend M.P.'s enormous Delhi apartment, we tried to come up with a list of women who'd succeeded in holding on to both a globe-trotting reporter job and a stable partnership. We expanded the list to include women we didn't know in person; still, we couldn't think of more than six names. Adding children to the formula narrowed the list even further, to a mere two. It was one thing to talk abstractly about how being a reporter overseas required a sacrifice. Seeing the hard data inspired a new round of soul-searching.

My friends and I came up with a code phrase to describe the stark life of the long-term female foreign correspondent: "Miserable Jen," as we'd nicknamed a journalist we knew in Delhi. She'd been reporting from overseas for more than twenty years, and her skin was leathery from sun and alcohol. At parties, she laughed too loudly and sometimes bragged about flings with her Afghan and Pakistani translators. Miserable Jen was the only foreigner I knew who'd caught dengue fever, a mosquito-borne disease also called "breakbone fever" because that's apparently what it feels like. When I'd tried to sympathize with her about it, she waved me off dismissively, saying she'd already had it twice before, in Africa.

Jen was one of the few reporters I knew who actively lobbied her paper to send her back to Baghdad after it became so dangerous that it was difficult to get out and do any real reporting. It was hard to believe it was still good for her career at that point.

"Maybe she likes Baghdad because the odds are good," M.P. joked.

M.P. liked to say "the odds are good, but the goods are odd" to describe the many opportunities for liaisons we had while living overseas. We'd all noticed what Geeta complained about: the paucity of single Indian men over the age of thirty. Married Indian men were more than happy to have affairs with *feringhee* girls, but that was not what we were after. The single expats we met in places such as Baghdad, Delhi, and Kabul were reporters, UN workers, and security contractors; it naturally followed that they were drifters, swashbucklers, or womanizers, generally uninterested in real relationships. Like them, we, too, were searching for bright flare-ups to grant us fleeting solace from the fear and sadness we so often witnessed and felt.

Miserable Jen worked hard and was often first on the story, but she no longer seemed to have any real interest in the places or people she covered. She'd get drunk and spit that she hated India and all its whiny inhabitants. Worst of all, Miserable Jen made other people miserable. After she left India, her translator told us that she'd often found her in the mornings passed out in her home office, a bottle of gin under the desk. When she came to, Jen would holler and throw things at her employees.

The sordid tale became a reverse source of inspiration to my friends and me.

"We will not become like Miserable Jen!" we'd promise one another, raising our glasses of overpriced imported red wine.

Most Westerners who visit India can agree that it inspires love or hate, or both. The German novelist and Academy Award–winning screenwriter Ruth Prawer Jhabvala said that some Westerners "loathe it, some love it, most do both." Jhabvala married an Indian and lived in India for most of her adult life, and yet her conflicting emotions about the place seemed to only grow stronger. In her 1957 book *Out of India*, Jhabvala wrote that she felt "strapped to a wheel that goes round and round," cycling between tremendous enthusiasm for India and thinking that everything in it was "abominable."

Expats often claim that the only way to get anything done in India is to be rude, and they may be repeating what they've heard middle-class Indians say. I think the extreme stratification of India's caste system makes it more acceptable to take advantage of people, because inside every interaction lurk station, caste, and wealth. Everyone I knew in India abused power, at least occasionally. Parvati brought out her "Delhi bitch" around government bureaucrats, rickshaw drivers, shop-keepers, and anyone else who got in her way. She had an affectionate relationship with her servant, Promila, but she wasn't above cussing her out for a minor infraction such as chopping the carrots before rinsing them. Another Indian friend would smack her driver on the head so hard that the *thwunk* would reverberate through the car whenever he got lost or drove too fast.

I had my own such moments; it wasn't for nothing that my Delhi friends called me "Demanda." At some point, I'd started to think it was acceptable to yell when things didn't go my way. Since that happens pretty routinely when you are an outsider in a developing country, I was quite often unhinged. Once, while waiting in the Lahore airport for information about the next flight out of Pakistan, I stormed up to the counter several times to holler that I needed to know what was going on. That part was not unusual; the reason I remember the event is because I eventually turned in aggravation to an expat journalist I vaguely knew who was standing near me and said, "No information about these canceled flights. Doesn't it make you want to kill someone?"

"I just try to think of something else," he replied coolly from behind his sunglasses.

I took a step back. It was a pitch-perfect rendering of what my phrase-coining friend M.P. called "third-world Zen." She'd spent seventeen years in Asia trying to hone this state of mind herself. It was harder in India, she said, thanks to the legacy of colonialism, which allows foreigners to be treated like high-caste dukes and duchesses. I'd often find myself whisked to the front of the line and escorted to the cleanest toilet, privileges that were easy to take for granted.

I didn't realize that the memsahib treatment had gone to my head, but my family and friends back home did. My aunt Susie once sent me a care package consisting exclusively of Buddhist books, a not-so-subtle prod to get me to calm down and treat people more kindly. One of the books suggested turning up the sides of your mouth, just ever so slightly, in what it called a small inner smile. I tried to practice that, sitting in the back of a rickshaw or walking through the market: smile my Buddhist half smile, try to think sympathetic thoughts, and take things less seriously. Of course, all I really wanted to do when I found myself lost again and late to another appointment was scream like a madwoman into the oven-hot air and smack the face of one of those ogling teenage boys.

Parvati was right when she warned me that I'd need to toughen up to make it in a harsh city such as Delhi, and that was even more the case in Kabul and Karachi. As I lay in bed listening to the sounds of a hostile city outside my hotel room window, I could almost feel myself growing another layer of skin. Soon, I imagined, nothing would be able to get through, and I'd become Super Reporter Girl—the hard-ass star of the movie of my life.

I got an inkling of the toll South Asia had taken on my personality when my younger sister, Jessica, came to visit me in Delhi. K.K. was away in his village that week, so we set out into Nizamuddin market to hail an auto-rickshaw. I dreaded this part of the morning, because Delhi rickshaw drivers consistently refuse to run the meter and always overcharge their customers, assuming that *feringhees*, even more than the rest of Delhi's population, are suckers. Parvati had taught me to bargain aggressively to avoid paying the extra fare, even if it required yelling and cussing in Hindi. After a couple of drivers named outrageous prices, I launched into an attack on one of them, using Parvati language: "You bloody *behen chode*! Do you really think you can charge that? Is this how you would treat your mother?"

The mother line—a crass exploitation of the importance of family connections in India—almost always worked. The besieged driver relented and waved us in. I let out a righteous huff, and Jessica followed me, looking intimidated.

We drove in silence for a few moments before she said, "You were really yelling out there, Miranda. How much extra was he trying to charge you?"

I was surprised by the disquiet in her voice. The bargaining session had seemed fairly routine.

"Not that much, but it doesn't matter whether it is five rupees extra or fifty rupees—"

She interrupted my customary rant against Delhi's dishonest drivers and cheating vegetable sellers.

"I know, I know, you've told me. It's the principle of the thing. But . . . it's still only a few cents. Who cares?"

I had no reply. After a moment, she asked, "What did you call him, anyway?"

"Oh. Um . . . I called him a sister-fucker."

It somehow sounded a lot worse in English. A few days later, Jessica told me, as perhaps only a sister can, that she thought I had been a nicer person before I moved to India.

Sometimes, I'd feel a surge of true memsahib anger at my maid. Once, Radha threw away a plastic jug of wildflowers I'd put out on the dining room table; I found them in the garbage, jug and all. When I asked why, her Hindi sped up incomprehensibly. That evening, when Parvati stopped by, I showed her the jug and asked what was going on. She broke into her trademark cackle.

"You put flowers in *that*? That's not a flower vase, that's a bathroom jug!"

I was tired of missing the joke and amusing everyone with my *feringhee* blunders.

"I know it's not a vase, but it's not something I use in the bathroom," I insisted.

"Well, I guess you use toilet paper, but the rest of us millions of Indians use these jugs to clean ourselves after we go to the toilet. That's the only thing this type of plastic jug is used for. Radha's Brahmin hair must have stood up on its end when she saw it on the table you eat off."

Compared to disinfectant-obsessed America, India at first appeared to be coated with filth and grime. But in fact, the dirt is neither uniform nor ubiquitous. Purity of the body is one of the most important aspects of Hinduism; even sweat and spit should be purged before praying or eating. Indians place a strong emphasis on personal hygiene, even if it isn't immediately apparent. Slum dwellers crap in the fields and let their kids wander barefoot through fetid alleys; still, each morning they wash themselves at the public tap with a carefully preserved strip of family soap. Every Indian woman has mastered the skill of rinsing herself through her sari. Only the middle classes wear deodorant, though, which makes for pungent experiences on packed trains. Some of the poor take the edge off their body odor by patting themselves with baby powder in the mornings, creating a ghostly effect as it sifts out of their clothes into a white sheen on their arms and necks.

Indians draw a bright line between "inside dirt" and "outside dirt" and have a strict code of conduct for distinguishing between them. Most families are willing to endure the stench of a garbage dump as long as their kitchen is immaculate. Removing street shoes inside is only one part of the code of conduct; when Radha saw me walking barefoot around the apartment, she'd demand that I put on my indoor *chappals*. The idea that I might step into the bathroom without shoes was repulsive to her, because she considered it the epicenter of filth. Many Indians reserve a separate set of *chappals* for use in the bathroom. No matter how much it is scrubbed, it can never really be clean; it is, after all, the place where the body's waste is expelled. Since only the lowest castes will touch latrines, they are often left to fester.

Mahatma Gandhi waged an unglamorous lifelong campaign to improve the conditions of India's toilets. The bathroom, he said, is "a temple. . . . It should be so clean and inviting that anyone would enjoy eating there." In a bid to eliminate the stigma of latrines, Gandhi required all the residents of his ashram to take turns doing Dalits' work. When he first imposed this rule on his household, even his wife, Kasturba, refused, saying it demeaned her high-caste status. He eventually convinced her to live by his principles, though he didn't have as much success with the rest of India. In my house, Radha resolutely ignored the bathrooms, so I cleaned the toilet bowls myself and paid Maneesh extra to do the floors.

When Parvati's mother came to stay with her, Parvati told me she actually had to keep her Dalit servant, Promila, out of her apartment. Her mother couldn't stomach having a filthy garbage collector inside a small space with her, and certainly not in the kitchen. Parvati had hired Promila to do the tasks of an untouchable—cleaning the stairs and taking out the garbage—and after a while moved her up to the better-paid tasks usually reserved for the higher castes—chopping vegetables and washing dishes. For Parvati, allowing a Dalit into her kitchen was a way to prove that she was no longer defined by the highly stratified society that she'd grown up in. But her mother was having none of it.

"She considers Promila filthy because she picks up garbage with her hands. In fact, my mom won't eat my food if Promila so much as enters the kitchen."

"What if Promila washes her hands when she comes in?"

Parvati laughed. There was a bitter edge to it.

"My mother wouldn't be satisfied even if she bathed in Dettol disinfectant for two days."

Promila had recently caused a bit of a scandal when she'd informed Parvati, and her other employers in the building, that she was not an untouchable. Her name, Promila, was not a Dalit name, she pointed out. While this was true, Parvati had heard Promila's husband calling her by the Dalit name Sushila. Parvati suspected that her servant was trying to disguise her origins to improve her lot in life. She didn't like being lied to, yet she couldn't help but admire Promila's bold ambition. She laughed as she told me that Promila would come by the apartment to try to irk her mother.

"She'll take my hand and say in this high, sentimental voice, 'Oh, *deedee,* don't you miss me cleaning and cooking for you?' My mother hates it. As soon as Promila leaves, she snaps at me, 'Go wash your hands! That garbage-collector girl is filthy!'"

Promila wouldn't have dared to try to disguise her caste if she were still back in her village, where the majority of Dalits live. Gandhi may have idealized the Indian village as "a complete republic" of enlightened agrarian life, but the Dalit leader B. R. Ambedkar called it "a sink of localism, a den of ignorance." The city was the only hope of escaping discrimination, he said. Of course, there is no way to know how many untouchables try to discard their identifying last names. Even if they don't, the city has an anonymizing effect, making it easier for them to avoid working as cobblers or street sweepers once they leave the rural areas.

"I was born a Hindu and I have suffered the consequences of untouchability. I will not die a Hindu," Ambedkar declared in 1935. Toward the end of his life, he—along with half a million other Dalits—converted to Buddhism in a public ceremony. In the decades since, many millions have followed his lead. Unless they clamber onto a bus to Delhi or Mumbai, though, Dalits are rarely able to transcend their caste. In their villages, they are known as "converted Dalits."

If my apartment had become the proving ground for Radha's caste pride, Maneesh was the standard against which she measured herself. The two maids would squat on the floor gossiping—though never as equals. Maneesh was careful not to interrupt Radha or disagree with her opinions, and Radha tossed out regular reminders of her innate superiority to Maneesh. When she found food in the fridge that was more than a couple of days old, she'd say, "You shouldn't eat this. I certainly wouldn't—give it to Maneesh."

Radha's disdain for her low-caste colleague was complicated by the fact that her life was not materially better than Maneesh's. Yes, Maneesh had to clean bathrooms and collect garbage, but Radha had to mop floors on all fours. Both were only a crisis or two away from irredeemable poverty.

The main difference was that Maneesh shared little of Radha's shame about her low status or lack of material wealth. She'd been asking me to come home with her for more than a year, and I decided to make the trip when she told me her niece was about to get married. Geeta shuddered when I told her my weekend plan. She found it hard to comprehend why I would spend my free time making anthropological excursions into the ugliest parts of India—and this time I wasn't even reporting a story. It also made Geeta nervous to think of the negative impressions I might come back with after inspecting the least-proud aspects of her country.

When we got close to Maneesh's neighborhood, we climbed out of the car and left it with K.K. The alleys in her area were too narrow for rickshaws, let alone wider vehicles. Maneesh lifted the edges of her *salwar* pants so they wouldn't drag in the mud, tugged her *dupatta* over her head, and led me down her lane. The familiar stench of sewage greeted us. Two bare-bottomed children were playing in the alley, naked except for a string tied around each of their waists. Their kohl-lined eyes and skinny frames gave them an unearthly aspect. They trailed after us, far more interested in the *feringhee* than they were in the sewage-splattered pig lying comatose nearby with a few granules of yellow grain stuck to its snout.

Someone had pressed green-brown henna handprints into the whitewashed concrete walls of the building, decorations for the wedding celebrations. Above the cement staircase, a battered gold paper banner read, in Hindi, "Bless this marriage." Maneesh, her husband, and their two teenage sons shared the place—three rooms, a bathing area, and a separate latrine—with her husband's brother and his family. It felt palatial compared to Radha's room. Maneesh's sons slept out on the patio at night, rather than next to her, as Radha's son did.

"I lived in a *jhuggi* growing up, made of mud brick with a hay roof. This is better," Maneesh pronounced.

I gave her sister-in-law a box of sweets to congratulate her on the wedding, and a young cousin brought us cups of *chai*. The milky substance had been boiled into sticky goo that caught in my throat. I tried not to cough as I forced it down. Maneesh squatted off to the side. I noticed she was as deferential to her sister-in-law as she was to Radha, laughing amenably at her jokes and offering no conversation of her own. There is a strict hierarchy inside Hindu extended families, based on the birth order of the sons. Maneesh, married to the younger son, ranked second in their shared home. Her status was depreciated even further because her husband contributed no income to the family.

After her sister-in-law left the room, Maneesh gave me an unsentimental, matter-of-fact description of her life.

"My husband is not good, *deedee*. All he does is lie around and get drunk. He's out gambling in the *bustee* now."

Maneesh was about fourteen when her father got her married to his neighbor's son, Om Prakash, a fellow Dalit. He'd worked cleaning floors in a public hospital in Delhi, but had recently decided it interfered too much with his drinking. Now, Maneesh said, he badgered her every night for money to buy hooch from the slum dealer.

"My husband always feels awful when he wakes up." She referred to Om Prakash in the usual wifely way by not using his name. "He complains that his head hurts and his body aches. When I tell him it's because he drinks too much, he starts slapping me around. But he beats me up even if I am quiet."

Maneesh wasn't making a bid for pity, simply stating the sorrowful facts as they were. Her concern was now for her sons, who seemed to be following Om Prakash's example: Both had dropped out of school after sixth grade and refused to get jobs. She didn't expect her sons or husband to show up to the wedding celebrations over the next few days.

"Everyone said giving birth to two sons was my good luck, but maybe not." She pushed herself up from her haunches. "This topic is too sad for the wedding season. Let's hope the bride's fate will be better than mine."

The bride was surrounded by visitors, so we didn't spend much time with her. In the car on my way home with K.K., a city bus lurched to a halt beside us. Delhi public buses are the cheapest mode of transportation; scarred and rusted like abandoned hulks at a scrap metal dump, they cruise through the streets as if they've been raised from the dead. This one had glassless window panes and bare metal benches; the outside was encrusted with red *paan* spit and greenish-yellow vomit stains. Inside, passengers swayed hip to hip in the vehicle's sickening lurch. All but the poorest classes avoid city buses in Delhi— especially women, because eve-teasing on board is almost inevitable. In the years I lived there, I only once traveled by public bus, and I was fondled by so many different hands during that fifteen-minute interval that I jumped off the first time it came to a full stop.

I imagined Maneesh wedging her tiny body into a sliver of space on one of these buses each morning, strands of hair flattened to her forehead with sweat. I wondered what she thought about as the bus pushed through the Delhi smog and traffic, taking her to another day of collecting other people's trash.

Radha had been glassy-eyed with a high temperature for days, but she refused to let me take her to the clinic, saying she'd already invested in a visit to her own temple doctor. She pulled a small brown-paper packet of unmarked white pills out of her sari blouse and, with some pride, informed me that his complex system of medication was too complicated for anyone else to understand.

Then she stopped showing up for work. Eventually, Joginder came by. She had cholera, he said, a severe bacterial infection that leads to such a rapid loss of body fluid that some patients die within days. Joginder was taking a collection in the neighborhood to help her get moved to a better hospital, because she wasn't getting enough rehydration therapy in the public facility.

When it comes to health care, India is rather like nineteenth-century America, where local healers, bloodletters, and ministers served as general practitioners for their communities. In modern-day India, mainstream doctors face competition not just from local quacks and temple doctors, but also from alternative doctors who have been officially endorsed by the Indian government. The Indian ministry of health has a branch specifically dedicated to such therapies: the Department of Ayurveda, Yoga & Naturopathy, Unani, Siddha and Homeopathy. With a name like that, even the acronym, AYUSH, is amusing. When I saw the hand-painted sign outside the building in Delhi, I thought it was a joke. In fact, it's just the Indian government's effort to cover all bases: Unani medicine for conservative Muslims, Ayurveda for South Indians, and homeopathy for the middle class. Almost everyone I knew in India would visit the homeopath before seeing a mainstream doctor. Geeta referred to practitioners of Western scientific medicine as "allopathic doctors," the dismissive term coined by the founder of homeopathy.

By my American standards, health care in India was fabulously cheap. I didn't even have health insurance in India, because I was certain I could afford to pay for whatever treatment I needed, and because almost no one has insurance, 80 percent of health-care costs are paid out of pocket. Indian companies manufacture generic versions of almost every medication, which keeps the prices down. Not only that, but few Indian pharmacists demand to see a prescription before doling out drugs.

Health care didn't seem cheap to my maids, though. Although Maneesh had cataracts in both her eyes, she couldn't afford the private hospital fees, nor could she bear the idea of joining the crowds outside the government-funded All India Institute of Medical Sciences (AIIMS), a prestigious medical college where she could get it done practically for free. At AIIMS, patients pay as little as twenty-five cents for treatment; almost four million people flock there each year. The streets around the hospital are filled with moaning piles of the sick. Having journeyed from their villages, they wait for treatment for days or even weeks. Inside, signs in English and Hindi above the hallway sinks plead, "Please do not clean cloth & utensils."

At the Kachhwa Mission Hospital outside Varanasi, where my great-aunt Edith worked in the 1940s and '50s, several hundred patients would cram into the compound every day. They were suffering from the range of urgent problems that regularly killed Indians seventy years ago—snakebites, tuberculosis, smallpox. Since Edith's day, the government has begun running regular vaccination programs in villages and has established a lot more rural clinics. Many are open only a few hours a week, though, which isn't much help to those Indians who continue to suffer from infectious diseases that disappeared from the Western world decades ago.

It was six weeks before Radha returned, heavy lidded and slow moving. Priya and I decided to tell her that she shouldn't cook for us for a while, since cholera can be transmitted through contaminated food. This seemed to make Radha worry that her sickness had undermined her superior status in our household.

"*Arre?* You had Maneesh cleaning for you while I was gone? Did she cook for you too?"

Priya reassured her that she had not abandoned her Brahmin principles and fallen so low as to have a Dalit make her food. Still, she pointed out that no Delhi apartment can go six weeks without a sweep, which only made Radha more catty.

"Well, it doesn't look as though Maneesh did much to improve it. She left dirty spots on the floors, and the dishes are greasy."

I made a disapproving face. Radha huffed off into the bathroom, where she spent the next hour kneading away at the pile of our dirty clothes, pushing her hair from her forehead, looking like nothing so much as an overworked *dhobi* laboring on a polluted riverbed. She made a show of meticulously dusting the bookshelves—her least favorite job—and when I put a hand on her shoulder to stop her, she snapped at me. Her eyes still looked feverish.

"How much more do you pay me than Maneesh?"

I wondered what this was about. Was Radha angling for another raise?

"Maneesh only collects the garbage," I reminded her. "You get paid more because you do way more work."

She swiped the bookshelf aggressively with her dusting cloth. I was about to walk away when she hissed, "It still isn't right to give her the recycling!"

So *that's* it, I thought. The recycling. In a country where everything is worth something, my yellowing newspapers and glass bottles were a valuable commodity. The Indian government doesn't run a recycling program, and it doesn't need to. The low-caste urban poor have created a complex private industry around discarded goods. Together, ragpickers, garbage sorters, and garbage collectors reuse and resell more than half of the country's plastic, whereas only about 10 percent of plastic in the United States is recycled.

In Nizamuddin, the recyclables collector was an old man with a Muslim beard, who rode on a clunky bicycle. By early afternoon, his rear basket was weighed down with old paper and plastic. My neighbors referred to him as the *han-ji* wallah—the "yes man"—because he called out *"Han-jiiii!"* as he cycled around the neighborhood, dragging the Hindi word for "yes" into a long, memorable solicitation. He didn't get my newspaper and bottles, though, because Radha had them as a condition of her employment. She'd lug the piles downstairs and cart them off herself to the local recycling depot.

If the world were fair, Maneesh would have been the one to get the recycling. Probably the only real perk of the job she'd inherited from her ancestors was the right to sell the valuables she found in the trash. I'd often see her separating our garbage into little salable piles on the pavement outside our apartment. In her pile of things worth keeping: a shampoo bottle, a cracked mug, rusty bobby pins. There was something very sad, and also kind of intrusive, about the care Maneesh took with the discarded objects of my life. I'd find myself thinking about her when I threw stuff away, wondering whether a sturdy plastic bag or piece of ribbon would make it to her pile. Sometimes I'd see them in their new incarnations—Maneesh carried a ripped cloth purse, once a gift from my mother, tucked into the waistband of her *salwar*.

When Radha was sick and Maneesh asked for permission to recycle the growing stack of old newspapers in a corner of my office, I'd been unable to refuse. Now I had to make amends. I asked Radha to sit down with me in the living room. As usual, she refused the chair and squatted beside me.

"I hope you know that you are essential to our household, Radha. We both really missed you when you were sick."

She shrugged like an offended teenager and looked down.

"I am in debt because of the hospital bills, *deedee.*"

I had already given Joginder money to help fund her hospital stay, but I felt inexplicably guilty. I offered to pay her what she would have earned from the recycling, and she nodded in grudging acceptance. Later, I saw her beckon Maneesh into the kitchen to explain the situation to the lesser maid in her imperious way.

"From now on, *deedee* says, only I get the paper and glass recycling. But I don't want to deal with the plastic bottles. They aren't worth much. Those, you can take."

CHAPTER 9

Seven Lifetimes

I was watching Geeta have her facial hair removed. She had a long list of beautifications to achieve at Madame X before her arranged marriage meeting that evening. It was her first in a long time, and she was nervous, so I'd agreed to accompany her to the salon for moral support. Geeta only occasionally brought up her stagnated husband hunt these days. When she was feeling lighthearted, she'd joke that Shaadi.com should give her an award for the longest-running matrimonial ad, or that her marriage meetings were keeping Madame X in business, if nothing else. She'd also started saying, more pessimistically, that she wished she'd married Mohan. Even though he was "bad natured," at least she wouldn't have had to think about marriage anymore.

Her father had come up with the latest Shaadi prospect—Ashok, a Punjabi who worked for a technology firm in California. That qualified him as an NRI, the acronym for "nonresident Indian." Since Indians first began emigrating to the West in large numbers, in the late 1960s, NRIs have registered right at the top of the husband hierarchy, even higher than engineers and doctors. Because they usually earned good

salaries, in dollars, they were considered the ticket out of an impoverished India. Now, of course, Indians no longer need to leave home for
a well-paid job with a multinational company; still, many Indians
persist in wanting to move overseas. Sixty-two percent of women
looking for a husband say they would like an NRI, according to a Shaadi
survey.

Geeta's interest in an NRI husband was different: She thought he
was more likely to be socially progressive than the average Indian boy.
Her evidence for this theory came mostly from Bollywood. In fact, her
model of an ideal husband was Shah Rukh Khan's character, Raj, in the
blockbuster film *DDLJ*. Raj, a second-generation Indian living in London, humbles himself to the heroine's family to prove that he is worthy
of her. In one scene, he is actually peeling vegetables in the kitchen
with the women of the house—unthinkable in preglobalized Bollywood.

Even more memorably, Raj fasts along with the women during
Karva Chauth, the annual festival when North Indian women refuse
food and water between sunrise and moonrise to pray for the health
and prosperity of their husbands. Geeta's mother had observed the
Karva Chauth fast every year since her marriage, and Geeta planned to
do so for her husband, too, even though she'd once noted archly that
there was no equivalent holiday during which husbands fast for the
health of their wives. Seeing Raj go hungry all day in the name of his
wife probably made Geeta overoptimistic about her options for an Indian husband.

More to the point, NRIs were more likely to be interested in marrying a girl over thirty, since they tend to be a little older themselves
when they embark on the marriage search. Because the families of NRI
boys usually expect their sons to marry Indian girls, NRIs make up a
full third of Shaadi's male members; the site has staked its business
model on the commitment among Indian families to marrying their
children to fellow Indians.

Ashok, whose online Shaadi handle was "NRIgroom," was clearly
taking advantage of the desirability of his overseas status. He had come
back to India on what Geeta called a "marriage pilgrimage"—his parents

had flown him back to the homeland to help him find a wife. It's a common practice among NRIs: The family sets up arranged marriage meetings with as many as two dozen girls, and their son is often engaged by the end of his two-week vacation in India.

Although Geeta referred to the marriage pilgrimage sardonically, I could tell she also found something comforting in its no-nonsense, pro forma attitude. At least this way, she said, she knew she was getting a boy whose family had committed him to an arranged marriage, which she hoped meant he'd be less ambivalent about the institution himself. In theory, Geeta had resigned herself to this type of marriage, but she still wasn't sure, and she was fed up with meeting boys whom she had to sell the idea to. She'd made a point of telling Ashok in an instant message that she was "on the arranged marriage track," and he'd messaged back that he agreed that love-cum-arranged was the best kind. That's why he wanted to meet Geeta with his older sister in tow, he said; marriages worked better if they were approved by the family.

As good as this sounded, it raised an issue. Geeta's parents couldn't come with her to the meeting—they had a family wedding to attend. Geeta couldn't bear the idea of sitting by herself opposite the boy and his older sister, as though he were the celebrity and she his agent. Determined not to give another boy the wrong impression by showing up unaccompanied for a marriage date, she asked me to come. A *feringhee* escort was better than none at all.

In trying to get married without a full protective network, Geeta found herself rewriting the rules. She was hardly alone in doing so, of course: Almost every young urban professional who goes for an arranged marriage in today's India changes it up somehow. But unlike many globalized Indians, what Geeta wanted, more than anything, was an acceptable tradition through which to make the most important decision of her life. She was looking for someone who fell between two worlds, and there simply weren't many of them out there: modern-minded boys interested in pairing off with a near stranger. Geeta used adjectives such as "conservative" to describe the kind of husband she wanted, but she also expected him to be sensitive and open-minded, meaning he couldn't ask for dowry or forbid her to work outside the home. In more than six years of arranged meetings, Geeta had only met a handful of boys who made the cut.

When Geeta told Sameena at Madame X that she wanted her back and arms waxed for the evening meeting, I forced myself not to smile. It still amazed me that Indian women were determined to rid their bodies of so much hair. On top of that, it scarcely seemed necessary: I knew that Geeta's date would be lucky to catch a glimpse of her arm above her elbow, let alone her back. Nevertheless, I settled in for a long day and decided to get my nails painted while I was waiting. I chose a light pink shade, which seemed to say "sister of the bride" or, perhaps, "lady chaperone." Watching the teenage stylist coat my nails with cheap lacquer, I felt a sudden qualm about my role that evening. Geeta had insisted that having me along would impress the NRI by demonstrating her comfort with Americans. But I was worried I would reveal the worst aspect of my Americanism and say something inappropriate. I wasn't exactly schooled in the protocol of arranged marriage meetings.

"I don't even have any clothes to match this girlie nail color, Geeta. Anyway, I need you to help me choose the appropriate thing to wear."

We had been talking about Geeta's outfit for weeks. Should she "go Western," as she put it, and don a skirt and blouse for the NRI? Or should she "do Indian" since it was a formal marriage meeting? If she went with the latter, should she don a contemporary tunic or go for a more conservative style of *salwar kameez*? There is a traditional point of reference for such questions, though unlike Emily Post's *Etiquette*, the classic guide to socially acceptable behavior in the United States since 1922, the manual for the marriage-age Indian girl has never been put to paper. The rules have simply been passed down through generations of Indian women, altered slightly for regional and religious differences: the appropriate attire for a girl's first meeting with a boy, what *mithai* she should serve, and which songs she should sing.

According to Geeta, the manual hasn't kept current the way the Emily Post franchise has tried to, with seventeen updated versions of the guide. The guidelines Geeta learned from her mother were almost defunct in today's changed cultural circumstances. At tonight's meeting, there would be no recital or homemade sweets—just cappuccinos in a hotel coffee shop. There was no absolute approved source to which to turn for advice on how a girl should dress for that. Instead, Geeta asked every girl her age she could think of, and they all concurred with her mother that she should "do Indian." Because the boy was bringing a family member along, they argued, she needed to counteract her unconventional escort with a traditional wardrobe—both for herself and for me.

When we got back to Nanima's apartment from Madame X, Geeta pulled open her closet and rifled around until she found what she was looking for, a *salwar kameez* suit with a high neck and a low hemline. It was more conservative than the Indian outfits I usually wore, and since I am more than a head taller than Geeta, it looked as though it would fit me badly. For herself, she chose a more fashionable outfit in orange and yellow. The tunic was fitted, with a shorter hem, and it was worn with tight *churidar* leggings rather than loose *salwar* pants—all important details that would signal she was a cosmopolitan girl. Geeta applied a narrow line of kohl under her eyes and just enough glossy lipstick to make her look pretty and not at all sexy.

"You don't think it's too tight, do you?" she asked, for the third time in ten minutes.

I reminded myself to be patient. At the meeting, her every aspect would be under the microscope. Ashok's sister would be making sure she'd described her skin tone correctly in her profile when she'd called it "wheatish to fair." She'd be noting how well Geeta spoke English and whether her purse matched her outfit.

Geeta seemed to have achieved the look she was going for: innocent Punjabi girl in the big city. As I took stock of my own image in the mirror, though, I felt a wave of exasperation. I looked like an awkward *gora* tourist dressed for a costume party.

"The guy lives in California, Geeta. Would it really matter if I wore jeans?"

Geeta looked at me as if I were missing a marble.

"We're not dressing for him, Miranda. This is about impressing his family."

• • •

When the heat of the day begins to drain off in the wooded areas of Lodhi Garden, the evening chorus of parakeets and swallows swells quickly to an almost deafening clamor. The park is one of the greenest parts of Delhi, but it is anything but peaceful. During walking prime time, the garden is a place for the city's elite to see and be seen. With middle-aged couples speed walking in matching sweat suits and lanky teenagers jogging with their iPods tucked into their waistbands, it could be a park in any affluent American neighborhood—if it wasn't for the grand marble sixteenth-century monuments, the women wearing brightly colored *salwar kameez,* and the kurta-clad politicians.

Parvati and I were usually too distracted by the activity around us to have heart-to-hearts on our evening walks. As a rotund man in flowing white garb strode past, a dozen aides and hangers-on in tow, she'd remark drily: "Member of parliament. You can tell the importance of a man by the size of his entourage." A few feet later, we'd be startled by a moaning couple behind a sari-draped bush or a knot of trees. Perhaps because she and Vijay were scrupulous about avoiding displays of affection, Parvati found these spectacles particularly offensive. She'd call out for the couple's ears: "*Hoo hoo,* another one? Do they really have nowhere better to go?"

Geeta had joined us in the park, determined to stay fit now that she was back on the hunt for a husband. We were certainly helping her in this effort—her legs were shorter than ours, so she had to scamper to keep up with us, which meant she was getting twice the workout that we were. Parvati refused to slow her pace; her policy was to endure but never accommodate Geeta, whom she considered a conservative elitist. The good-natured Geeta appeared not to notice Parvati's disdain: She was puffing along behind us, straining to hear my longer-legged friend's story about Promila, her Dalit maid who denied that she was a Dalit. The latest turn of events was that Promila had taken to refusing to do untouchable tasks. She and Parvati were at a standoff about her job description, which meant Parvati's bathroom hadn't been cleaned for weeks.

"Who does she think she is?" Geeta piped up behind us. "Tell her to do the work you pay her for, or get rid of her! There are millions of people in Delhi who would be happy to clean your toilets."

I shrank into my skin. Parvati cycled through her own bouts of frustration at her misbehaving servant, but she also admired Promila for trying to buck the caste system. Parvati also hated hearing sweeping generalizations about caste, such as Geeta was prone to make—she refused to tolerate them from anyone aside from her mother.

She wheeled around to face Geeta.

"See, this is why India is stuck in the dark ages. Even educated people are stuck with medieval ideas!"

Geeta looked startled by the ferocity in Parvati's voice. She was a punchy Punjabi, though, and she braced herself against the assault.

"Parvati, what I am saying is quite simple. You pay her to do certain tasks, and she thinks she's too good for such work. If she is so much better than other Dalits, then she should prove it. She's had plenty of opportunities. Already there are quotas in government jobs for the lower castes."

Parvati's eyes narrowed, and I wished intensely I hadn't suggested we all go for a walk together.

"How many Dalits do you work with at your company? Just name them. How many."

Geeta faltered: "I'm not sure. But . . . that's not the point. Chances are there for them. If they want to apply for the job, they can."

"Then why don't they?" We were attracting glances from the speed-walking couples. "Do you think they'd still want to pick up garbage if they had the opportunity to work in an office? You think they prefer that, just because it is their traditional work?"

Like the battle over affirmative action in the United States, the debate in India about job quotas is a hairy one. Geeta was making the mainstream argument: that the quota system had created a "creamy top layer" of low-caste beneficiaries who now had an unfair edge over the higher castes. Parvati's position was less popular: that affirmative action hadn't yet helped the worst off, and wouldn't unless the government extended the quota system to include elementary school education.

Digging deep into their argument, the two of them ignored my attempts to make peace; in fact, they ignored everything I said, until I gave up on the walk and led us out to Parvati's car. Geeta's face was still twisted with anger when Parvati dropped her at Nanima's. She slammed out of the car. Parvati and I had planned to go out together after the walk, but I felt awkward about it now, because it looked as though I was choosing sides.

I could tell that Parvati was trying to pull herself together as she drove us out of Nizamuddin.

"Sorry about that. Even though she has bloody backwards ideas, she's your friend."

I mustered the nicest smile I could. I'd given up trying to influence how Parvati behaved—if that's a bad idea in any friendship, it was utterly counterproductive with her. In any case, I had a feeling something was going on with her these days. The last couple of times we'd met, she'd come alone.

"Are you and Vijay fighting?"

This had become a fairly standard question in the years since we'd become friends. Parvati's confrontational personality and Vijay's propensity for whiskey-sodden gloom made for an explosive combination. I'd become somewhat inured to their hollering matches outside the Press Club or in Vijay's apartment after dinner, and the occasional climax of Vijay storming off. After one of these fights, Parvati sometimes went weeks without speaking to him. It was probably for the best that they couldn't share an apartment.

They both seemed content to accept the turmoil as the way things were. Vijay was pretty hotheaded in general, which was one reason he'd taken up boxing as a hobby. He spent a night or two a week at the extremely low-budget, cramped, and smelly men's boxing gym in their neighborhood. At first, I thought this hobby seemed incongruous with Vijay's string bags and Marxist politics, but as I got to know him better, I realized it was all of a piece. Boxing was a great way for him to purge his angry energy. It didn't entirely work, though. He was notorious in Delhi journalism circles for walking out during editorial meetings if the management of his newspaper refused to take a stand on an issue he believed in, or if he thought his boss was ordering him around too much. Parvati had more than once talked him down from quitting. After a bad fight, Parvati would remind me—a little defensively—that she'd never met anyone with his passion for music and poetry, or his rigorous commitment to socialist ideals. That stuff made his terrible temper worth bearing, she said.

Luckily, Vijay rarely directed his angry outbursts at me. It only happened once, late at night; the three of us were having a nightcap at a hotel bar after an embassy party, along with a British reporter I'd started an affair with. It was a new and awkward relationship; we both had significant others back home, and no one other than Parvati knew that we were dating. I don't know whether Vijay had figured it out, but if he had, it probably only worsened his mood, already blackened by the foreigners and elite Indians around us.

"All these privileged *choots*. Screw this bloody globalizing Indian government. Selling us off to any foreign government that's buying. We're at the beck and call of the U.S.!"

In his booze-addled blur, Vijay made a fabulous leap of logic: He tried to blame my British friend and me for the Iraq war. At first we laughed, but it was not a joke; Vijay's yelling soon got us evicted from the bar. It took him more than two weeks to call me and acknowledge that I wasn't personally responsible for the actions of my government.

Parvati's fits of pique were not as irrational, though they were more often directed at me. She was the dominant force in our friendship, and I rarely contradicted her: I considered myself the Maneesh to her Radha. When I refused to go along with her plans or do favors for her, it sometimes turned ugly. Once, she called late at night to ask for the cell-phone number of an acquaintance at the U.S. embassy, whom she wanted to talk to for a story. When I told her it was too late to call him, she hung up and refused to speak to me for more than six months.

In the time I had to stew over the incident, I decided that she was right in thinking me ungenerous—I should have just given her the number; what did I care if she woke up the guy? Still, I was shocked that she could hold a grudge about it for so long. One evening, she showed up unannounced at my apartment with a bottle of Seagram's Blenders Pride. I was so happy to hear her voice that I swallowed my pride and buzzed her upstairs.

I needed Parvati's intensity and independence—especially if I'd been spending a lot of time with Geeta. My own inclinations lay somewhere between theirs, and it seemed to me that only with them both in my life could I achieve some kind of equilibrium.

Still fuming about Geeta's conservative views, Parvati tugged her seat belt across her body as a police car appeared beside us at a red light.

"Bugger off, you bloody cops." She looked at me a moment later, to acknowledge that she was overreacting, and her tone lightened. "This has been a bad week. I'm feeling really tense."

I was surprised; this was a vulnerable moment by Parvati's standards. The light changed, the cop car sped off, and eventually she spoke again, gazing straight ahead at the road.

"You know, I've been wanting to talk about something with you. Shall we go somewhere?"

She drove us to Khan Market, an upscale shopping spot that was central to my existence: It contained the ATMs that allowed me to withdraw money from my American bank account, the pet shops that sold cat food, and the well-organized grocery stores that I relied on for expat luxuries like peanut butter and soy sauce. Parvati and I liked to meet at Café Turtle, a bookstore and coffee shop—though never with Vijay, because he'd refuse to order even a cup of tea at such places, on the grounds that the *chai* at outdoor stalls cost a tenth of the price.

Parvati found a table outside so she could smoke. We had the patio to ourselves. She collapsed in a chair, looking worn out, and took a long drag of her cigarette.

"Vijay's college days were really exciting for him. You know how he was a student leader and all."

I turned back from the view of the bustling Saturday market and the green of Lodhi Garden beyond. Vijay often boasted about how he'd chaired meetings and led protest marches in his student days. He'd shown me photos of himself in those days, thinner, longer haired, and fiery. I imagined him surrounded by girlfriends in college, though he'd never directly said anything to give me that impression.

Parvati had occasionally mentioned boys she'd dated before she met Vijay; but his discomfort with the topic was on another order of magnitude. We'd been friends for years, and he still scarcely acknowledged his multiyear commitment with Parvati to me. Sidelong references to my relationship with Benjamin made him uneasy, too. Sometimes, if Parvati was feeling mischievous, she'd tweak him by making a bawdy joke. He'd promptly remove himself to the kitchen to pour another drink, and she'd whisper loudly, "Isn't it cute? My boyfriend is as modest as a blushing Bollywood bride!"

Parvati was looking at me steadily now, and her next comment brought me back to the present.

"His college days were passionate times. In fact, Vijay got married in college."

The last of the evening light picked up the green flecks in her eyes, giving them an urgent glitter. Everything I'd thought about her, and their relationship, and even India, shifted a little in that moment. Parvati lit a second cigarette off her first.

"Her name's Divya. She was his college girlfriend—very beautiful, he is always saying, and very intense. I guess she wanted to get married, and he went along with it. It was a love marriage. I don't know that many details, though. He doesn't like to talk about it, which is hardly surprising."

"What happened?"

"Well . . . they're still married." The words hung in the air for a moment before Parvati picked up the thread again. "I mean, they have been separated for a long time. But she didn't want to do a divorce; it was too shameful. So he agreed. He won't ever officially divorce her now."

After the split, Divya left Delhi and moved back to her hometown, Jaipur, several hours' drive away. A decade later, she had yet to acknowledge to her family that her defiant love marriage had collapsed. Her family continued to go along with the ruse, perhaps preferring it over the humiliating truth. Vijay had explained this choice to Parvati by reminding her how difficult it was for women who break the mold. First Divya had married against her family's wishes, and now the marriage had fallen apart; if they found that out, it would surely only vindicate their conservative beliefs.

When Parvati told me that Divya had started contacting Vijay again, I couldn't help but think that Divya was probably holding out hope that he would one day return to her. Parvati seemed to read my thoughts.

"I don't think he loves her anymore. I really don't," she said. "I think he takes her calls because he feels so guilty about how it ended."

"So . . . what happened?"

My astonishment had rendered me incapable of articulating a different question. Flustered, Parvati smoothed the free strands of her hair with her hands.

"You know Vijay. Not many people can put up with him, and I think she was a pretty moody girl, too. But how can I know? He hasn't come to terms with it himself."

I remembered that Vijay hadn't spoken to his parents for years, and that he'd told me that his relationships with his siblings were rocky. Maybe this explained it. My mind was careening all over the place. The right thing for him to do, I thought, was to initiate an official divorce; even if it would take years, it was the only way to be respectful to Parvati. Of course, that was an American idea, born from a culture that actually lauds couples for ending unhappy marriages. Not so in India. Even in Vijay's liberal circle of journalists and activists, a divorce could render him a social outlier. No wonder his relationship with Parvati was secretive and turbulent, I thought.

I considered how I would feel if I were relegated to the status of mistress in the eyes of society. I was pretty sure I'd be paranoid about what people thought of me, even in my significantly more tolerant world. I didn't have Parvati's mettle to battle worries like that. It also occurred to me that Parvati might have adopted a stance against marriage and kids because she was, in any case, unable to have those things with Vijay—though I would never have suggested such a thing to her. In fact, now that I knew the backstory, I wished I hadn't quizzed her so aggressively about Vijay early on in our friendship. She'd finally told me the whole truth, and I had no idea what to say. Parvati had run out of words, too. She stubbed out the last cigarette of her pack and drove me home.

During my first years in Delhi, I rarely caught more than a glimpse of the air-conditioned, generator-supported world of the elite. Because I'd shown up in India without a foreign correspondent's salary or contacts, I didn't meet the kind of people most of my colleagues socialized with—industrialists, government officials, film stars. Over time, I found myself scheduling interviews at five-star hotels and dining out at the aptly named Diva restaurant. I had to force myself to put it out of my mind that I was blowing the equivalent of Radha's monthly earnings on a plate of pasta and a glass of wine. In fact, I learned to celebrate how far my paltry public radio salary would stretch in India. It seemed amusing that my servants considered me the epitome of wealth, but in a way, I was. Having secured a steady job and salary, I could even have moved into one of Delhi's luxurious gated enclaves, but I found them to be disturbing reminders of class and clout in the status-obsessed political capital.

When I began shambling after the five-star denizens I was forced to learn a whole new set of Delhi rules—starting with the vehicle I was seen in. If I took a rattling taxi to an interview with a government official or an important businessman, I'd have to hope that he wouldn't catch sight of me climbing out of it in front of the building—because if he did, I knew it would be a struggle to be taken seriously. As for rickshaws, they aren't even permitted inside the gate of most Indian hotels and government buildings. I'd often been dumped at the bottom of a hotel driveway and forced to approach the entrance on foot—undoubtedly the least classy way to arrive at an appointment in a city where no one other than beggars and dogs walks between destinations. The hotel porter would gingerly hold open the door for this sweaty, uncouth *feringhee,* his mustache twitching disdainfully.

One of the best things about hiring K.K. was being able to turn over to him the stress of dealing with my vehicle status. I'd call the taxi stand in the morning and describe my day's appointments, and he'd choose a car accordingly. Having driven Delhi's elite for fifteen years, K.K. was better qualified than just about anyone to be a vehicle snob. As co-owner of Nizamuddin Taxi Stand, K.K. liked to remind me, he had access to "all many kinds of top-class cars." On important days, he'd show up in a Honda City, because foreign-made vehicles confer the greatest status on their passengers. No matter what appointment I had, though, K.K. outright refused to drive an Ambassador, the classic Indian car, first made in England but manufactured in India since 1948. Like the flowing white kurta uniform, the Ambassador remains an essential accessory of Indian government ministers. But to K.K., as to many of the aspirational classes, the car was nothing more than an unwelcome reminder of India's shoddy socialist days, when the best way to acquire wealth was to bribe a corrupt government bureaucrat.

K.K.'s personal vehicle of choice was the Tata Indigo, an Indian-made sedan marketed as "the working man's luxury car." He deemed this vehicle acceptable for most of my evening social events—partly because it was equipped with a DVD player. He kept a stockpile of Bollywood movies for the nights he waited for me while I mingled at some work-related cocktail hour. With hundreds of embassy officials and Indian businessmen filling the lawns of multimillion-dollar colonial homes, such parties ran late into the night.

It took me a while to get used to the dozens of uniformed servants flitting across the lawns, proffering predinner kebabs. I'd never experienced anything like it in my rumpled academic family. It was always a relief to clamber back into the car and ask K.K. to drive me over to Parvati's tiny apartment, where the blinking tube light needed to be replaced. I'd have a similar sensation when I showed up at the dinky Fitness Circle after an indulgent Sunday brunch at an ostentatiously decorated restaurant with other Western reporters, as if I was living two lives and neither of them was exactly real.

When I complained to a wealthy Indian friend about it, he was unsympathetic.

"That's India. This country is totally irreconcilable. There's only one thing to do: Reconcile yourself to it."

What astonished me was that India's *poor* had reconciled themselves to it. In my first couple of years in India, I routinely wondered why there hadn't ever been a true caste- or class-based revolution. Eventually I decided that it could be explained by the Hindu belief in dharma and reincarnation. Many of India's poor are simply getting through this life in the hope and expectation that in the next one, it will be them in the back of the Mercedes and the rich man will be crouched under a plastic tarp in torn clothes. It makes it easier to accept things as they are, and it certainly creates a powerful incentive to live a moral life. Dharma didn't make the daily inequalities okay for me, though.

I reserved a special dread for the traffic triangle near Nizamuddin, a gathering point for Delhi's maimed and impoverished, which I called Hell Corner. Once, when an aggressive, brawny adolescent beggar girl tugged at my purse through the rickshaw, I actually slapped her across the face. I don't remember whether I hit her hard, but what I do recall is her laughter, loud and bitter. In bed that night, I remember thinking, I have reached an all-time low: I actually struck a beggar child. I felt sadder about myself and the world than I had in a long time. After that, when I was driving through the intersection with K.K., I'd urge him to floor it through a yellow light to avoid getting stuck. I couldn't force myself to do as other passengers did and ignore the beggars with a straight-ahead stare.

One evening, Parvati and I got caught there at a red, and she rolled down her window to hand out a few coins. Like most middle-class Indians, she made regular donations to beggars; it's an essential social duty in both Hinduism and Islam. A woman with a badly burned face approached the car. I hated how the toddler in her arms had learned to mimic her imploring gestures. Parvati told me that most of Delhi's beggars belong to street rings and hand over their earnings to gang leaders at the end of each day. The leaders force the women to carry babies and sometimes deliberately disfigure the children, she said; they keep the kids hungry so they are more likely to cry. Looking out at the assembled miserable on the corner that day, Parvati seemed as perturbed as I was.

"Just look at this! Handing out rupees to whoever comes up to the car isn't a good solution. We should come up with a better system, a way to decide who to give to."

For starters, Parvati declared, no more donations to women holding babies—unless the women also bore obvious signs of domestic abuse. We should stop giving to the plucky street kids, because they were almost always attached to a gang, she said. We agreed that lepers and the limbless should always get our coins. Even though many of them also work for the mafia, they have little choice other than to beg, we reasoned.

It was a completely arbitrary notion of right and wrong, of course, but I was glad to impose some kind of order. The new rules made me feel good about contributing to the skateboard beggar, my longtime favorite on Hell Corner. He'd lost both his legs to some terrible accident, and his beard had a lot of gray in it. He scooted himself between the wheels of the stopped cars on a self-styled skateboard with fierce, determined energy. Because he couldn't reach the car window, I'd drop the coins onto the street, and he'd scramble to pick them up before the light changed. Even if the cars were moving toward him to get across the light, he always touched the coins to his head in a gesture of thanks.

Geeta guided her little car through the pandemonium of Hell Corner and turned into the well-groomed driveway of the Oberoi hotel. We waited in the lobby, perched stiffly on uncomfortable pastel-print chairs. I averted my eyes from passing guests, hoping I wouldn't run into one of my sources, clad as I was in my village-girl costume. I wondered whether Ashok's family was part of the social elite, or whether they'd chosen the place as a conceit. With dowry at the center of marriage negotiations, money is an unavoidable aspect of Indian matchmaking. Presenting an image of wealth is one way to push the girl's family for higher dowry gifts. Geeta's liberal Punjabi parents were extremely unusual in insisting that they wouldn't pay dowry at all; that was how it had been for generations on Geeta's mother's side. Still, if Ashok's people had aimed to impress Geeta with their choice of venue, they'd succeeded. She twiddled a strand of her hair into a strange curl that I didn't have time to fix before they were standing in front of us.

The boy was short and pleasant looking in an unremarkable way. It was his glitzy sister who caught my attention. One glance at her expensive silk tunic and Italian shoes and I knew Geeta had miscalculated—these people were more upscale than we had anticipated. Next to her, I looked as though I'd been milking cows all afternoon. She introduced herself as Maneka, proffering a carefully manicured hand; I wanted to hide my own ten-rupee nail job behind my back. With a flick of her tinted hair, she glided down the hall to the swanky coffee shop, and we followed.

Inside, I told them I would get the drinks—I figured it was appropriate, since I was sort of playing the role of Geeta's father. Standing at the stainless steel counter, I thought how different this atmosphere was from the Barista coffee shop where Geeta had met Aditya, the hand-holder. Barista's best-selling items are American-style brownies and sugary smoothies; customers at the Oberoi expect espresso drinks and fresh almond croissants.

I glanced back at the table. It looked as though the meeting was off to a bad start. Geeta was twisting her hair again, and Ashok was straight backed and tense in the wrought iron chair opposite her. It was a weird, contemporary version of the feudal village scene, in which prepubescent boy and girl are seated on opposite cushions, hands and eyes lowered, as their fathers negotiate their futures over their heads. I clonked my knee against the marble table as I sat down, spilling our drinks, and promised myself I would keep my mouth shut.

Maneka seemed perfectly comfortable, however. With a crisp copy of Geeta's bio-data laid out in front of her on top of a manila folder, she conducted the meeting as if Geeta were one of thousands of long-shot candidates for a coveted job.

"Where did you go to school?" "What rank did you graduate?" "How long have you been working in Delhi?"

Gone was the Punjabi princess I knew; Geeta responded obediently without raising her eyes from her interlocked fingers. Her voice was so low I had to strain to hear her. When Maneka asked about her cooking skills, she looked up at her from beneath her eyelids like a coy fifties Bollywood starlet.

"Well, I love making the Punjabi favorites. My father always praises my *paranthas*. In fact, he says they are better even than my mother's. I am not sure whether I should believe him, though." She giggled a little, showing off that infectious Geeta charm for the first time since we'd sat down.

I knew she hadn't made a *parantha* in years; her ability to praise herself under duress and to stay on message was impressive. Even today, many matrimonial ads call for a "homely" woman, a term that means "domestic" in Indian English. Geeta's task was to prove she was a nurturing caretaker, neither careerist nor over-Westernized, but she also had to be careful not to come off as unsophisticated to her savvy interviewer.

When Maneka finished her inquisition, she turned to Ashok as though he were her errant celebrity and she his public relations guru.

"Any follow-up questions?"

Ashok forced himself to raise his eyes to Geeta across the table, and I got a good look at him. He was probably a nice, easygoing guy in real life, I thought. Scrutinized by three pairs of eyes, he seemed to struggle to come up with a reply.

"Well . . . I guess I would like to ask you some things about your personality. Like . . . what is your favorite color?"

He was not being ironic. Here was a grown man asking his potential wife a question that hadn't been asked of me since grade school, and Geeta leaped in with a coquettish answer, as though she'd been waiting for the question all evening.

"Well, I'm wearing orange. So probably you can guess it is a favorite color of mine. What about you?"

Ashok, a technology analyst with an MBA degree, had a little speech about his favorite color, too.

"Many boys like blue or green, but I think I like brown, because it is the color of most people's eyes." Was this a subtle stab at flirtation? His next question confirmed it. "You have lived in Delhi all these years, so I was wondering what you do for fun. I don't even know what people do when they go out at night here anymore."

A shadow passed across Geeta's evenly composed face. I could imagine she was thinking that there was no correct answer to this question. She didn't want to seem like a village naïf, but admitting she had a social life could open up all kinds of problematic questions: Did she go out with boys as well? Had she ever had a "friend"?

"Not much. I can't go out very much because I have to watch Nanima. She's my main social activity, I guess! And I sleep a lot on weekends. Ask Miranda, she knows how much I love to sleep."

I nodded knowledgeably in agreement, my one and only contribution to the conversation so far. But Ashok pressed on, making me wonder what his real motivation was: "You don't go to clubs or anything? I'm only asking because that's what we do in California—you know, groups of guys and girls together."

My palms were sweating. I avoided Geeta's eyes, but nothing could have distracted her. The girl has fortitude, I thought to myself.

"Sometimes I go to a movie with a girl from work. Not often, though. I have a simple life."

Maneka had shifted her gaze from Geeta to her brother. Her lip was twitching with barely disguised hostility. She picked up her cup and took a final sip of her latte before filling the silence that followed Geeta's answer. Her eyes remained on her brother, though, as she addressed Geeta.

"In the United States, people do things differently. And I'm sure you know that even here in India people have all kinds of relationships. But Ashok's tired of all that clubbing-clubbing. That's why we are looking for an arranged match."

A hint of triumph flashed across Geeta's face.

"Actually, I too believe in the arranged way. I think it works better than a love match. I guess you can say I am quite traditional."

But the meeting was over for Maneka. She tapped the paper into the folder.

"Of course, my brother has many good proposals. As you know from his bio-data, he is making a high salary in California. He has an MBA from a top university, and our family is well connected." She stood up. "So you can imagine that we have plenty of families expressing interest. We'll contact your father if we want to pursue."

Ashok gave Geeta an apologetic glance—or perhaps it was smug?—
and he and his sister swept toward the hotel's front entrance. Geeta
and I took the side door out to the lot where the "self-driven cars" are
parked. She navigated us into a line of sleek chauffeur-driven vehicles
waiting to exit the hotel driveway. I ran through the meeting in my
mind, trying to decide whether it would upset Geeta to talk about it.
When I couldn't hold out any longer, I spat out: "What was up with her?
Was that normal?"

Geeta looked a little surprised at the strength of my reaction.

"She was just being protective of her younger brother, Miranda.
Plus, she probably felt like she had to act the way her father would have,
you know? It's weird for everyone, doing these meetings in a pretend
traditional way. No one knows how to act."

"I wouldn't have expected her to ask you so many questions about
your cooking. She seems way too modern to be asking all that stuff."

"Yeah, I was a little surprised about that, too," Geeta replied mildly.
"Obviously they want a conventional type. But if you thought that
meeting was bad—you have no idea. It's so much worse when the parents are there. Maneka didn't even ask about my past. And plus, the boy
was nice. You should see some of the *moorks* I have met."

"So you liked Ashok?" There was surprise in my voice. He'd seemed
kind of confused and cowardly.

"He was cute and seemed to have a nice nature. But I'm pretty sure
they want a girl from a rich family."

"They seethed money. We should have made them buy the coffee!"

Geeta shot me a smile as we swerved out into the city traffic. The
Hindi pop on the radio was a dull throb between us.

"You know what? Maybe Ashok has a girlfriend back in California. I
bet that's it—his family won't let him marry her." It sounded like a plot
from a melodramatic TV family drama, but Geeta's conviction grew as
she spoke. "That would explain everything. I bet his family is pushing
him to do an arranged match, and that's why she didn't ask about my
past—she didn't want to risk having to answer the same kinds of questions about him."

A familiar song came on the radio. It took me a moment to identify which movie it was from—was it *DDLJ*? Or *KKKG*, that movie we'd recently seen with Amitabh Bachchan? Then I realized: It was from *KHNH* (Tomorrow May Never Come). In the video for the first love song, the lovers frolic through Times Square as they realize what they are feeling. As corny as the scene is, it always made me think of Benjamin driving me through Manhattan on his motorcycle one Sunday morning, when the streets were empty and it felt as though the whole city belonged to us. It was strange to remember that hopeful, fresh-faced time, from here inside the calloused body of Super Reporter Girl.

I'd recently returned to Delhi from covering the Indian Ocean tsunami and its aftermath. When the quake hit, the day after Christmas, I'd abandoned my family vacation, deaf to my mother's pleas, and taken the first flight out to Sri Lanka, where the death toll was rapidly rising. Sri Lanka is a tiny teardrop-shaped island nation off the southern coast of India, and the tsunami had turned it inside out. Along the southern coast, train tracks were twisted up into tree branches like a roller coaster gone wrong. A woman's nightgown fluttered like a pink flag above a fisherman's leveled shack. The bloated, stinking carcasses of buffalo floated in ocean lagoons. In the relief camps, everyone was drunk on moonshine.

"Why should I talk to you? My whole family is dead. What can you give me?" the fishermen would ask.

I'd give them the stock journalist answer—that hearing their story could help influence the U.S. government to send more aid. There was truth to this reasoning, but it still felt like a cheap lie. After weeks of reporting on the disaster, I'd started to lose faith in the very mission of journalism. In a hotel bar in Colombo, the capital of Sri Lanka, my journalist friends talked about where the "sexiest" part of the story was. What they meant was where the most bodies were. I felt as though we were all competing with one another to squeeze painful tales out of as many victims as we could find and get the grisliest stories first.

In one relief camp, my driver—who doubled as my translator, to save money—helped me interview a man who'd lost everyone except for one lanky preteen daughter, who crept over to me as I talked to him and put her head in my lap. I stayed stroking her hair long after I finished talking to her father, even though my driver had been agitating that we had to find somewhere to stay for the night before it got dark. When she sat up, my jeans were damp from her tears. I gave her money, even though I knew I shouldn't since I planned to use her father's interview on the radio. In spite of the intimacy of that moment, I can't even picture her face anymore. It has run together with all the other lyrical, brokenhearted Sri Lankan faces.

My friends emailed from New York, saying they'd been hearing me on the radio and were envious of my exciting life. It was hard not to roll my eyes at my laptop screen. I'd spend hours crouched under the mattress with my microphone on damp and moldy sheets, in a sweaty attempt to re-create the sound of a radio studio as I voiced my stories. I'd been wearing a single pair of jeans and sweatshirt for weeks, and I'd lost so much weight they hung off me. I felt as though I was filled up with the ghosts of all the unknown drowned. I spent most evenings in half-abandoned guesthouses, the coffee and bags of flour floating in a filthy pool of sea backwash in the kitchen, starving dogs panting in the lobbies. I made all kinds of friends, knowing I'd probably never see them again.

By the time I got back to Delhi, all I wanted to do was lie in the dark with my cats. My mother sent worried emails suggesting that I could be suffering from post-traumatic stress disorder. I told my editors that I was going to stick close to home for a while. Saying so felt like a failure; having laid claim to a huge swath of Asia as "my patch" of reporting ground, I felt as if I was neglecting the purpose of my existence if I wasn't roaming around searching for stories. I'd left everything else behind—my reporting had become my whole identity.

That was especially apparent as I faced the final disintegration of my relationship with Benjamin. Even though I'd known that the only possible action was to choose between him and India, I'd delayed doing so, afraid that opting for the latter was tantamount to resigning myself to becoming Miserable Jen. I didn't want to leave a job I loved for a man I wasn't sure I could trust, but I didn't even know how to voice that to him. Instead, I'd argue that I wasn't yet ready to move back to New York, where any job I could imagine would feel like a dull grind. Besides, Delhi felt like home by now. Not to Benjamin, though—it was too hot, life was too hard, and he couldn't get enough work to justify it.

In the meantime, I'd been defiantly dedicating myself to everything *but* Benjamin: resolutely creating a community for myself in India, obsessing over my reporting, and turning to love affairs whenever I was bored or sad. I told myself he wasn't right for me—but now and then, the thought struck me that he might not be entirely to blame. It was possible that I was too itinerant, independent, and cold to hold down a relationship with anyone at all.

One morning after I got back from Sri Lanka, I donned my running shoes and a pair of sweatpants over my shorts, so as not to expose my legs on the walk over to the Fitness Circle. I hadn't seen the gym ladies in months; I thought their easy banter would be a welcome break. Once I got there, though, I realized that I couldn't deal with their questions and wished I'd brought my iPod. Leslie came up behind me as I was stretching. I flinched when she touched my shoulder, and she peered at me kindly.

"You look tired. Usha could give you a massage if you'd like. It always makes me feel better."

I swallowed. My face felt bloated from the pressure of holding back my tears. If I took the massage, I was liable to start weeping right there on the smelly gym mats. Then the ladies would flock over to comfort me, *tsk*ing sympathetically.

"She misses her husband."

"It's terrible to be alone here without any family."

As much as I'd hate to admit it, I'd know they were right. I wasn't ready to open up to all of that.

Benjamin came through Delhi soon after, on his way back to the States from Thailand, where he'd gone to write a magazine story about the tsunami. I hadn't seen him in seven months, during which time I'd lost track of, or stopped caring about, who had violated our constantly shifting relationship rules. Something was different, though; for the first time since I'd met him, I didn't want to hear about his adventures, didn't care what he'd seen and how it had inspired him. It must have been the same for him, too, because when he hugged me hello, he seemed to be holding back from me. Standing in his arms, I felt suddenly quite clear that all we'd had was a romantic ideal. We'd worn it out like a pebble rubbed too long for good luck.

In the morning, Radha discovered Benjamin on the office floor, but to my relief, neither she nor my housemate asked why my husband had been banished from the bedroom. I don't think I would have known what to say. The world seemed very large. I was floating softly above its surface, looking down at all the people I'd known. They were all safe inside their houses, I imagined; they had plans and partners and a sense of themselves.

My thirtieth birthday loomed over the months that followed Benjamin's final departure, only heightening my self-pitying state. I didn't want to believe that turning thirty drew a red line across my life, as it had across Geeta's, but it did seem to announce that it might be about time to grow up. It was hard not to think of adulthood as a lockdown, in spite of my efforts not to see the world as a binary place in which you had to choose between being either young and hopeful or grown-up and sensible. And the evidence was mounting that my current lifestyle—tromping around Asia, covering conflicts and having affairs—was not sustainable. I found myself doing battle with India's marriage obsession: I could feel it seeping into my skin, this urgent need to settle down and find a match.

Much to my dismay, my friends in New York were growing up, too. Each time I went back, I'd half expect everything to be the same as I'd left it, and would inevitably be piqued to discover that my friends now had priorities other than downing weeknight margaritas at our favorite Mexican bar in Brooklyn and making dinner of the free chips. Their jobs and boyfriends were more serious now. I'd missed the weddings of four close friends; soon they'd start having children, and our friendships would dwindle down to nominal acquaintanceships. I knew there was a chance this would happen with age anyway, but surely the distance didn't help. When I tried to tell my friends about my life, it came out sounding more chaotic than I'd expected it would. I didn't know where I wanted to live, or how. They thought I was brave, but I could see something else behind their eyes, too, something very different from admiration.

Boarding the plane back to Delhi, I usually felt more relief than anything else. I thought about how I'd felt sorry for my great-aunt Edith as a child, when my mother told me that she'd been allowed to visit home only once every five years, and that the journey back home to England from India had taken her six weeks by ship. Marriage and children were impossible, and I don't think Edith kept up with many people in England over the four decades she lived in India, other than her siblings and fellow missionaries.

I'd always considered this a wrongheaded sacrifice, made in pursuit of a half-baked ideal. Only now, as I breathed a sigh of relief at my aloneness, did the thought strike me that Edith might not have wanted those things at all. After all, hers wasn't an especially religious family, and she'd joined the Bible Churchmen's Missionary Society against her father's will. She'd chosen a life apart from everything familiar. Perhaps the trappings of a late-twentieth-century British life felt like a prison to her, and the experience of leaving everything behind had freed her missionary soul.

Listening to the song from *KHNH* in the car with Geeta, I was overwhelmed with emotion—which was not entirely inexplicable. I'd figured out that Bollywood romances fit well with my predilection for the dreamy and the passionate. Their sentiment is much like that of the Merchant Ivory film *A Room with a View,* for instance, which I'd cried my way through more than a dozen times. Watching Bollywood helped me escape the disparaging patter in my head and reminded me of the transcendent sensation of falling in love—with Benjamin, with India.

Toward the end of *KHNH,* we learn that Shah Rukh Khan's character has sacrificed his chance to marry the girl he loves. Although they are destined to be together, he takes fate into his own hands, because he knows he is going to die and he wants to protect her from widowhood. I could see why Geeta was tempted by the idealized vision of love and the notion that there was one soul out there fated for her. I couldn't think about Benjamin without blaming myself for not making it work, but Geeta had an easy out—she could shift the responsibility onto a higher force. If she didn't get the hero in this lifetime, she could tell herself that she'd find him in the next one.

Benjamin used to recite Robert Frost to me when I was sad:

I'd like to get away from earth awhile
And then come back to it and begin over.
May no fate wilfully misunderstand me
And half grant what I wish and snatch me away
Not to return.
Earth's the right place for love:
I don't know where it's likely to go better.

Maybe Frost was wrong. At the end of *KHNH*, Shah Rukh Khan's character is on his deathbed, having surrendered his heroine to another man. He tells her new husband that he is laying a claim on her, overriding the Hindu belief that a marriage ties a couple together for seven lifetimes.

"Naina is yours in this life," he tells him. "But in every life after this—every other birth—she will be mine."

In the heady fantasy world of Bollywood, nothing is more romantic than rediscovering your true love on the other side of death. But maybe there was more to this reincarnation stuff than silly fantasy, I thought. Like Edith, I'd chosen India—but perhaps our path really does choose us, as many Hindus believe. Perhaps I should stop trying to mold my future into the shape I thought it was supposed to be and accept the life I had. I turned up the volume, and Geeta and I belted out the song the rest of the way back to Nizamuddin.

CHAPTER 10

A Modest Dowry

The topic of marriage inspired uncharacteristic cynicism from Usha, the otherwise cheery yoga teacher at the Fitness Circle.

"There's no marriage in India without dowry," she told me. "The boy always asks for dowry—usually he demands it. And if the girl's family can't pay, there's no wedding."

When I told her that Geeta's father had said he would refuse to pay dowry on principle, Usha snorted dismissively: "Good luck to her finding a husband who'll go along with that!"

There had been no such high-minded ideals in Usha's own, low-caste Hindu family. Their dowry problem had been more typical: They simply couldn't afford to get Usha married. Her father had worked on and off as a tailor and furniture repairman; like more than 90 percent of the Indian workforce, he'd had neither an employment contract nor regular hours, no unemployment insurance, and no promise of a pension. Her mother's life sounded almost Dickensian. She gave birth to twelve children at home on her charpoy. "No birth control in those days," Usha said, grimacing. Only half of Usha's siblings had survived past infanthood—which, some sociologists say, partly accounts for why Indian women used to have so many children. Like most women of her time, Usha's mother had never visited a "ladies' doctor," as gynecologists are often called in India, and never had a checkup during any of her pregnancies. She eventually died in childbirth, as do almost a hundred thousand women every year in India.

After her death, Usha and her older sisters had to drop out of school to take over the cooking and cleaning; Usha never completed the fifth grade. Her brothers left school soon after, to start earning for the family when their father fell ill. He died, and her brothers had to dispatch Usha's four older sisters before they could start looking for a match for her. By the time they got to her, she was twenty-two, already considered "a little old" in her community, and they'd spent all the dowry savings on the older sisters. They were forced to lower their sights for Usha, which meant her first prospects were a stream of undesirables.

One suitor, a village boy, arrived with eight family members in tow. Usha said she was immediately turned off by the women's polyester-blend saris and the cheap metal bangles clanking up and down their arms. Still, she acted as a marriage-age girl should, lowering her gaze modestly as she carried out homemade snacks on a plastic tray for the guests. She presented several plates of fried vegetable *pakoras*, sickly-sweet *mithai*, and *chai* in her brother's best teacups, made of porcelain. The boy's escorts hungrily polished off the plates of food before turning to the work at hand: inspecting the girl. They complimented Usha's narrow waist and small hands, then *tsk-tsk*ed aloud about her uneven complexion as though she couldn't hear their commentary.

"Why does the girl have these blotches on her face?" one demanded of Usha's oldest brother. He had no answer, so she continued. "It's unfortunate. The skin is fair, but these sunspots are not good. A girl's skin should be smooth."

The women informed Usha's brother that they "always check the girl's feet," and requested that she remove her sandals. Usha, who was otherwise following the manual for the demure marriage-age girl to the letter, couldn't help but raise a skeptical eyebrow. Discussing her skin tone was par for the course at such a meeting, but she'd never heard of a foot test. It was hard not to chuckle at the women's self-important provincialism as they described their obscure village tradition. If the girl's big toe and second toe were equal in length, they informed her, it meant she would get along well with the boy. If her second toe was longer, she would try to dominate him, and his family would be able to ask for more dowry.

Usha reluctantly slipped off her sandal and pulled up the leg of her *salwar.* The women crowded around her, pushing over one another to get a peek of her feet. Then came the cry: "The girl is good!" Usha's first two toes were the same length. The family promised to return the following evening with an official proposal.

Usha says she gave her brother a pleading look after they left.

"Don't worry, I would never give you away to such superstitious village louts," he promised her. "They would be lucky to get you for *free.*"

The free part was a joke, of course. The idea of a wedding without dowry was even more laughable than checking a woman's feet to determine whether she'd make a good wife. Dowry is as essential today as it was centuries ago in many Western cultures. Because marriage in India is still considered a negotiation between families, it includes a complex symbolic exchange of goods and prestige.

Thousands of years ago, dowry was supposed to act as a sort of buffer for Indian women, who are more vulnerable after marriage because they become a part of the groom's family. Dowry was a way for the natal family to pass on some inheritance to their daughter and ensure that the girl wouldn't be completely dependent on her husband. In practice, though, most of the gift went to the groom's family, rather than to the bride herself. Dowry served other purposes, too. It was a way to sweeten the deal for the boy's family, since the girl was expected to marry up and often hailed from a slightly lower-status family. It was also a way to compensate for the economic burden of bringing a new bride into the groom's household.

Dowry has been illegal for forty years, but, like child marriage and caste discrimination, the law has done little to eradicate it from Indian culture. In fact, dowry expectations have broadened and increased in recent years. The practice first originated among upper-caste Hindus, but in recent decades it has become obligatory across all castes. Ironically, this has happened even as women have achieved more choice and economic freedom. In today's globalizing India, parents routinely begin saving for dowry as soon as a daughter is born. Most Indian-owned banks have special "daughter funds" or wedding loan programs. The best sales—especially on big-ticket items such as electronics—are found during the wedding season. Stores do not necessarily advertise the lower rates as "deals for your dowry shopping," but they don't have to. The Indian government recently declared that it would toughen the Dowry Prohibition Act by requiring couples to submit a formal list of gifts exchanged during their wedding ceremony. If that happens, though, families will surely find a way to get around this bureaucratic requirement, as with every other; the government is filled with corruptible officials who'd accept a small cut in exchange for failing to note down the full amount offered to a groom's family.

Dowry has much more serious consequences than petty corruption. The worst of them is the epidemic of harassment and bride burnings, or dowry deaths, in which a wife is abused or killed by her husband or his family. A 2009 study in the British medical journal *The Lancet* found that young Indian women are more than three times as likely as young men to be killed by fire—deaths often related to domestic abuse. One married woman dies by fire almost every hour, according to the Indian government. Brides in hospital burn wards often tell police that they were set on fire by husbands or mothers-in-law after months or years of dissatisfaction over dowries. The families claim that the bride's sari caught fire or that a tank of cooking gas exploded as she was cooking. Reports of "stove-bursts" or "kitchen accidents" in the newspapers, I learned, are allusions to murder.

In the months after the foot test suitor came calling, Usha had three other possibilities. The first asked for a car, the second a motorcycle, and the third a great deal of cash. Usha's oldest brother was getting worried—not least because his younger sister was living in his cramped home until he found her a match. When an aunt suggested a Dalit boy, he didn't dismiss the idea out of hand, even though there was a yawning social chasm between his family and this boy's. Usha's family

ranked low on the caste rung, but untouchables do not even register in
the system. Because caste is inherited from the father, few non-Dalit
families would consider marrying their daughter into one—after all,
what kind of parents would knowingly consign their grandchildren to
a life of untouchability? But the aunt explained that this boy didn't hail
from "a family that cleaned": the boy's father worked in a cycle repair
shop, a respectable enough vocation, and that made it seem a little less
dishonorable to consider him.

There was an added incentive: The untouchable family would have
little power in the dowry negotiations. Usha's brother quickly worked
out a deal. When Usha moved into her new home, she brought with her
what she considered a "modest dowry": a bed, sofa set, fridge, TV,
sewing machine, and kitchen utensils. That's not to mention the
mandatory clothes and electronic items that her family presented to
the groom's side at the ceremony. All told, Usha's brothers borrowed
close to five thousand dollars for the wedding—hardly a modest sum
for an impoverished family.

Radha started fretting about Pushpa's dowry as soon as her older
daughter hit puberty. When I met her, Pushpa was a shy sixteen-year-
old, meticulous about her studies and about her long black hair. Each
morning, she'd use a drop or two of palm oil to brush it straight and
shiny. At first, Radha had boasted about how Pushpa loved school and
what good grades she got, but now she was occupied by new concerns.

"It's time for the girl to get ready for marriage, *deedee*. I can tell she's
going to give me trouble about having to leave school before she graduates, but she's already had many years of school. It's time for her to
move on."

Radha had made it known to her daughter from an early age that she
could give her only two guarantees about her future husband: He would
share her religion and caste, and he'd help usher her into her years of
womanhood in comfort. Pushpa was more nervous than excited about
her looming marriage. Like everyone, she'd heard stories about abusive mothers-in-law, and admitted to me that the prospect of going off

to a new home frightened her a little. She'd never have dared tell her mother that, though. Nor would she have admitted to her mother that she sometimes watched Shah Rukh Khan films with her girlfriends and imagined finding her own love match. The world of love-cum-arranged was unthinkable for Pushpa. As far as Radha was concerned, her daughter's husband would be chosen by the *pujari,* and even being selective about a boy's "nature" was an indulgence they were unable to afford. It would be enough of a challenge to find a boy for Pushpa who met the basic criteria without demanding an extraordinary dowry.

Radha's worry wasn't whether the girl was ready; it was how to fund the wedding. It had never crossed her mind to plan an event within her means. If she was to secure for her daughter an alliance that would get her out of the slums, she expected that she would have to meet the groom's family's higher standards for the nuptials. Weddings are, in general, the biggest lifetime expense for Indians of all income groups. Middle-class Hindu weddings mean a guest list tipping into the thousands and two full weeks of religious rituals, parties, and dinners—in other words, lifelong debt. In today's India of conspicuous spending and Bollywood glitz, the richest grooms arrive at their weddings in helicopters; their banquets feature extravagant flourishes such as spurting chocolate fountains. Indians spend an average of thirty-two thousand dollars on a wedding. That's seven thousand dollars more than the average American spends, even though Indians earn only 10 percent of the American per capita income.

One morning, Radha marched past me into the kitchen, her jaw set. She had the morning's vegetables in one arm and a plastic bag with a change of clothes in the other. I opened my mouth to say hello, but she spoke before I could get the word out.

"I can't chat today, *deedee.* I have to hurry."

She rushed through the *jaroo-pocha*—sweeping and mopping—and worried aloud as she chopped the vegetables. I was half listening as I made my way through the stack of the day's papers, tearing out articles that might be useful story ideas.

"Pushpa is slim, pretty, and well behaved. My relatives say that in the village, she would already be married. *Ay bhagwan.* Families in the

city are asking for such high dowry these days. And now the girl is saying she doesn't want to marry before she finishes school. Does she
think we can just choose when it happens?"

After she finished the floors, Radha disappeared into the bathroom, where I heard her washing herself under the tap—the shower-
head intimidated her as much as the TV remote. She emerged in a
clean sari, a fine dusting of baby powder creeping up her neck and already congealing into white lines in the damp folds of her neck. She
tugged her *pallu,* the loose end of her sari, over her head so that it covered her hair, and announced that she was going to visit the priest at
the neighborhood Hindu temple.

Even though the temple was just a few paces from my apartment,
for years I didn't know it was there. It didn't look like much: a tumble-
down structure perched in the center of an overgrown courtyard with a
few Hindu swastikas painted on the outside wall. Inside, marble idols
of the gods—almost life-size and dressed in handmade outfits of saffron and gold—lined a marble-floored room. The resident priest,
Dharamdev Shastri, was a bombastic, balding Brahmin. His large forehead was painted with white and orange lines displaying his caste and
religious rank; he wore a long, loose shirt and *doti* cloth the color of
cream. When Dharamdev walked, which was rare, it was with a shuffle.
He spent most of his day cross-legged behind a low desk, watching the
tiny green parakeets flit through the courtyard.

Like almost everyone in Radha's limited world, Dharamdev was a
migrant from the Madhubani region in Bihar. In fact, he was related to
Radha through her late husband, though that was not apparent from
the reverence with which she treated him. Dharamdev was highly educated by the standards of Radha's community: He held a college degree
from a Hindu Sanskrit college. The Bihari immigrant community had
been coming to him for religious advice since he first took up in the
temple. As far as Radha was concerned, there was no one with greater
moral authority than he, which was why she'd come to him for help in
finding a match for her daughter.

When she got back from the temple, she squatted in front of me,
her face flushed, to tell me about the visit in feverish detail. Radha had

never considered placing a classified ad for Pushpa—she wanted to marry her the village way. Back home in Madhubani, weddings are brokered either by relatives or by the local *pujaris*, who operate efficient matchmaking businesses out of their temples. The priests keep a running list of the marriage-age girls and boys in the region and align couples from nearby villages—so as to minimize cultural differences and to prevent marriages within the same line of descent. Dharamdev welcomed the opportunity to continue the tradition in the Delhi temple, because he earned ten dollars a pop for matchmaking duties and *puja* ceremonies. This was his only source of income other than donations to the temple, and a good incentive to be efficient in aligning boys and girls.

Radha abased herself in front of the priest, and only when he repeated impatiently that she should sit up did she settle herself cross-legged in front of him. He pulled out a large, yellowed ledger book, the kind used by Indian government bureaucrats. Seeing the pages filled with handwritten notes, Radha said, made her heart flutter with the seriousness of the hallowed task she'd embarked on. She sat breathlessly before him for what seemed an eternity as he flipped through the pages. After a while, he fingered a page in the ledger, drained the tin cup of water on his desk, and placed a pair of large-framed reading glasses on his nose.

The boy he had in mind was, naturally, a Brahmin from Madhubani. He'd recently graduated from high school and was making decent money in an office job, Dharamdev said, reading from his notes. The boy's family and nature were good.

The catch was that he'd already found another girl for him. The problem was not with the boy but with the girl, Dharamdev added quickly. His idea was that Radha's daughter might be able to take this girl's place—if Radha was willing to accept the astrologer's date, that was. Radha assured him that she was happy to marry her daughter off on whichever date he named, and then asked, in her most obsequious voice, whether he could tell her more about the issue. Dharamdev seemed reluctant to go into detail, but after a moment, he sighed, removed his glasses, and leaned back against the wall.

The boy's family, he said, had visited an astrologer to find out the auspicious time for his marriage, and they'd been told he must marry within the next two months, ideally on April 20, to be exact.

"Of course, the astrologer's date is unchangeable. I went to great trouble to find a family who would agree to it, and then they changed their mind. They complained that it was too soon for the girl. I tried to tell them this was God's date, but no use."

Dharamdev said he'd advised the boy's parents to abandon the match. Radha was nodding sympathetically. She could see that her respected *pujari* felt he'd failed and that the boy's family probably blamed him for arranging an unsuccessful match. Radha leaped to assure him that she agreed that the girl's family was clearly in the wrong. "How could they think their own schedule was more important?" She bowed her head. If given the chance, she said, she'd gratefully accept the fate he had in store for her daughter.

A week later, Dharamdev sent a message to Radha's *bustee:* Pushpa's alliance was fixed. The boy's family had agreed to the match. Radha didn't even know the boy's name yet, but I had never seen her as happy as she was the following morning.

"Oh, *deedee,* this is a gift from God. They are a very good family. The father is working in a nice shop. The boy earns a huge salary at his very fancy job. He is a 'mobile-in-charge.'"

The English phrase clattered against her mouth. I doubt she knew what *mobile-in-charge* meant; I certainly didn't. But she knew that the boy earned more than one hundred dollars a month and that any job with an English title implied social capital. Radha, who had never owned a landline or a mobile phone, was going to marry her daughter to a boy in a position of authority in something to do with phone technology. It was evidence that she'd succeeded as a mother: She'd managed to secure a better life for her daughter.

Radha's gleefulness was disconcerting. But she soon reverted to her more customary state of pessimism: "I only pray that nothing goes wrong before that." In two weeks, she said, the families would meet

for the first time at the engagement ceremony, where they would negotiate the important details of the alliance, including the dowry. In a nod
to the relative liberalism of city life, the *pujari* had deemed it acceptable for Pushpa and the boy to "see each other" at the engagement. In
today's Bihar, Radha informed me, bride and groom are rarely permitted to meet before they have completed the wedding rituals. At this
citified engagement ceremony, Pushpa and her husband-to-be could
sit together in the same room, although they wouldn't exactly "meet":
They were not to look directly at or speak to each other.

What was worrying Radha now—because there always had to be
something—was that the groom's family would decide that her daughter's status was too far below theirs. Making her way across the living
room floor with a rag, Radha enumerated all the reasons why the boy's
family might nix the match.

"First of all, *deedee,* I am a widow. And we cannot invite them to our
house for the meeting, because our house and area are not good. And
then—I wash floors and clothes for a living. If they see the calluses on
my hands, they will think I have the hands of a sweeper!"

Inevitably, when Radha complained about her job, I felt like a colonialist memsahib responsible for her degradation and humiliation.
The specter of my missionarying relative Edith would rise up before
me, her hair pulled back into a severe bun, her Bible in hand. I lamely
offered that she could try moisturizing her hands to smooth out the
calluses before the meeting.

Radha sniffed at me. "*Arre,* it would take months to get soft hands
like yours. Anyway, the *pujari* will be there, and I can't lie about what I
do in front of a religious man."

She dunked the floor cloth into the bucket and wrung the water out
hard. I returned to my newspaper until she spoke again.

"Well, if I say I'm a cook, I won't be lying—right? Maybe I don't need
to tell them that I mop floors. I will tell them my boss is a foreigner.
That will make it seem better."

This congratulation for my American birth emboldened me to pipe
up again.

"I think any family would be impressed by a mother who's worked so her children can go to school. You should be proud of what you've done."

Radha looked embarrassed by the compliment. She also knew better than to believe that their admiration for her values would outweigh their disdain for her untouchable's occupation. "Maybe, *deedee*. But no Brahmin family would want the daughter of a sweeper in their family—not even a Brahmin sweeper."

She turned up her mouth sardonically at her little caste joke; there is not supposed to be any such thing as a Brahmin sweeper. Then she heaved the bucket of dirty water into the bathroom to dump it down the drain.

When Radha came to me with a submissive and downtrodden expression on her face, I knew something was up. The expression didn't suit her.

"*Deedee,* you know my daughter's wedding is going to be very expensive. . . ."

I looked up and asked how much she wanted. My tone was sharper than I'd meant it to be; perhaps I'd learned something about servant management from Geeta and Priya after all. She cut the coy act and reached inside her *choli,* the intimate safekeeping place for the most important pieces of her life. She unwrinkled a scrap of paper, on which was written, in Babloo's careful handwriting, "10,000 rupees"—almost two hundred fifty dollars. When Radha saw the surprise on my face, she tried to explain.

"In my day, *deedee,* in the village, dowry demands were much lower. But now people see money everywhere. The boy's family is sure to ask for at least double what I make in a year. Also, I have to pay for the wedding, with no one to help aside from Joginder. I don't want to deny my daughter the match that the *pujari* says will bring her a good life!"

She insisted she would take the money as an advance against her salary, but we both knew that she'd never be able to repay me and that the guilt-ridden memsahib would give her whatever she asked for in any case.

I ran into Joginder in Nizamuddin market a few days later, and he stopped me to talk. That was unusual: Joginder was usually in too much of a hurry for idle conversation, and especially with me, because I required slow and careful Hindi. It took particular effort today because Joginder had inserted a wad of *paan* into his mouth only moments before I saw him, to judge from the size of the packet and the sharpness of the odor. He raised his volume even higher to compensate.

He'd started a collection for Radha's wedding fund, he said; had she approached me already about helping her out? I nodded, a little annoyed, because I assumed he was going to try to get me to lend her more money. In fact, Joginder wanted to gossip. He confided that he didn't approve of Radha's extravagant wedding plans. It wasn't the dowry that he took issue with—she had no choice about that—but he did think she was planning an irresponsibly spendthrift wedding. I realized that he was collecting money for her only because he considered it his brotherly duty. I'd never heard Joginder say anything negative about his cousin-sister before and wondered what had happened that he was voicing it to me now.

"Radha is the kind that needs to show off. She will be inviting so many guests and giving expensive saris-saris to each one. She'll insist on special food instead of the simple rice *dal* that villagers are used to." He repositioned the *paan* to the other side of his mouth. A dribble of red goo escaped down his chin, and he wiped it away unselfconsciously. "She wants to prove to everyone from the village that she is having a good life, because they all know her husband is dead and her in-laws have abandoned her."

Joginder didn't share Radha's superiority complex—although, he reminded me, he was himself high caste, "the Ram caste, just one rung below Brahmin." A few years ago, he said, he'd found Radha a well-paying job as a cook for a family of wealthy meat-eating Hindus, and she'd turned up her nose at the job. It still made Joginder angry that she'd said she wouldn't defile herself by cooking meat.

"She thinks like an old-timer. If she insists on working only in pure-pure veg houses, she will always be poor. But when I tell her this is why she's living in the *bustee,* she doesn't care."

I could imagine Radha's response: Joginder wasn't himself a Brahmin, she'd say, so he couldn't understand.

We were still standing on the street. Passing rickshaws whipped up dust storms around us, and I could feel sweat streaking under the waistband of my *salwar kameez.* A group of young guys leaned against the fruit stand, passing a small, rusty knife between them to peel open guava fruits. Each time they split open the pale green skins to reveal the soft white innards, the tangy smell stung my nostrils. As they sucked the white meat out of the skins, they eyed me almost unblinkingly with the idle, vacant curiosity of the overworked and exhausted. I wondered fleetingly whether I had any wifely cachet left with the Nizamuddin crowd. Joginder hadn't asked about sahib in a while. But his thoughts were on higher matters now. He was in a mood to muse on the globalizing India.

"You know what, *deedee?* Radha hasn't realized that things have changed. Caste isn't so strict anymore, not even in the villages."

Joginder said that as a child in Bihar, when a cow or buffalo died in the fields, the villagers would call for one of the local untouchables to cart away the carcass. "Now they say the world has changed and they shouldn't have to do the dirty work their fathers did," he told me.

In Delhi, caste rules had broken down even further: Radha didn't like to acknowledge it, but her own children had of course played with kids of unknown caste origin. In the city, they all knew people who had taken up different occupations than their parents and grandparents. There was simply no way to monitor it anymore. Still, I told him that as far as I could tell, caste remained important to many people in Delhi, not just Radha.

"Well . . . that's because there are some ways it hasn't changed at all, *deedee.* When it comes to marriage, caste matters more than anything else. I'm glad that India is modernizing. I like having a cell phone and seeing American TV. But there are some Indian traditions that are important, and they shouldn't ever change."

"Marriage is about honor, *deedee,*" he continued. "If my daughter joined a family from a lower caste, no one from my village would come to the wedding. They wouldn't even accept a drink of water from my house afterwards, because they would consider us contaminated. And that's how it should be."

Radha knew her daughter would have to drop out of high school to marry the mobile-in-charge, but that was an easy calculation to make. She'd sent her daughters to school to make sure they didn't have to mop other people's floors; this was just a different route to the same outcome. A good marriage was a more efficient way to guarantee that Pushpa would be "well placed" in life, because it eliminated the uncertainty right away.

But Pushpa was ashamed and confused when her mother told her she wouldn't be able to take her tenth-grade exams. Radha had always insisted that she go to school every day, and now she was commanding her to quit showing up for class because she had too much to do in the weeks before the wedding. When Pushpa suggested that she'd like to finish school after marriage, Radha was quick to disabuse her of that notion: "I can't imagine any family that would allow it."

Joginder knew Radha was probably right about that, which was why he thought she should have waited another year before approaching the *pujari*. He spoke about the importance of "the education of the girl child" with the evangelistic fervor of a man who has come to an unexpectedly progressive decision on his own.

"I make no difference between a boy and a girl," he'd say. "If my daughter wants to get a job, she should. I will find a family that agrees."

Joginder's older daughter, Rekha, was Pushpa's age. He didn't plan to marry her off for several years, though; in fact, he told me proudly that he might allow her to take a one-year computer course after high school. He planned to raise the topic of Pushpa's education at the engagement meeting, in the hope of influencing the boy's family. Since he was Radha's closest male relative in Delhi, he was expected to be at the meeting to help negotiate the dowry.

Radha couldn't bring herself to disagree with a male relative to his

face, so instead, she paid a visit to Joginder's wife. She told me later
that she'd found Maniya in her usual spot—on her charpoy in the afternoon shade, shelling peas with practiced speed. Maniya was half
watching her ten-year-old son's heated game of cricket in the alley
with the other ragtag neighborhood kids. They used a stick for a bat and
a rock for a ball, which had made for some serious black eyes in the
past. Radha sat down heavily beside Maniya on the cot. Although she
was tired from her morning's work, she didn't pause to complain about
her swollen knees as she usually did. Joginder's disapproval had been
weighing on her for days; she got right to the point.

"I've always believed it is best to get girls married when they are
young. That's the way our people have always done things."

Maniya had heard Joginder rant about Radha's decision, so she
knew where this was heading. While she wasn't sure she agreed with
her husband's opinion that girls were the same as boys and couldn't
help but think that she herself hadn't needed an education to be a good
wife and mother, it was her duty to agree with her husband. She had to
prepare her words carefully, though, because Radha was her closest
confidante, and she didn't want to isolate her.

"My husband never even saw a photo of me before we were married.
But things are changing now. The villages are almost as modern as the
city."

Radha wasn't to be thrown off course.

"Maybe so, but do girls wait until they are eighteen to marry there?"

"Probably not. But here in the city, girls even go to college before
marriage. Rekha told me, and you see it in films, too."

Radha was unsmiling: "If it keeps on like this, girls will be the age of
a grandmother by the time they become a mother. It makes no sense!"

"Think of it this way—if you had gone to school, you could have gotten a better job when your husband died."

"That's different. That's my fate," Radha said, in the pitiful tone of
voice she reserved for speaking about her widowhood. Maniya refused
to take the bait.

"You are still marrying your daughter into a good family despite that. We only hope for the same for ours. Every parent knows it is marriage, not a computer course, that determines a girl's happiness."

Rekha, the daughter in question, was crouched over a bucket at the other end of the alley, rinsing out an enormous batik-print bedsheet under the outside tap. Her mother had always decreed her "too tall" for her age—whatever her age—because she'd never been able to wear family hand-me-downs. Now that she was a teenager, Rekha's relatives would shake their heads sorrowfully when they saw her: It's much harder to marry off a tall girl, they'd say.

In spite of this physical disability, Rekha's parents believed she had good dharma. She'd proved it the previous year, when she was having trouble preparing for her exams. Without electricity in the porch-shack, she'd been unable to study once the sun went down. When Rekha told her teacher, he took up her cause. He called Mago-sahib, the man who for twenty-one years had been Joginder's overseer, and asked whether he couldn't find a little more space for the family, at least in the weeks before Rekha's exams. The call apparently shamed the landlord: He told Joginder that he'd allow him to stretch his living space into an interior room of the house.

For the first time in their lives, Joginder and Maniya had legal electric power running through their home and were able to sleep in a separate area from their children. Maniya hung her saris on a hook on one wall, brightening the corner with streaks of yellows and reds. On another wall, she nailed up a calendar, a free offering from the Nizamuddin tailor shop, which had a different Hindu god on each page. When Rekha did well on her exams that term, Joginder took it as evidence that girls should be encouraged at school.

He recited this tale of good fortune at Pushpa's engagement meeting, but the father of the groom only nodded distractedly.

"Yes, we too believe that school is important. But my wife will need the girl to help in the house. That's the first duty of a daughter-in-law."

The groom's father moved on to more pressing matters, asking his son, Shivshankar, to tell them about his job. The boy explained that *mobile-in-charge* meant that he managed cell-phone towers for Airtel,

India's biggest wireless provider. After the wedding, the family explained, Pushpa would move in with her in-laws in Delhi and Shivshankar would make the twenty-hour train ride back to Patna, the capital of Bihar, where he lived for most of the year in a company guesthouse. The groom's parents turned to Radha and began quizzing her about her daughter's nature and the dishes Radha had taught her to cook. They had a long list of their own Bihari favorites that they wanted to be sure Pushpa could handle.

When Pushpa told me about the meeting, she said she didn't once lift her eyes from the lap of her red celebratory sari. She was listening intently, though. She knew she'd soon be responsible for using the right amount of mustard seeds for her in-laws' meals. Only a few weeks from now, she would be forever linked to the stranger who sat only a few feet from her. Pushpa resisted the urge to peek at him, so for all she knew, he could have looked like a crooked character. Or, she said, he might have even looked like Shah Rukh Khan.

Listening to his high-pitched voice, though, she somehow knew he didn't. It quavered with nervousness, and she imagined his face was tight and pinched. Pushpa gave her *pallu* a tug to be sure no hair was showing and reminded herself that it was time to grow up. From now on, no one must know how she felt. Beneath her scarf, her carefully oiled hair gleamed, even though no one could see its sheen.

CHAPTER 11

The Boy Will Do

Ramadan was not a good month for the Fitness Circle. Since Muslims are not supposed to eat between sunrise and sundown during the holy month of fasting, they try to exert as little energy as possible. Banks and some government offices set up napping benches for Muslim employees during lunch hour; some shops just stayed closed. For those gym ladies who were getting up before four o'clock to prepare the family's morning meal, the rest of the day was pretty much a wash. Membership shrank by half, and Leslie could barely stay afloat.

Azmat still showed up to do *jaroo-pocha,* but her own exercise regime, such as it was, fizzled out entirely during the holy month. She'd catnap on the mats for a while, then amble over to the treadmill to talk to me.

"Why are you working to stay slim and trim if you already have a husband?" *Slim and trim* was one of Azmat's most frequently used English phrases. I'd inject as little enthusiasm as I could into my smile, hoping to discourage further conversation so I could keep up my pace. She rarely got the hint and would continue gamely on.

"I don't know why you bother. Your husband isn't even in Delhi now—you might as well relax." A little while later: "You're really sweating a lot, *deedee.*" This remark allowed her to transition to a favored theory: "Foreign ladies sweat more than Indians. Everyone notices it."

I'd restrain myself from pointing out that if she and the other gym ladies engaged in taxing physical activity, they, too, might perspire.

Eventually, bored by my lackluster responses, Azmat would wander away, eyeing the empty doorway ruefully. When a black burka would block the light at the door and one of the ladies would clomp down the stairs to join her, she'd brighten immediately. They'd sink onto the mats and make what Azmat called "time pass chat" to kill the dull, hungry hours. A common topic was whether they would lose weight this month. Azmat had been disappointed that in past years, she'd actually gained a couple of pounds during Ramadan, because she'd eat so much in the evening to compensate for the day of hunger.

At sunset, the mosque in the Nizamuddin *bustee* sounded a siren throughout the neighborhood, as loud and jarring as an air-raid warning: the signal that it was time for Muslims to say *namaaz* prayers and break the fast. One evening, I followed the wail into the *bustee,* where Azmat shared an apartment with six of her nine siblings. She'd advised me that I'd be unlikely to find the place on my own—if locating an address in Delhi's middle-class neighborhoods is a challenge, it is virtually impossible amid the tiny lanes of the *bustee.*

Azmat met me on the *bustee* outskirts. She was clad in a black, sequined *salwar kameez* edged with bright orange stitching; a matching *dupatta* covered her hair. The material was gauzy, but opaque and unrevealing. Still, she looked positively flashy compared to the burka-clad women around us. Azmat had often informed me that her brother, Mehboob, was unusually liberal in not making her and her sisters cover their faces in public. He'd warned her that she'd lose this freedom after marriage.

"He says he probably won't be able to find a boy for me who won't make me wear burka. I'll be tripping all over the place! You can't see anything in those things, *deedee.* I'll probably have to give up my job at

the Fitness Circle after marriage, too. So I'm just enjoying my freedoms now."

As she led me through the maze of narrow lanes, I had the sensation
of falling down a rabbit hole into a world distinctly different from my
own India of chauffeur-driven cars and movie tickets. We were only a
few steps away from my orderly neighborhood, but the passageways of
packed mud had narrowed, and I fell behind Azmat because we couldn't
fit two abreast. The brick and cement houses were piled haphazardly
on top of one another on either side, like teetering castles of cards—
cluttered with plastic water tanks, satellite dishes, and laundry lines.

A couple of scraggly goats were tethered to a pole in an alleyway,
snapping greedily at a pile of scraps. They looked as if they needed
more than another two weeks of fattening; that was all they had left
before they'd be slaughtered for the Eid feast at the end of Ramadan.
When the siren finally stopped, the sound echoed for a moment in the
air, and then the *bustee* was charged with a new energy. Vendors shut-
tered their stalls of essential oils, strings of beads, and religious
books, and joined the men streaming toward the mosque. Others, too
hungry to sit through formal prayers, were cramming into kebab
shops.

Azmat's apartment smelled like stewing meat and onions. We all sat
cross-legged on the plastic sheets that she and her sisters had laid out
on the floor, with the food in the middle, like an indoor picnic. Azmat's
brother said a quick prayer, and they passed out dates to break the fast.
They presented Rhemet's special chicken *biryani* rice dish with great
fanfare; this was the dish that Azmat believed would guarantee her older
sister a swift match. There was also a dish of ground lamb and wheat
called *haleem*, plates of cut fruit sprinkled with salt and pepper masala,
and rose-flavored vermicelli in syrupy milk. The family ate efficiently,
breaking their concentration only to heap more food onto my plate.

In the digestive silence that followed, one of Azmat's brothers returned to the topic of Rhemet's *biryani*. "The whole neighborhood
knows when Rhemet is cooking. The aroma is so fragrant that it makes
people long to taste it."

"Any boy who does will surely want to marry her!" chimed another brother.

Rhemet looked down with forced modesty, and everyone chuckled, as at a joke that has been told many times before. I noticed that none of the three sisters, not even outgoing Azmat, spoke much around their brothers. They addressed them not by their first names but more respectfully, by the Hindi words for "older brother" or "younger brother."

When the brothers headed out to visit a relative, Azmat's familiar, chatty self reemerged. She moved to the daybed and patted the space beside her for me to sit down.

"You know we still haven't found a match for Rhemet or me yet, Mirindaah. That com-*pooh*-ter way didn't work."

I nodded, and she pointed toward a huge blowup of a couple in wedding regalia. It was the only decoration in the room.

"That's our brother in Mumbai. He was the first in the family to marry—and he chose a girl he went to school with. Not arranged." She looked at me significantly as she said these last words in English, anticipating that I'd be impressed. That did not mean, however, that she'd want the same for herself, she was quick to inform me: "It's not good for a girl. The family should pick her match—that's the right way in my community."

Azmat wanted a straightforward alliance, but spending time at the Fitness Circle had made her consider making some changes. Now that she'd befriended women who worked outside the home even after marriage, she'd decided that she'd like to find a husband who would allow her to do the same—or, at the very least, who would permit her to take a tailoring course so she could work from home. Mehboob told her that was probably too much to ask; he was not optimistic that they'd find a boy who'd be willing to invest in a sewing machine.

When I asked her to tell me what else she'd like in her husband, she smiled coyly. Apparently, Azmat often whiled away the unsociable hours at the Fitness Circle imagining her dream spouse. Her ideas sounded far from dreamy to me, though.

"The most important thing is that the boy come from a good family, where everyone lives together under one roof and shares their income.

He also shouldn't have any bad habits: no smoking, no drinking, and no *paan*. I don't want him to take a second wife, no matter what the Koran says."

Rhemet joined us in the living room. I was pretty sure she'd been listening in from the kitchen as she washed the dishes. Although she was the shier of the two and usually allowed Azmat to speak for the both of them, she sounded like a reproachful older sister now.

"You know you aren't likely to find all those things in one boy."

Rhemet realized that if Azmat held out for the perfect husband, her own marriage could be further delayed, since Mehboob had decided to combine the two events. As a result, her own wish list was even more modest than her sister's.

"I'm looking forward to socializing a little after marriage. It isn't appropriate for single girls to mingle outside the family. And I guess I'd like to improve my appearance, too. Maybe my husband would take me to get the mole on my face removed." She laughed as though she was embarrassed about this self-indulgent aspiration and added, "It doesn't matter, though. We'll both be content with any boy our brother chooses for us. Now that our parents are gone, he knows best."

Azmat wasn't so easily quieted.

"Well, our brother thinks it is okay to have more modern ideas, Rhemet. He says it is acceptable to talk to the boy or even meet him for a date before the engagement."

She used the English word *date* proudly, a cherished signifier of upward mobility.

"He does say that," Rhemet concurred. "But I don't think I could— I'd be too nervous."

Azmat reminded her that Mehboob's own wife, Hena, had been reluctant, too.

"Now Hena says she's glad she met him before they got married, because she knew what to expect in the marriage. Most girls are terrified on their wedding, because they don't know whether the boy is nice or not. But she didn't have to be worried, she said."

Hena was the first girl in her family to go on a premarriage date. Even though the event was chaperoned by Hena's sister and her husband, who sat at a separate table within eyesight, it was a radical move for a conservative Muslim girl. Mehboob chose the venue—Yo! China, a Chinese fast-food chain restaurant whose ridiculous name apparently appeals to middle-class teens. Although the place was far from romantic, the loud piped music and non-Indian cuisine made an important statement about Mehboob's aspirations. The appeal of the globalized lifestyle worked their charms on the girl.

"Hena told me that our brother asked about all kinds of unheard-of things. He even asked whether she liked the idea of marrying him. Can you imagine? She didn't know what to say! He told her he didn't want to marry her unless she wanted to. Eventually, she became bold enough to tell him yes."

Recalling the story of her brother's match, Rhemet seemed to recover from her irritability. She pulled a pink-covered album from the sole bookshelf in the room.

"Our brother's wedding photos. We never get tired of looking at them."

Rhemet flipped the album open to an image of Mehboob, exuberant in a cream-colored *sherwani,* the formal brocade coat typically worn by Indian grooms. I couldn't see Hena's face in any of the images because her gaze was always lowered, but Azmat informed me that she'd worn blue contact lenses that day, to make her look "even more beautiful."

Rhemet flipped through quickly. The best part was toward the back: the honeymoon pictures. The section opened with a shot of an ornate canopied bridal bed that the family had decorated with mounds of rose petals. This intimate picture led into dozens of even more private photos of the newlyweds. Apparently, the honeymoon, just as much as the wedding, is family property in India.

Both Hena and Mehboob were clad in revealing Bollywood clothes in the shots of their week together in Goa, a strip of India famous for its beaches. Gone was the loose *salwar kameez* Hena usually wore; she'd transformed herself into a saucy Mallika-style starlet for her honeymoon. To judge from Azmat and Rhemet's reaction to the album, it is just par for the course to do so. In one picture, she modeled painted-on-tight jeans and a 1980s-style cropped jean jacket that exposed her midriff. Mehboob strutted beside her in a bomber jacket and knockoff designer jeans. They looked like stills from a romantic Bollywood film: The couple posing stiffly in front of their palm-tree-lined hotel; standing, not touching, in their flashy outfits beside a waterfall; and strolling barefoot in the surf. I mentioned how different Hena looked, and Azmat laughed.

"That's why they took so many snaps. She'll never wear any of those clothes again. It was purely for the honeymoon."

I paused at one of the last photos of Hena on the beach. She was pointing at the words "Mehboob loves Hena" scratched into the sand.

"It was an arranged match, right? They had just had one date?"

"Yes, but they'd already been alone in Goa for a few days. Of course they felt love by now!"

Azmat's chuckle was startlingly bawdy.

Geeta's father didn't hear from Ashok's family, and she took out her frustration on Shaadi, refusing to sign on to her account for more than two weeks. When she finally went back online, an instant message box popped up.

"Hi Geeta—It was very nice to meet you in Delhi. I am sorry my family wasn't in touch." It was Ashok. She was trying to decide whether to respond when another line pinged through. "Actually my situation is a little complicated. I have a girlfriend who I am trying to get married with. Our families are giving us trouble." Silence for a moment. Then he wrote, "Anyway, bye!"

Geeta closed the message box, feeling more vindicated than angry. It was just as she'd thought. Energized by the knowledge that Ashok might have worked out had his situation not been "complicated," she resolved to take fate into her own hands. She'd have to do as Radha's and Usha's parents had: compromise on the match. In the online matrimonial world, this meant expanding the criteria on her Shaadi profile to include non-Punjabi boys. She wasn't willing to go so far as to include those from another caste or religion, but even so, she decided not to tell her parents what she was doing. As eager as they were to get her married, they would hate to imagine her raising children who didn't speak their mother tongue.

Geeta received several new emoticons expressing interest right away, including one from a guy with the no-nonsense profile name "groom4marriage." His Shaadi profile identified him as "32 yrs, Hindu, Brahmin, software consultant, USA." When Geeta told me about him, she couldn't remember where he lived; whether it was New Jersey or California didn't mean anything to her. What mattered were the specificities of his Indian origin; still, she didn't find that out until after several instant-messaging sessions. Shaadi protocol demands that the boy and girl play it cool for the first week of online correspondence. Only after that do they start to ask the leading questions of the marriage oriented.

When "groom4marriage" revealed his real name—Ramesh Murthy—Geeta definitely didn't play it cool. She called me right away to tell me that his name made clear what his profile did not: that he was from South India.

"My God, I can't believe I've been chatting to a South Indian all this time!"

She made it sound as though she'd been talking to an alien. Although there are major cultural differences between South and North India, it didn't follow that she'd be more worried about the guy's home state than about the fact that he currently lived in a different country.

"He may be an NRI," Geeta tried to explain, "but these boys move back home when they get married. And his home place is Bangalore, where everything is different—food, culture, language, even the women's saris. I probably have more in common with a Muslim from the North than I do with a Hindu Brahmin from Bangalore."

This was quite a statement for someone who had grown up fearing Muslims. Geeta hadn't been taught to be afraid of South Indians, though—just to consider them strange and humorous. She said she'd known only two South Indian kids in Patiala, and they'd been mocked for their long names and funny-sounding mother tongue. It was hard for Geeta to get past the stereotyped image she held of South Indians as dark-skinned, mustachioed weirdos with heavy looping accents.

I gently suggested that she might not want to give up on Ramesh Murthy quite yet, though, since he fulfilled every one of her other pre-requisites. And over the next few weeks, Geeta showed an impressive capacity for open-mindedness toward the South Indian. Usually, when I stopped by Nanima's in the evenings, I'd find her on the sofa watching TV with the old woman, each of them sipping a mug of hot *haldi* milk, tinted orange with tumeric powder, which Geeta said helped digestion. Now, though, Geeta's evenings of what she called "time pass" were over. Instead, she'd be hunched in front of her old desktop PC, poking out messages to potential husbands one finger at a time.

After a few weeks, she told me that they had moved from instant messages to phone calls—a sure sign that things were getting serious, according to Shaadi's rules of courtship. Geeta said they would some-times talk past midnight, and joked that she was losing sleep willingly for the first time in her life. She seemed disarmed by it all.

"It's crazy that I have so much in common with a South Indian boy, Miranda. He wants to know everything about my life. You know what he told me tonight? He said I should always be treated like a princess."

I should have been happy for her, but I felt protective. There were too many similarities to Ashok, who'd gamely agreed that an arranged marriage was a good idea, even while he had an American girlfriend back home. Geeta hadn't told her father about Ramesh yet, and I couldn't help but think about the questions he might have asked: What do we know about this boy? Who is his family? How can we trust him?

I was also a little peeved that my friend was disappearing into this virtual relationship. Geeta didn't have as much time to hang out as she used to. I was ashamed of my ungenerous feelings. Geeta had been looking for a husband for almost a decade. Was I so selfish that I be-grudged her the first guy in ages who seemed to have potential? Per-haps I was afraid she'd leave me floundering in Nizamuddin, without her troubles to distract me from my own loneliness.

I guess she could tell that I was lukewarm about these new developments, because she sounded sheepish when she told me that she had an appointment at Madame X in the morning.

"Ramesh is coming to visit—but he's not on a marriage pilgrimage. First he'll visit his grandfather in Bangalore, and then he'll be coming up to Delhi to meet me—only me."

Geeta had consented to meet Ramesh alone for lunch, rather than an evening activity, when he came to town. She felt okay about going unescorted, she said, because she'd already given him her antidating speech.

"I told him firmly, just one date. We've already done the chatting. So the only reason to meet is to decide whether a marriage will happen."

Geeta's voice sounded exultant on the intercom. I heard her newly bought heels clip perkily on the stairs as she made her way up. Inside the apartment, she plunked a wooden mask down on the living room table. Her face shone.

"See this? Ramesh brought it all the way from Sri Lanka. He loves to travel. You won't believe it: At the end of lunch he said he wants to bring me to Sri Lanka. He said he has feelings for me!"

Her words were flowing out in a stream of non sequiturs. As grizzled and cynical as I was feeling, I couldn't help but grin at her. They'd talked for two hours, she said. She'd been relieved that he didn't have a heavy South Indian accent and was at pains to reassure me that he did not "look all South Indian," as though I'd been as concerned about this as she had.

"He's not all dark and scrawny with that horrible curly hair. In fact, he's quite fair. Maybe it's because his mother's family comes from the North of India."

I asked what else they'd talked about, and Geeta said she couldn't remember, sinking back from her perch on my living room chair. Over the next hour or so, she'd sit suddenly upright, recalling scraps from their conversation: He never watched Hindi films, for instance, and loved Hollywood.

"In fact, he has American taste in most things." Geeta sounded satisfied about this. "He will only wear American clothes, like Banana Republic and Tommy Hilfiger, and some other brands that aren't even *available* in India."

"He sounds like a modern-minded guy. So . . . did marriage come up?"

Geeta shifted in her chair. She'd been enjoying the afterglow of her date until I broke in with reality.

"Of course it did. In fact, Ramesh said three times he wanted to marry me. But I stayed quiet. You know . . . he doesn't look the way I imagined my husband would. He's not tall or Punjabi. It just . . . complicates things that he is from the South, that he is so different. I don't think I'm ready to make the decision."

"What about being able to tell that you want to marry someone in thirty minutes?"

I was just ribbing her, but Geeta didn't see the humor.

"I guess that's only if I *don't* like a boy. Deciding to like someone takes longer—the risks are much more. Maybe Ramesh is already liking me too much, but something isn't right."

When Geeta and I watched an old movie, we'd chuckle at how the 1950s Bollywood heroine lowers her eyes when the hero proposes marriage. A girl can never say yes the first time: It's one of the rules of courtship laid out in the unwritten marriage-age girls' manual. She will raise her eyes ever so slightly to signal that she means "Absolutely yes! Oh my God, yes!" I had to watch a great deal of Bollywood to realize that coyness is the way the pious virgin shows that in fact she wants to embrace the hero in a verdant field of mustard. I couldn't tell whether Geeta was acting the part of the reluctant bride because she felt she should, or whether she had genuine reservations.

Either way, Ramesh was prepared to wait. He'd told Geeta he'd stay in Delhi for the next week, during which time he dedicated himself to wooing her: He sent her flowers every day and peppered her with compliments and requests to meet him one final time. Even the Punjabi princess seemed a little overwhelmed by Ramesh's extreme courtship. "What am I supposed to *do* with all these roses?" she said. It might have been frightening for Geeta to be treated as she'd always dreamed,

because it seemed like evidence that she was fated to marry this South
Indian boy.

I doubt Geeta slept or worked much that week. She told me she'd
been leaving the office early every evening and spending hours on the
phone with Ramesh. But although he was staying with relatives just a
couple miles from Nizamuddin, she didn't see him again until the day
before he left. She called me before she agreed to meet him, eager to
hear that it was the right decision.

"Ramesh has been trying to convince me all week that we should
have one final premarriage meeting. What do you think? Once more is
okay, right?"

I'm sure she could hear my smile in my voice.

"I don't know, Geeta . . . wouldn't that be a second date?"

She sighed.

"No, Miranda, it's absolutely not a date, and the first one wasn't either. You know that! I have a very serious decision to make, and I think
I need to talk to him in person once more to decide."

So I told her what she wanted to hear. She made me promise to
come over to Nanima's the following night, so I could ensure that the
old woman didn't embarrass her when he picked her up.

I was waiting there as arranged when Ramesh rang the doorbell.
Geeta was still getting dressed. She'd been having trouble deciding
whether to "go Indian" or not for this meeting. Her friends had pointed
out that there wasn't much point in her trying to look traditional on a
second, unescorted date, but it still felt wrong to her not to dress like a
traditional, modest bride-to-be. Her anxiety was contagious. Nanima,
her maid, and I were all hovering outside her room, and we all jumped
at the sound of the bell. I sent them back to Nanima's bedroom and
smoothed out my hair in the mirror before pulling open the door to the
South Indian.

I was startled by how good looking Ramesh was, with finely chiseled
features and intelligent eyes. He was well dressed, too: His jeans were
a baggy American style rather than the slum-cut tighter fit generally
favored by Indian men. He stood in the living room, wiping his hands
on them, until I gestured awkwardly to the sofa. Geeta was right:

Ramesh spoke English with an American twang, drawing out his vowels the way Indian call center workers do after they've been trained to sound un-Indian when they take computer support calls. Ramesh also used obvious Americanisms, such as "you guys" and "dude," more often than seemed strictly necessary in twenty minutes of casual conversation. After sitting down, he informed me that "the American lifestyle" had made a big impact on him during his college years in Edison, New Jersey. Afterward, he'd found a job as a computer programmer so that he could stay on. He proudly listed the "American food" he'd learned to cook, omelets and pasta, and his favorite restaurants, Pizza Hut and Burger King.

Growing impatient with the fast-food theme, I asked Ramesh what else he liked about American culture. He had something more substantial to say: He'd been impressed by America's ethnic diversity and civic values, he said, and by community associations, neighborhood cleanups, and crime-watch campaigns. Ramesh went to pains to emphasize that he'd made non-Indian friends in college.

"I didn't want to live in an Indian ghetto, you know? In college, black guys, white guys—we all hung out like we were the same. I didn't know their family backgrounds, and they didn't know mine. In India, people are so concerned about whether they are the same as other people."

I was impressed by his bluntness. Ramesh was thirty-two, with a younger brother and sister who were both already married, and he said he'd only just started thinking about marriage—which was also unusual. I decided to take advantage of the time before Geeta emerged to do a little reconnaissance about his plans.

"Do you plan to stay in the States?"

Ramesh wiped his hands on his jeans again.

"I don't know. When I lived there I felt really American. But after some time, I started to think that I am a little different from American guys—at least in the relationship way. Americans come in and out of romantic affairs easily. We aren't like that in India. Here, nothing is more important than family. And that's how I feel."

It didn't exactly answer my question, but it was the right response for a marriage-age boy, and Ramesh knew it. I felt sure then that Geeta would marry this guy. As she clip-clopped out of her room wearing "Westerns"—slacks and a blouse—I gave her the escort's approving nod.

Geeta came over that evening after the date so we could rehash the conversation we'd had hundreds of times.

"Ramesh thinks love and marriage should go together. I wonder whether there's something wrong with me."

"Well, you always said that love will come later," I said, trying to quell my Super Reporter Girl urges, even though I felt as though I'd said this many times before.

"What if it doesn't, though? What if I never feel it for him? I don't even know what love *feels* like!"

"I think you need a drink, Geeta."

When I offered, Geeta usually demurred, saying she was too petite to handle alcohol. She agreed tonight, though, and I poured us each an Old Monk rum and mixed it with seltzer water to cut the sweetness. Geeta accepted the glass without acknowledging that she'd taken it. She was staring out over the balcony. The neighborhood *chowkidar*s had begun their nightly racket, blowing their whistles and clanging their clubs against the metal railings of the gates. We were accustomed to the racket of the overenthusiastic Nizamuddin watchmen. It was their habit to make enough noise to ensure that the whole neighborhood knew that they were out on their rounds. The watchmen wanted us to know that they were earning their keep, even at the cost of keeping everyone awake.

"I always thought that if it was the right boy, I would just know . . . but I don't feel sure at all. I don't understand how Ramesh can say he's already in love with me."

"Okay, Geeta. If you're not feeling sure about marrying him, why don't you try to imagine whether you *could* love him someday?" She shrugged her shoulders. "Well, are you attracted to him?" I continued.

Geeta wrinkled her eyebrows.

"Girls don't think like that in India, Miranda. Remember, it's not like *Friends* here."

I couldn't help but think that we were in trouble if the definitive word on sexuality, for Geeta, came from *Friends* reruns. Still I pressed on, emboldened by the rum. Geeta hadn't ever talked about sex, or anything to do with her body, with anyone: not with her mother, her female cousins, or her friends. I struggled to come up with the right vocabulary to use with her.

"Well, what about Amit? You told me you thought he was cute. Did you ever flirt with him?"

"Are you kidding me? He's my boss, and he's married, Miranda!"

My pop sex-therapy session wasn't going as well as I'd hoped.

"All I mean is that even if it doesn't mean anything, sometimes we flirt with guys just because they're attractive and it's fun to. It doesn't have to mean anything. It's just a function of male and female energy."

Geeta took a thoughtful sip of her drink.

"I don't know, Miranda. Amit is cute, and because he is Punjabi, automatically we understand each other's jokes and references. We have a rapport, I guess. But Indian girls don't think about flirting around like that. At least, we're not supposed to."

"Especially not with your boss, I guess," I added.

"Even if he wasn't my boss it would be that way! Any kind of flirting seems bad to me. Only now, with TV and everything else, love and sex have become part of how we think in India now. That's totally new, though, and most girls still don't know how to deal with it. Very honestly, Miranda, we're still pretty naïve about all of that kind of stuff."

In spite of her stated naïveté, I decided to plow ahead with my lesson in the womanly arts. I winked at her.

"Well, no matter what happened before, once you get married, you'll realize that you can have a lot of fun. I bet you'll wonder why you waited so long to jump into the sack."

Geeta let loose a giggle.

"I think you've had enough rum, Miranda!"

But I was just getting started. I hadn't ever met a thirty-something virgin before—not that I was aware of, anyway—and it seemed like a problem I should help her correct.

"When I was seventeen, I used to joke with my high school best friend that we were the Last American Virgins, because it felt like we were."

Geeta gulped, imagining me a sex-obsessed American teen. I was enjoying the shock on her face.

"Actually, we were pretty average. I looked it up. Most Americans lose their virginity when they're seventeen. You've waited more than fourteen years longer than that, so my theory is that you're going to have a lot to make up for when you get married."

Geeta held up her hand, laughing.

"Enough, Miranda. Don't tell me anything more about it. Now I know why Indians don't talk about sex to their daughters. We would want to have it all the time!"

Instead, Geeta steered the conversation back to the issue she was obsessed with: the love versus arranged marriage conundrum. She'd obviously turned the corner on her feelings for Ramesh. If, before, she'd been suspicious of any boy who wouldn't insist outright that he wanted a traditional arrangement, she was now trying to justify Ramesh's views against the institution. She spoke in the assertive voice that meant she was trying to convince herself of something.

"Ramesh says he's been living in the U.S. too long to have a pure arranged type. He wants to have a connection with the girl he marries. In fact, he wouldn't even consider ours to be an arranged marriage, if it happens. It feels more like love to him, because we have connected."

I tried not to look skeptical. Ramesh seemed like a *filmy* type, someone who liked the idea of love enough to convince himself he felt it—even if he'd only met the girl twice. Of course, I was a pretty *filmy* type myself, so I should know. Geeta, unconcerned about whether I was paying attention, was still talking.

"His family has been begging him to look for a girl for years, and his father kept sending him bio-data for all these girls, but he wasn't ever interested. He said they all looked the same. When he went on Shaadi and saw my picture, it was love at first sight. . . . Just the same that happened with me! I have met so many boys, thirty or more, and he was the first I liked."

I was surprised by Geeta's ability to completely rewrite her own romantic history. In the days following their second meeting, she began acting as though all her doubts about her future had disappeared. She found a way to mirror the narrative that Ramesh had come up with— a story line in which they had discovered each other after many lost years—as though to convince herself that their match was fated. In this version of their love story, she was alternately a girl giving in to a determined suitor and a princess accepting her destiny. I could see the appeal of the fairy tale. Geeta had resolved not to do as so many of her friends and family members had and make the familiar Indian calculation about a match: that the boy would do.

CHAPTER 12

Too Much Passion for This World

Parvati was hungry. We'd both been working late, and I'd invited her over on her way home, but she called from outside my apartment to tell me there was a change of plan.

"I need some real food, Miranda. Not *pasta.*"

She pronounced the word with the disgusted emphasis that most Indians reserve for words such as *boyfriend.* I restored my unsatisfying Western cooking to the fridge and slid in next to her in the passenger seat of her car.

Parvati drove us to her favorite *parantha* stall. In the parking lot of the *Times of India* building, two grease-spattered, spindly armed teenagers labored over an enormous, blackened stove to satiate the late-night crowd with thick fried breads. We pulled up wobbly plastic stools and balanced leaf plates on our knees. I was full before I could even finish the Frisbee-sized thing. When I wiped my lips, a long line of *parantha* grease smeared across the back of my hand like the trail left by a slug across a leaf. Parvati tossed her plate into a nearby trash can, where it was ravaged by a stout rat. I shuddered and folded my legs under me on the stool.

Parvati's mind was elsewhere. The bare bulb hanging from the *parantha* stall cast a slash of light across her face.

"Remember how I said Divya had started contacting Vijay again?"

I nodded, feeling my pulse increase as she fixed her gaze on me. I could never tell what it was going to be with Parvati. She fostered un-predictability and drama in her life, and right now she looked as though she could say anything.

"Suddenly she was calling him all the time. Vijay didn't tell me what was going on until a few days back. Divya had a baby." Her eyes, meet-ing mine, were dull. "He told me it's not his. He says it's the baby of some boyfriend of hers, but now the boyfriend has left and she's just alone with this baby."

"Wow." It took me a moment to register the implication of what she'd just said, and then a moment longer to eliminate the skepticism that immediately followed. After all, a lot of men have told a lot of girl-friends that some other woman's baby isn't theirs. Parvati either fully believed that the child wasn't Vijay's or was determined that I should believe that she believed it: Either way, it was clearly not up for dis-cussion. I struggled to come up with the appropriate response and finally managed, "Does she have people to help her? Is her family in Jaipur?"

"Yes, they're there, but that's also complicated. They assume it's Vijay's—everyone thinks they are married and that he's not around much because he works in Delhi. I don't think anyone knows about this other man. She's been begging Vijay to come and help her, and he fi-nally agreed to attend some family event with her. It's crazy." Parvati al-most chuckled—though not quite. I felt a wave of resentment toward Vijay.

"Has he told her about you?"

"Yeah. She knows I'm his girlfriend—in fact, she wants to meet me. Vijay says she knows they are finished, she just can't admit it to her fam-ily. I don't worry about his feelings; I can tell that he doesn't love her.

Vijay doesn't respect many people other than me, honestly. We fight, but he knows his life would be much more chaotic if I wasn't in it."

I nodded in agreement, remembering how well she'd cared for Vijay when he'd had chest pain and heart palpitations the prior year. He'd started feeling unwell after working out at the boxing gym, and then felt progressively worse. Parvati had spent hours on the phone that night, trying to get him an appointment at AIIMS, Delhi's highly esteemed research hospital. Then she took a week off work to take him to various appointments. When they were told that Vijay had danger- ously high blood pressure, she'd dedicated herself to helping him cut down on his smoking and drinking. They'd been spending less time at the Press Club in an effort to avoid the whiskey-sodden political argu- ments and dozens of cigarettes that inevitably accompanied a night there. She'd convinced him to take a break from boxing, too, because the doctor said it was too much of a strain.

The pair of them had adopted an uncharacteristically Zen-like new regimen. Parvati had convinced Vijay to take evening walks around the neighborhood with her, and to read at home with a glass of *nimbo panne* instead of whiskey. I was sure that I could already see a difference in Vijay's manner—on more than one occasion, I'd seen him ignore po- tential provocations from friends who stopped by and started talking politics.

Thinking about this made it more difficult for me to come to terms with the new information.

"Wait—he's actually in Jaipur with his wife and her baby now? Why?"

Parvati glanced over at the next table of *parantha* eaters, a loud group of newspapermen telling dirty jokes. They were paying us no more attention than they were the rummaging rats, which had now multiplied from one to several.

"He feels guilty. He says there's no one else to help her. She lost a lot of friends when they split up."

I was still suspicious.

"So . . . he's sleeping on the sofa or something while he's there?"

"You know how weird Vijay is about this kind of stuff. Dealing with women, even in normal situations, makes him intensely uncomfortable. You know as well as I do, Miranda—the man is not suited for anything other than an idealistic life of the mind. I imagine he's staying as far away from her as he can. I almost feel sorry for him."

"He has too much passion for this world," I said, reciting Parvati's own line back to her; she often used it in the wake of one of his storming-off scenes.

She gave me a feeble smile.

"Yeah, my boyfriend has way too much of *everything* for this world. He's too kind, really—he feels responsible for messing things up for Divya."

I said I was sure that if I were in this situation, I'd be feeling much less solicitous toward both of them. Parvati pushed her hair back with her hand.

"I was angry, too, Miranda, believe me. As you well know, I'm not some Mother India martyr type. But there's no point in being angry. I've chosen to be with Vijay. He's made unconventional decisions, and you pay a high price for that in India. But Divya is paying an even higher price than him."

Parvati stared into the tottering pile of greasy leaf plates in the trash can beside us. Her forehead was creased with tension.

"You know how much I complain about the neighbors and my family prying into my life. But now I've been thinking about what it's like for Divya. I mean, my God, lying to everyone all the time about everything: It must be exhausting. Seriously, I can't imagine a worse fate."

A few weeks later, Parvati called with an "urgent request": that I meet her at the outdoor clothing market near her apartment that afternoon. It didn't make sense: Parvati hated shopping—especially there, because the cheap cotton *salwar kameez* suits leaked color and wore thin after a couple of washes. She was determined to bend me to her will, though, begging, "Come on, you can't have that much work to do. It's a Saturday."

I gave in when I realized that she must have a good reason, even though she refused to explain on the phone. Parvati didn't often make requests of me. After fighting with Vijay, she'd wait a couple of days before she called. When she did, she rarely wanted advice or sympathy; she preferred to play it down. I don't think she was proud of her relationship upheavals, and talking about them made her feel too vulnerable.

Parvati met my taxi on the outskirts of the market. She was restless as I paid the driver, tapping her *chappal*-clad foot on the concrete, pulling a cigarette out of her ten-pack of Gold Flakes, and lighting it with quick, nervous fingers. Her hair was uncombed, little strands fluttering out of the braid that she usually pulled together tidily before going out in public. When I was done, she gestured me urgently to follow her into her parked car.

"What's going on, Parvati?"

"I know I'm acting crazy. But just listen. Divya's coming here." She lowered her voice as though someone might hear her through the sealed windows. "She's got her baby here, too, and I said I would help her buy some things for it. Vijay isn't coming. It was just going to be the two of us. But I got all freaked out about it earlier and thought that I needed to have someone here with me."

Divya had been in town only a day, she said. She was staying in Vijay's guest room over the weekend, baby and all. She'd apparently come specifically to meet Parvati. It seemed strange—especially for socially conservative India. I was having trouble picturing Vijay cloistered in his apartment with girlfriend, wife, and child. Parvati said they'd dealt with the awkwardness by getting rollicking drunk. They'd ended up singing 1950s Bollywood tunes—which was a good conclusion to any night, according to Vijay and Parvati.

"Considering what a bad situation it is, and all the potential for discomfort, it's actually been okay. I had some good chats with her last night. She's an interesting girl, and I feel like I could actually be her friend if it wasn't for all this. I think this hardship has been a strain on her. She seems unhappy and somehow a bit . . . off. It's like she laughs a little too much, you know? Nervously."

"That's sad," I said.

"Yeah, it is—*she's* sad, in general, actually. And I know I shouldn't say this, but I think something about the situation has affected the way she looks and acts. All the stress and strain of being alone and lying about her marriage—it makes sense that it would have an impact."

"Explains what?"

"Well, those good looks Vijay was always telling me about. She used to be this gorgeous girl with smoldering dark eyes, but not anymore. I don't see it."

I snorted in spite of myself. It was a bitchy thing to say about a woman in trouble, but it broke the tension. I didn't know how to respond to Parvati's uneasiness about the strange situation with Vijay's unusual houseguests. Neither she nor I knew how to act when she felt vulnerable. I changed the topic the only way I could think of—by asking questions.

"Did you know she was coming?"

"Not until two days back. I guess she'd been telling Vijay she wanted to come for some time, and he finally agreed, so she got on a train on the spur of the moment. She's impulsive like Vijay that way."

"It seems strange she would make so much effort to stay in touch with him if she didn't have feelings for him."

Parvati cracked her window and flicked her cigarette butt out. A blast of hot, dry air shot into the air-conditioned car, and the effects of that single beam of heat stayed for a few moments after she rolled it back up again.

"Probably she does. But I've made damn sure she knows she can't have him. Maybe she's trying to be friends with me instead of trying to compete with me. I guess that's good, right?"

Parvati saw a figure approaching the car and waved through the windshield.

"This is her. I told her to find me in the parking lot."

We watched Divya as she approached, reluctant to leave the cool air until absolutely necessary. Through the windshield, I could see that she had wide-set eyes and broad features, the kind of face that might have once been striking. Now, though, her eyes were sunken and her features sagged with extra weight, making her appear older than she was. That impression was exaggerated by a tragic slash of red lipstick across her face.

The bright makeup seemed shocking, because I'd become accustomed to the homogeneous, conservative style of dress among women in India. It's rare to see dramatic or showy shades of lipstick on anyone other than low-caste villagers or prostitutes. It was unnerving to see a thirty-something middle-class woman with red lips; and all the more so because Divya had an infant slung across her chest. Even under the best of circumstances, a woman in her late thirties carrying a child draws surprised and judgmental glances in India, because that is considered old to have a baby.

The woman walking toward us was not what I had pictured when Parvati first told me about Vijay's stormy college love affair. There was something tragic about her moving slowly in the heat, weighed down by the swaddled infant. I wondered whether Parvati was right about her being "a bit off," because it was hard to believe that she wasn't self-conscious about her makeup. Parvati was apparently thinking the same thing.

"I don't know why she does her face up like that," she said through her teeth, so that Divya couldn't read her lips through the windshield. She was almost at the car now, but Parvati continued. "I feel sorry for her, having to carry that baby everywhere. I know that most women want children—and I am just different that way, because I don't—but I *really* can't imagine having one on my own like that. With no help, and everyone looking at you and imagining the worst . . . *Ay baba.* Come on, let's take the poor woman shopping. It's the least I can do for my husband's wife, right?"

She gave me a sardonic grin, and we climbed out of the car into the scorching sun of the parking lot.

Geeta's father was so eager to talk that he called her before he even boarded his flight home from Bangalore.

"I won't be able to eat for a week, *betee,*" he said, and she knew the visit had gone well: There's no better way to demonstrate warmth in

India than to lavish food on your guests. Before he told her about her potential in-laws, Nitin Shourie paused to describe, in mouthwatering detail, Ramesh's mother's *obbattu,* a thin, fried chapati filled with cane sugar and coconut.

"You won't find a better family than his, *betee.* This is our chance. I'm going to tell your mother that we should bring this boy in and treat him like a Punjabi."

Geeta was a little surprised by her father's enthusiasm. When she'd broken the news about Ramesh, her mother had been so upset that she'd refused to speak to Geeta for several days. It had fallen to her father to summarize their objections.

"All these years your mother has waited for a son-in-law, and now you're going to marry a stranger and move to the other end of the country, where all their habits are strange to us. How will you be happy down there, *betee?*"

Their disapproval had made Geeta edgy and flustered for weeks; she kept leaving her keys in the car and forgetting to renew her prepaid credits on her cell phone, so she'd be unable to make calls for days at a time. When it rang, she'd plow frantically through her bag to find it. She lay awake at night, even on weekends—her most prized sleeping time—second-guessing herself and mourning the angst she was causing her parents. Only when her father finally came around and told his wife that they owed it to their daughter to meet the boy's family was she able to relax.

From what Geeta could conjecture, the visit had been uncomfortable at first. For starters, the families spoke different regional languages: Geeta's, Punjabi, and Ramesh's, Kannada, the language of their home state, Karnataka. It wasn't an issue for Geeta and Ramesh, because, like most middle-class Indians of their generation, they could rely on English to bridge the regional gap. Not so for their parents. When the two mothers met at the engagement, they wouldn't be able to utter a word to each other beyond *Namaste.* The fathers could speak just enough English to show off a little, though not enough to form full sentences; they relied on Hindi to communicate with each other, even though Ramesh's father had barely spoken it since high school.

Keshava Murthy was a man of large gestures. His was a prominent business family, and his youngest son's engagement seemed the kind of occasion that warranted great rhetorical flourish. I'm sure it must have pained him to be unable to communicate smoothly with the girl's father. He tried to make up for it in other ways. He donned expensive, designer-made kurta suits and embellished his poor Hindi with expansive arm gestures in an effort to signal his acceptance of the cultural differences that lay, unmentioned, between the two families.

Each man had something to prove. Geeta's father was determined to demonstrate to the wealthier, more successful man that he was an upstanding Brahmin whose daughter would make a kind and caring addition to the Murthy family. Keshava, for his part, needed to show that he could create a superior life for Nitin's only child in his multi-room mansion. He was confident about the advantages he could offer.

He considered it a great accomplishment—his own—that his extended flock still lived together under one roof. If Geeta married into the family, she'd move in with Ramesh's parents, grandparents, brother, brother's wife, and their two kids—not to mention a couple of widowed aunties who always seemed to be around. This was evidence, Keshava thought, of how safe the other man's daughter would be.

It was Nitin's first visit to Bangalore. Before the benefits of the economic boom of the 1990s trickled down to the middle classes, Indians rarely took vacations at all. If they did, they traveled by train, because it wasn't until the early 2000s that air travel became remotely affordable. That's when the Indian government liberalized industry regulations to allow low-cost private airlines to enter the market and make air travel available to more than business travelers and the rich. Since the train journey to Bangalore took forty-two hours from Patiala, it was an unlikely destination for a Punjabi family.

In any case, the city had only recently become a place worth visiting. For most of Nitin's life, Bangalore had been best known as "the pensioners' paradise." It was only in the nineties that Bangalore created incentives to draw in technology companies. They worked: Soon, practically every U.S. software company had research and outsourcing operations there. Bangalore became the world's back office and out-sourcing capital. For years, it was the fastest-growing city in India.

Keshava assumed his relatively provincial guest would be impressed by the steel and glass of the new India. He expounded grandly on Bangalore's opportunities and the tens of thousands of college graduates who flock to its green corporate campuses. Nitin tried to act impressed, but what made the biggest impression on him was the pollution. He was shocked by the hours they spent in traffic, competing for road space with busloads of technology workers and aspirational multitudes on scooters. "I think I'd rather live in a pensioners' paradise than booming Bangalore," he joked later.

Keshava Murthy was unaware of these sentiments and dedicated the rest of Nitin's visit to showcasing his proudest achievements, with a tour of the factories of Murthy Electronics Manufacturing, the refrigerator-parts unit that had been in the Murthy family for three generations, and, of course, of his luxurious home.

Because Nitin had spent his career as a state-employed doctor, the family had lived in a government-allotted apartment that spoke of India's socialist past—gray concrete floors, gray concrete façade, every unit grayly identical. In Nitin's social circle, there was a certain prestige to dedicating your working life to what Indians refer to as a *service job.* Because Indian government employees are well respected and underpaid, they pride themselves on living the self-sufficient, frugal lifestyle that Mahatma Gandhi advocated. In fact, Gandhi's vision was not that different from the ancient Brahminical ideal of centuries ago, when the priestly caste eschewed worldly needs to educate others about the principles of Hinduism. Geeta still sometimes described her father as being "correct for our caste," a phrase that probably came directly from him.

But in an era of fast-rising prosperity, Nitin's moralistic lifestyle was out of fashion. Of the two fathers, only Keshava had learned to adapt to the India of global corporate values and seven-figure salaries. His friends headed thriving car dealerships and textiles companies. I imagine Nitin shuddered a little when the other man clapped him on the back and declared, "This is the era of big money in India, dear Nitin-*ji*! For the first time, we Indians are able to earn serious money—why shouldn't we?" Keshava seemed not to share Nitin's Brahminical qualms about money—he was proud of his prospering family business.

Geeta told me how Ramesh justified his father's capitalist instincts to her. His father had never been motivated by raw financial ambition, he said, but rather by a desire to grow his great-grandfather's business. To Keshava, upholding the family name seemed the noblest of goals, which was why he'd never been able to understand his son's decision to stay in America for as long as he did. Ramesh's college and career achievements were blunted in his father's mind because he had attained them in New Jersey, apart from the family.

He'd been trying to cajole Ramesh into the family business for years now. Keshava's wife, Savitramma, had hoped to pull her son back in by marrying him off to a girl from a local Brahmin family, but, much to her surprise, the boy had refused to consider any of their matches. He'd made them wait for years and now he'd picked a complete stranger—a working girl who lived alone in Delhi—and he was set on her. Soon after he returned from Delhi, Ramesh had sat his parents down and made a pact with them: If they let him marry the girl he chose, he'd come back and work for Murthy Electronics Manufacturing. If they gave him trouble, though, Ramesh said, he might just return to New Jersey. It was close enough to a threat to anger Keshava, but his wife reminded him that it could be worse. Their son might have shown up with an American girlfriend in tow; they'd all heard such stories. At least this girl was Indian and would understand the importance of the family.

By the time the two fathers met in Bangalore, both were resigned to the alliance, which was why they were making such an effort to ignore their cultural differences. Nitin did his best to suppress his aversion to the Murthys' extravagant lifestyle, reminding himself that Geeta would enjoy having expensive saris and her own car and driver. Keshava kindly overlooked the other man's shabby bureaucrat's clothes and his old-timer views on caste and money. For the most part, it worked. Nevertheless, the Murthys' money—and the Shouries' lack of it—necessarily complicated the nuptial negotiations. Nitin knew that if he expressed moral distaste for the dowry system, Keshava was likely to assume he was trying to get out of the marriage because he couldn't match their expectations.

Nitin waited until the end of his second day in Bangalore to suggest to Keshava that they take a stroll on their own while the women prepared dinner. Outside in the balmy evening, it took only a moment for Nitin's fears to be confirmed: The other man clearly did not share his distaste for dowry. Nitin had to backpedal to save his daughter's best—and perhaps only—shot at a good marriage.

"Of course, government salaries are modest. But like any father, I have saved for my daughter's wedding. I hope you won't think that our dowry principle is a matter of money. I would of course want to send my daughter in comfort to your house. Gifts for the couple and the family—that goes without saying—we would never want her to be a burden to you."

"No need, no need," Keshava said, though of course there was.

Nitin, I'm sure, was trying to rescue something of his pride.

"The part we would like to avoid is the dowry *negotiation*. My wife and I think it seems . . . indecorous. Educated people should avoid this bargaining. Such behavior is more for the lower castes."

"Of course, *ji*, of course."

Nitin later told Geeta that Keshava had answered him as if he were comforting a child, patting his arm as they walked back to the house.

"We are in complete understanding, *ji*. We will not make demands. You simply give what is comfortable. It's not the money that matters; it's the family. Family first."

I was sure something was wrong when Maneesh stopped showing up for work. She'd never missed a garbage-collection day before—not without telling me first that there was a Hindu festival or family event she had to attend. When she finally rang the bell to my apartment after a few days' absence, my first thought was that her husband had seriously hurt her. She had dark circles under her eyes, and her *salwar* didn't match her *kameez*, as though she'd dressed without thinking. Seeing the concern on my face, her legs buckled beneath her. She fell to her haunches on the living room carpet and wailed, "*Ai-o deedee!* I have a fever!"

Radha rushed out from the kitchen, and the two of us stood there together, stunned by this tragic display from our cheery garbage collector. I wondered whether she was actually ill or whether it was that she lacked the vocabulary to express sadness or fear. I'd noticed that Maneesh sometimes described her emotions in physical terms.

"My husband is very ill. *Ai-o,* he is in the hospital!"

Radha and I exchanged a glance. Few Indians of their poverty level would pay for treatment if they had any choice about it; the drunken Om Prakash would surely never spend good booze money on a hospital visit unless it was serious. Maneesh wiped the tears off her face ferociously, like a child, and drew a shaky breath.

"He's been sick for a couple of months, *deedee,* and last week, his legs swelled up and he couldn't eat. So his brother took him to the hospital in a rickshaw. They had to wait outside for a whole day before the doctor saw him."

Radha *tsk*ed sympathetically. She knew what it was like to watch your husband die in Delhi's public hospitals.

I sat down next to Maneesh and put my hand on her arm. In a culture where women rarely touch anyone other than their children in public, the gesture seemed extremely intimate after I made it. I think Maneesh was in too much of a state to notice.

"Where is he now?" Radha prompted.

"I don't know for sure. My brother-in-law and sons are with him." Maneesh raised her head to look at us. "What will I do if he dies?"

"Widowhood is a terrible fate," Radha said, and followed it with a bleak invocation of God: *"Arre bab."*

I shot her a reproachful look. "If they took him to the hospital, I'm sure he'll be okay."

Radha couldn't understand why I would say something she saw as clearly untruthful; platitudes were not a part of her vocabulary. She leaned toward me and said, in a loud whisper, "Maneesh's husband does nothing but drink and shit. He doesn't even eat anymore. People have been expecting him to die for years."

Maneesh had of course heard her, and nodded miserably in agreement.

"It's true, *deedee*. I'm going to be a widow. I'll have to spend the rest of my life in mourning."

"When you say goodbye to your husband, you surrender everything worth living for," Radha told her, just for good measure.

I gave Maneesh bus fare. Radha poured leftover rice and lentils into a plastic bag for her, and she accepted it gratefully. I watched from the balcony as she limped down the block toward the main road, her shoulder bones poking out of the back of her *salwar kameez*. Her husband was dying, but the intensity of Maneesh's sadness still surprised me. It sounds cynical, but in the slums, death always hovers close. Nearly four million babies die within a month of their birth every year in India. Maneesh had told me that "two or three" of her siblings had died when she was young; she wasn't sure exactly how many.

It also seemed that Maneesh might actually be better off without Om Prakash. She'd told me that he often drank away all the money for vegetables and she and her sons would eat their evening chapatis with nothing more nutritious than chilis. Still, in a society in which marriage is a requirement, her husband provided the outline of her life. No one in Maneesh's community would believe for a moment that her life would be easier if she lived alone, even though everyone agreed he was a crooked character. As Radha put it, a life without a husband is scarcely a life at all.

The classical Hindu texts decree that upper-caste widows are supposed to teeter between life and death once their husbands have left the land of the living. Centuries ago, Hindu widows frequently took their own lives by committing sati, throwing themselves on their husbands' funeral pyres during cremation ceremonies. Sati was the greatest sacrifice a wife could make for her husband; the women who did so were honored like saints. At Mehrangarh Fort in Rajasthan state, the maharaja's widows left impressions of their handprints in the fort's inner walls before they killed themselves on his pyre when he died. That was 1843: The British had made sati illegal fourteen years earlier.

The practice is no longer commonplace. When, in the 1980s, an eighteen-year-old widow was burned alive in her red wedding sari on her husband's pyre, the country was horrified. There were infuriated panel discussions about "backward India" on English-language TV shows, and the uproar eventually caused the Indian parliament to toughen the laws against the practice. Nevertheless, it is a testament to the strength of tradition in India that the police couldn't prosecute anyone. The community closed ranks around the family, calling the woman a martyr and refusing to reveal the circumstances around her death. During the years I lived in India, I read about several possible sati cases, but the authorities couldn't ever confirm whether the women had chosen to throw themselves on their husband's pyres or had been pushed.

"Woman is as foul as falsehood itself," wrote Manu in the first Hindu law book. Although he ranked women almost as low as untouchables, even he did not command widows to immolate themselves at their husbands' funerals. He merely decreed that traditional Brahmin widows should immolate *pleasure* from their lives after their husbands' deaths. They were banned from remarrying and instructed to shave their heads; wear nothing other than white, the color of mourning; and survive on one meal a day. Even today, some families force the widow to live out the rest of her life in deprivation and prayer in an ashram. It's a convenient way for them to free themselves of the burden of caring for their daughter-in-law.

Radha's in-laws had banished their dead son's wife to the city instead of an ashram. And once in Delhi, Radha had imposed upon herself the strict rules of Brahminical widowhood with the zeal of a true martyr. She never wore colorful clothes, a *bindi* dot on her forehead, or bangles on her arms. Radha fasted during every Hindu festival without fail, and even on normal days she ate only one meal. Her food was without spices or chili and her morning *chai* was without sugar.

Because Maneesh was an untouchable, outside the Hindu system, the strict laws governing widowhood shouldn't have applied to her. But the lower castes have increasingly adopted high-caste practices in recent years, because mimicking upper-caste rituals often feels like advancement. Adopting the stark life of a Brahmin widow could hardly have seemed empowering for Maneesh, though.

The next time I saw her, she came to tell me that the doctor had sent Om Prakash home to die on his charpoy, because his liver and kidneys had failed. The women of the house had gathered around Maneesh after his death to ready her for the thirteen-day mourning period. They rubbed the red *sindoor* out of the part in her hair; the powder had first been applied by her husband during the wedding ceremony and had signified that she was married. They pulled the *mangalsutra*, the gold necklace that is another traditional symbol of marriage, off her neck. They held her arms down and smashed the bangles off them, leaving violent red marks on her wrists. Maneesh said she was sobbing as they removed her toe rings, because she knew they would be pushed onto the dead toes of her husband.

In the other room, Om Prakash's brothers bathed his emaciated body and decorated it with garlands of orange and yellow marigolds. Maneesh's elder son had his head shaved to symbolize his grief before collecting Om Prakash's ashes from the cremation ground. He couldn't afford to travel to Varanasi, which Hindus consider the most auspicious place to scatter the ashes of the dead; instead the men of the family took a taxi to Haridwar, a secondary holy city along the Ganges, carrying the ashes with them in a tin carafe.

Along the banks of the fast-flowing river, hundreds of candles inside leaf baskets floated downstream, like so many prayers to the gods. The men chanted a prayer and tossed Om Prakash's ashes into the water. Back in Delhi, the female relatives dressed Maneesh in a white sari and submerged her into the Yamuna River. The largest tributary of the Ganges, it was supposed to purge her of the sins of the living world.

When Maneesh returned to work a widow, her face was gaunter than before. She had an abstracted, reflective attitude about her.

"I feel like I am dreaming all this. When I did the rituals, it felt as though I had died, too. Everything seemed familiar. I guess that's because I was doing what widows always do."

To Maneesh, widowhood wasn't a way to prove her saintly virtue to the world, as it was for Radha; it was just further evidence of her bad fortune. She wasn't ready to accept that her days of womanhood were over. I couldn't tell whether she was mourning her husband or her new status as a widow, but perhaps they were one and the same.

"I always loved wearing bangles and anklets, *deedee*. I always had toe rings and colorful outfits, even if they were inexpensive ones. But now see." She gestured sadly at her plain white *salwar kameez* and unadorned arms. "My sister-in-law warned me that if I wear anything more than this, everyone will say, 'Why is that widow going around like a bride?' There are new rules for me now. When I attend my relatives' weddings, I cannot sing with the other women. I have to sit at the back, because it's a bad omen for a girl to see a widow at her wedding."

Maneesh's sister-in-law had also warned her not to chat to any men in the *bustee*, because that would spark rumors that she was on the hunt for a second husband. The community didn't expect Maneesh to feel much sorrow at Om Prakash's death, but even if they assumed she'd want to remarry, that didn't make it socially acceptable. Until the nineteenth century, remarriage was actually illegal for Hindu widows, and the cultural prohibition remains.

I could tell that the topic was making Maneesh uncomfortable. She wanted me to know that she'd only consider it if her brother-in-law kicked her out and she needed somewhere to go. She had a good relationship with her husband's family, but nevertheless, her brother-in-law would have to be very kind *not* to eject her from Om Prakash's home after his death.

Maneesh seemed determined to find something sacred in the memory of Om Prakash.

"He was useless, *deedee*, but he was the man I was married to. We were together since I was very young. When I sit alone after I finish my work, I will always think of him."

She told me that she'd mark his death anniversary every year by making a meal for the birds. She'd cook a rice pudding called *kheer* and serve it, along with fried *poori* bread, on small plates made of leaves. She'd put the food out on the terrace as an offering to the gods in the name of the man she'd married. The next morning, in the smoggy dawn of the slum, Maneesh would climb onto the terrace and clear away the remains left by the crows.

CHAPTER 13

Curves

Geeta decided to shop her way into believing in her marriage. She showed up at my apartment one Saturday morning after a visit to Madame X, clutching a long list of things to buy. She'd been working on it all morning with Sameena, she said, while getting her nails done. "I don't know how I will do it all before the wedding!" she said dramatically, handing me the list.

Her face showed none of the worry of recent months, though; in fact, I think Geeta relished the shopping challenge before her. If it had been my list, I would have been truly stressed out. She had to find two weeks' worth of fancy outfits for the wedding period; ten days of honeymoon wear; and an entire trousseau for her new life at her in-laws' house. Her mother would help her find the equivalent of her wedding dress, the *lehnga choli* that she'd wear during the final cere-mony, but she was on her own for the rest. Geeta circled the words "honeymoon outfits" on her list and tapped them with her pen.

"I can't imagine anything worse than looking for bikinis or under-clothes with my mother."

From my brief experience of Pooja Shourie, I had to concur. It was hard to picture Geeta's mother, a reserved and frugal woman, in the lingerie section of a Delhi boutique. I thought of the first such outing I took with my own mother, age thirteen, having convinced her to buy me a training bra because all the other girls had them. In the fitting room, enduring the humiliation of my mother's eyes on my bare chest as I tried on bras I did not need, I'd wished I'd asked a girlfriend to come to the mall with me instead. I could imagine that the experience would be similarly uncomfortable for Geeta, age thirty-one, particularly because India has no tradition of mother-daughter outings to Victoria's Secret. Underwear is considered private and embarrassing, and sexy lingerie is a relatively new phenomenon.

In fact, until recently, bras were the exclusive preserve of the upper middle class, and even today, the poorest Indian women do not wear them. Radha used tight-fitting sari blouses instead. Geeta's mother had owned no more than two or three bras her whole life, washing them carefully by hand every week. For decades, she and the rest of India's bra-wearing minority had a choice of only two brands. Geeta's mother picked Groversons' "Paris Beauty," in either white or beige. I assume the worldly name appealed to the upwardly mobile, although the sensible, polyester-blend garments didn't evoke Parisian couture in any way apparent to me.

But the days of Groversons were over. Geeta had access to a wider diversity of brassieres than her mother and grandmother could have dreamed of. I knew, because in my effort to avoid wearing dowdy Indian bras, I'd discovered a couple of places that sold imported Asian and European underclothes. When the British chain Marks & Spencer opened an outlet in a Delhi mall, I actually called my mother to tell her. She could understand my excitement, having first taught me the joys of M&S bras.

An American friend had recently told me an Indian-run boutique, Curves, boasted a specialty in "adventurous intimate wear for Indian tastes." I thought it would be fun to check it out for Geeta's honeymoon needs—though I knew Parvati would laugh at me for trying to participate in Indian wedding traditions. My displays of what she called "*feringhee* enthusiasm" for India-specific activities always cracked her up.

Apparently, Delhi ladies were not yet taking advantage of the new openness in the Indian bra market. When we arrived at shopping prime time, midmorning on a Saturday, the entrance to Curves was deserted. Faced with the large CURVES sign over the building, Geeta faltered, and I had to remind her that teddies and thongs were essential to the honeymoon experience. She squared her jaw.

The building *chowkidar,* a lanky guy clad in a ratty security guard uniform, was sharing a bidi on the street outside with some other guards. It looked as though he passed most of his hours this way. When he saw Geeta and me moving toward the shop, he made a lunge for the entrance and all but shoved us aside on the staircase in his ardor to sprint up ahead of us so that he could do his job and pull open the door.

Inside, incense and Sikh *gurudwara* chants filtered through the empty store, imbuing the racks of swimsuits and underwear with an unlikely religiosity. A portly Sikh man charged over.

"Good hellos! Hello hello!" he shouted in heavily accented English, shattering the calm. He introduced himself, but I quickly forgot his name; to Geeta and me, he was always Mr. Curves. He had an exaggerated bravado and seemed to have been born without the Indian modesty gene that usually applies to all matters sexual. Mr. Curves lost no time in informing us that he "had a strong interest in the bras for the curvy ladies of India." He gestured toward his wife, who had come up behind him, and she modestly acknowledged her curvaceous figure with a slight curtsy. He sent her off for glasses of water and drew an hourglass figure in the air with his hands.

"Why did I get this interest? Why do you think?"

The two of us were still lingering awkwardly at the entrance to his store. I took care not to look at Geeta so I wouldn't laugh.

"Because I wanted for the ladies to be comfortable! India is a very great country, but the ladies of large bosoms were never feeling nice. That's why ten years ago I began making my designs. And today, the Delhi ladies are catching up with my forward ideas. Now too many ladies are coming to buy my intimates. Too *too* many!"

The evident untruth of this made me wonder what Geeta must be thinking.

"Do you only carry bras for full-figured women?" I ventured.

"No no, madams. We are also importing bras for all kinds of ladies. Look in my store, you will see sexy-sexy designs from Thailand, from Germans, from . . . many other countries. The ladies are loving us too much. And their gents are loving us even more."

He gave us an unsubtle wink, his head wobbling-nodding comically. I sneaked a look at Geeta. She looked as if she was dying to get away from this lusty salesman her father's age. In a bid to save our outing, I suggested that Mrs. Curves might show us around, rather than her husband. Before he scuttled out, Mr. Curves handed us each a plastic keychain in the shape of a female figure and embossed with the store's name. Geeta's lip curled with disgust—I knew Maneesh would pluck the keychain from the garbage the following morning.

Geeta dragged behind as Mrs. Curves led us through the store, not wanting to appear eager to get her hands on the lacy G-strings we could see lining the back walls. We passed an aisle of maternity clothes, which, Mrs. Curves informed us, was new.

"Ladies used to just go to the tailor as their bellies grew. That's what I did—just had a slightly bigger *salwar kameez* tailored every month or two. But now that women are working in offices, they are needing to look professional. They are wanting better choices, like the slacks with expandable elastic waists we are selling here."

I could tell Geeta had stopped listening; we'd had arrived at the wall of underwear. She gazed in wonderment at racks hung with satin girdles, string bikinis, and a series of transparent bras edged with fake fur. It was an impressive display, considering that jeans and a T-shirt is considered a racy outfit in most parts of India. Mrs. Curves offered a sympathetic smile to Geeta's stunned expression.

"Some of the Asian and French styles are quite wild. But these days, Indian girls are wanting this kind of fetish wear after the wedding . . . to surprise their groom."

I thought of Mehboob and Hena's saucy honeymoon shots and wondered what she'd been wearing underneath that cropped jean jacket. Mrs. Curves pulled out a black silk bustier; the matching underwear of the set featured a fire-red flower on the crotch. Geeta looked at the price tag and gasped.

"What? Do girls really pay so much money for such a tiny thing?"

Mrs. Curves seemed well prepared for this reaction.

"Yes, *betee*. A lot of ladies come in and say '*Hoo hoo!* Why spend all that money on something when you're just going to take it off!' But their daughters, if they are modern girls"—she looked pointedly at Geeta—"they've seen intimate wear in films and music videos. They want to have fun with these sexy pieces."

The sales pitch had the desired effect on Geeta, who was determined to be a modern bride, whatever that might entail. She informed our saleswoman that she, too, was in the market for "fun items" for her honeymoon—although she'd probably choose something a little less "forward" than the underwear with the red-flower crotch.

"Congratulations, *betee*. I thought you must be doing your marriage. And where is the honeymoon happening?"

This was a question Geeta loved to be asked. Her honeymoon destination was irrefutable evidence that she was an adored bride of the globalizing India. Her husband wasn't taking her somewhere predictable and domestic, such as Goa, but rather to Thailand, on what would be her first-ever beach vacation and only her second-ever trip outside of India. Thailand is just a four-hour flight from Delhi, but nondomestic travel is still rare for all but India's upper crust. Mrs. Curves reassessed Geeta with an approving eye.

"Veeery lucky girl!"

Geeta acknowledged this statement with a regal nod. Glancing around again at the wares, though, her confidence faltered again.

"Actually, I don't know what I need. What do girls wear at the beach in Thailand? I only have one or two minis. Do I need more? And bikini . . . I am not sure I am brave enough. What Indian girl even knows swimming?"

Mrs. Curves was accustomed to the shopping traumas of brides-to-be.

"Hardly any Indian girls have learned to swim, *betee*. Of course, that

doesn't mean you can't wear a bikini. But many Indian girls are too shy
to be wearing something so skimpy in public. Only in private they wear
the sexy-sexy numbers."

Geeta looked relieved.

"Maybe I'll skip the bikini, then." She gave Mrs. Curves a sidelong
glance. "You are also Punjabi, right?" The saleswoman nodded as
though this was self-evident. "So you know that in our tradition, the
new bride should discard her old clothes before she moves to her in-
laws'." Mrs. Curves nodded again. "My mother wants me to do things
the Punjabi way, even though I am going to marry a South Indian . . ."
Geeta's sentence dribbled out, and she looked at Mrs. Curves, whose
eyebrows were raised skeptically.

"Accha?" she said, using the word for "really" archly. "You are marrying someone from different community? Hmm, I guess modern
girls have all kinds of love matches these days."

I felt a wave of annoyance, but Geeta was accustomed to other people weighing in on her personal life. Her focus was just to ensure that
our saleswoman was aware that while she was a modern girl, she also
had traditional bona fides.

"Actually, I am not having a love match. It's love-cum-arranged."

Worried that the day would disappear into a lengthy discussion of
marriage—a topic I was now totally sick of—I jumped in to change the
subject.

"I didn't know that you had to replace all your old clothes."

To my relief, Geeta turned to address me.

"Yeah, everything. I'll give them to my cousins or the servants. You
see why I have so much shopping to do—it all has to go."

"Who pays for all of it?"

"My father, of course. He's been saving since I was born, Miranda.
He transferred the money into my account as soon as he got back from
Bangalore."

The mention of money set Mrs. Curves straight. Reminded of the
dollar value of collecting on Geeta's wedding wardrobe, she was happy
to abandon her moral qualms about a cross-cultural love match.

"Let's start with the intimates!" she said.

Geeta turned to the task at hand.

"Okay. I should mention that my fiancé has told me about his preferences. He says nothing in silk or red. He doesn't like such styles. He mostly prefers black lace."

I must have looked as shocked as Mrs. Curves did. Although Geeta talked to Ramesh every night, I hadn't considered that their conversations might ever drift into the realm of sex.

"He told you that?" I said.

Geeta nodded with forced nonchalance and wandered away, toward another rack of underclothes. Mrs. Curves's eyebrows were up in the air again. For a woman who spent her days hawking racy underwear, she had a flawless expression of moral superiority.

"*Hoo hoo,*" she said to Geeta's retreating back. "Boys these days— they are having all kinds of experiences before the wedding. I suggest you buy some adventurous numbers!"

One morning, I found Usha and Azmat, Leslie's two employees, in intense discussion on the gym mats. It was raining hard outside, so there were no customers in the Fitness Circle. They were conserving electricity by sitting in the light of only one fluorescent bulb; even the radio was off. As I came down the stairs, shaking off my umbrella, Usha leaped up to turn on more lights. Her guilty expression made me curious; surely something was going on.

"What have you ladies been talking about?"

"Oh, nothing, *deedee,*" said Usha, avoiding my eye.

But Azmat nudged her: "Usha-*deedee* was just explaining sex to me." They dissolved into cackles as she said the English word.

I sat down. After much embarrassed laughter, Usha capitulated.

"I was telling Azmat that I didn't know about it either until my wedding night. I mean, I knew something was going to happen, and I knew it was called 'sex,' but I didn't know how it worked. When my husband came near me, I backed away."

"You mean that no one told you about it? Not even at school?"

The ladies laughed at my naïveté.

"School! That's the last place you'd learn about such things, *deedee*."

Azmat said that when she first got her period, she'd assumed she was dying. Her sister found her hunched over the toilet, afraid to move.

"Later, my mother told me that this always happens when girls get older, and that I should use a rag in my underwear. She didn't exactly explain it, though. She never told me that a girl's period is related to sex."

"I didn't know I would get my period before it happened, either," Usha added. "When it happened, I fainted from all the blood." She paused. "It's not good that things are this way in India. I don't want my daughter to be as ignorant as I was."

Even after years with the gym ladies, Leslie was regularly startled by how little they knew about their bodies. In an effort to remedy the situation, she'd bought a subscription for the gym to a wholesome Hindi magazine called *Grihshobha*. It is essentially a low-budget version of *Woman's Day* with more moralizing articles about good hygiene and safe sex.

All the gym ladies had read the articles about birth control, Usha said.

"It's the thing every married woman worries about. We used to be too shy to talk about it, but once someone brought it up to Leslie, we started asking questions. All of us have the same problem: We don't have enough money for more than two or three children."

"It's not popular to have lots of children these days," Azmat piped up. She didn't like to be excluded from a gym conversation, even if the topic, such as this one, was not relevant to her life. Usha, on the other hand, had given it a lot of thought. Although she had never visited a ladies' doctor, she was proud to tell me that she'd discussed birth control with her husband. She had a well-thought-out take on the importance of birth control these days—it was because things were different in the globalizing India, she said.

"Our parents had lots of kids, but things have changed. Now we want to send our children to school and give them a good life."

Azmat was about to speak, but stopped herself and looked to Usha for permission, who nodded somewhat reluctantly. "Usha-*deedee* told me that her husband agreed to use condoms, just like *Grihshobha* says husbands should!" said Azmat.

Usha had long been the envy of the group for her husband. He had a well-paying job in a clothing shop, he rarely complained about Usha taking a job "outside," and one year he'd even shown up at the gym with flowers on her birthday, a gesture that sang of Bollywood romance. After that, whenever he came up in conversation, the Fitness Circle ladies would describe Usha's husband with the English words "very-very nice."

The news that he didn't mind wearing condoms had inspired some cattiness among the ladies, though. It was easier for Usha's husband to do so because he was a Hindu, some said, but it wasn't acceptable for Islamic men. Azmat said the discussion about the legality of Muslims using birth control tended to be heated. One of the ladies had insisted that Islam forbids couples to "stop a baby from happening"; another suggested that this rule had been loosened by Islamic leaders due to the rising cost of living in India. They turned to Leslie, but she was at a loss. She suggested they consult a religious elder, but it was hard to imagine the ladies working up the nerve to ask an imam for sex advice.

Geeta and I made our way to the closest Barista. She stuffed the shopping bags under the table so that no one could see the Curves logo and sank into her seat, looking exhausted and small. When the server came around, she ordered a brownie, saying she needed to boost her energy.

"*Ay baba.* This is just the beginning! I think I'm going to have to quit my job soon." When I smiled, she added, "I'm serious, Miranda. You don't think I can get all this shopping done on the weekends, do you?"

To me, it seemed Indian brides had it pretty easy. They aren't responsible for dealing with their own wedding arrangements; their families take care of everything from the caterers to the honeymoon arrangements. But they have different pressures. Geeta's mother had insisted that she move back to Patiala three months before the wedding, when she would leave her family to join another, and, of course, she was responsible for coming up with a new wardrobe, which I was learning was no small task.

Geeta's shopping challenge was made more complicated by her

fiancé's expectation that she look the part of an Americanized bride. As Geeta liked to remind me, Ramesh would be happiest if she dressed in jeans every day. The irony that her husband-to-be, a love-cum-arranged match, was more liberal than her conservative and controlling college boyfriend, a pure love match, helped Geeta convince herself that she was making the right decision in marrying him. Yet it didn't make it easier to decide how to dress in her new life.

Whatever Ramesh said, Geeta knew that a jeans-clad daughter-in-law was unlikely to be acceptable to his conservative South Indian family. New brides are always expected to dress decorously. Ramesh had acknowledged that his mother and aunts dressed in formal South Indian saris and gold jewelry every day. In Geeta's family, her mother and aunties wore *salwar kameez,* more casual garments that allowed for greater mobility than saris. And they clearly spent less time on prayer and cooking than the women in the Murthy family: Many of them held jobs as nurses or teachers, while none of Ramesh's relatives had ever worked outside the home. Geeta would need suitcases' worth of tidy matching outfits and wifely saris to fit in.

It would be a shift, because Geeta was proud of her identity as a professional woman. She was only mildly ambitious: She'd worked for the same company for eight years in Delhi and hadn't considered moving to a bigger firm because she didn't want a taxing work schedule. What Geeta loved about her working life wasn't so much the work itself as much as the lifestyle: wearing stylish suits and driving herself to work in the mornings. Blasting Red FM on the stereo and honking her horn at bad drivers on the Delhi roads were a part of it, and so was the occasional night out with girls from the office.

Because she'd always associated working with singledom, I doubt Geeta considered staying in Delhi after she got married. Both she and Ramesh seemed to take it for granted that they'd move in with his family in Bangalore. I'd assumed that she would find another job after marriage, though. Ramesh was probably as close to Shah Rukh Khan's character in *DDLJ* as a thirty-something girl could hope to get, and he'd said he liked modern, professional girls. But Geeta had no plans to look for a job in Bangalore. It turned out that while she wanted a sensitive-minded NRI boy, she was also looking forward to an easy, family-oriented postnuptial lifestyle.

"I'm going to have plenty to keep me busy after marriage," she said to explain her decision to me. "I'll have to focus on adjusting to Ramesh's family. Just think—I've only once visited Bangalore. I don't know anything about life there. I'm going to have to learn to speak Kannada. And even if Ramesh says he wants me to hold on to some of my Punjabi traditions, I'm sure his family will want me to do things their way."

Hearing Geeta get specific about her new life made me realize how very different it would be after she married. It was hard to imagine making so many sacrifices for a relationship. My mother forfeited a graduate school scholarship and an art history career to be with my father, and left her family in England to marry my dad. She'd always told me not to compromise my own life too much. I'd grown up believing I'd regret it if I altered my life goals for a man.

I'd also convinced myself that choosing between a relationship and a career was an outdated baby-boomer quandary. In New York, few of my girlfriends would have considered changing their careers—let alone abandoning them—for the sake of a relationship. It might have something to do with the kind of people who move to New York, but there had also been a profound generational shift. Most of my friends believed, as I did, that the gains of seventies-era feminism should have protected us from this conflict.

It wasn't that simple, of course. Although my sense of myself was rooted in my independence and my journalism career, I didn't want my life to be restricted to that realm. Deep down, I worried that I'd lost my one and only shot at coupledom by choosing the Super Reporter Girl life over Benjamin. I couldn't voice the thought to anyone, though—it seemed too awful to say.

Luckily for her, Geeta didn't share this aspect of my identity crisis. She didn't seem to find it discordant to plan to be a professional woman while single and a housewife once married, and part of me envied her that. I'll never forget something that a film critic in Mumbai once told me during an interview about Bollywood heroines. Although

actresses are now able to portray modern girls, she said, such characters tend to be split between their pre- and posthusband selves.

"Women in movies seem to forget that they have professions once
they fall in love," she said. "A girl gets engaged, and she's suddenly
singing songs and shopping. After marriage, the center of her existence becomes the man and his family. That ideal is very Indian."

She could have been referring to Geeta's life. Maybe Geeta had
based her identity on what she saw in the movies, or maybe Bollywood
has so deeply penetrated Indian culture that it has redefined social
stereotypes. Either way, it seemed that Bollywood had indeed prepared
her to be a perfect Indian bride.

Geeta's single decade had been a terrible strain on her relationship
with her mother. It wasn't for weeks after Nitin returned from Bangalore that he could convince his wife that a South Indian boy was better
than no boy at all for their daughter. Eventually, Pooja called Geeta. She
didn't mention the match; she just told her daughter she'd paid a visit
to the safe deposit box at the bank that morning to look at the family
wedding jewels.

"There is so much gold waiting for you, *betee*. I can't wait to see you
dressed like a proper Indian bride."

A few weeks later, Pooja made her first of many trips to Delhi to
begin the hunt for the *lehnga choli* in the city's upscale wedding boutiques. Geeta said it was strange to relax into spending time with her
after years of being on guard against scathing remarks. Her mother was
startlingly even-keeled, and after a couple days together, Geeta felt
comfortable enough to confide her apprehension about fitting in with
Ramesh's family. Her mother let pass the opportunity to make a snide
comment about how Geeta had chosen to marry a stranger.

"It is never easy to join a new family, *betee*," she said instead. "Even
if it is a well-aligned match, the girl has to change to fit in with her husband and new parents. It was hard for me, too."

It hadn't occurred to Geeta that her mother might have had trouble
getting used to her father's family. Of course, it wasn't the kind of thing

a mother would confide. But now Pooja seemed to feel an urge to link herself to her daughter's experience and prepare her for married life.

"I came from the same community as your father, but I still had to figure out how much sugar he liked in his *chai,* and whether to chop one or two onions for the korma. My mother-in-law was very particular, and it is the girl's duty to learn these details. If you don't, the family may feel they made a bad choice. Then anything could happen."

When Geeta told me about this foreboding conversation, I couldn't help but think of a scene from *DDLJ.* The heroine, Simran, is sitting with her mother at an open bedroom window, through which we can see the Punjabi mustard fields and the sun setting behind. Simran has confessed that she is in love with Raj, the Westernized Indian in a motorcycle jacket. Her mother has a stark message to deliver.

"I, your mother, come to take you from your own happiness."

She is weeping as she tells Simran that she has to forget about Raj and marry the man her family has chosen for her.

"You know, my father used to say there's no difference between man and woman," she continues. "When I grew up, I realized what a lie that is. At every step, as sister, daughter, mother, I went on sacrificing my own happiness. When you were born, I made a promise never to let that happen. . . . But I was wrong, Simran. I had forgotten that a woman doesn't have the right to make promises. She is born to be sacrificed for men."

Geeta stirred the ice in her drink with her straw. Something was bothering her, though we'd been sitting in the Barista for almost an hour before she'd tell me what it was. Eventually she cleared her throat. A few nights ago, she said, Ramesh had whispered into the phone that he wanted to talk about something intimate: her past. The words had sent a familiar chill down her spine. Until then, Ramesh had insisted that a girl's "innocence" didn't matter to him; when they'd first met, he'd told Geeta that he thought it seemed "backwards" to make virginity into such an important attribute in a marriageable girl. Now, though, he just had to know. He promised it wouldn't have any impact on the wedding, but Geeta, horrified at the prospect of having to tell him about Mohan, allowed her silence to eat up the conversation.

In a bid to make her more comfortable, Ramesh offered to tell her about his own relationship history. Geeta remained frozen, even after he informed her that he'd had an Indian-American girlfriend in New Jersey. The admission was rare—boys are rarely quizzed about their pasts during arranged marriage meetings—and none of Geeta's friends had ever asked a boy about prior girlfriends. Still, his candor didn't set her at ease, and hearing her cry down the phone made him more nervous than he needed to be. Eventually, Geeta whimpered out the story of Mohan. Although she quickly told him they'd never been "involved," Ramesh was not satisfied.

"He asked me for all kinds of details—did we kiss and all other questions. He really wanted to go into it. I said, 'I am a very honest person, and I'm not going to lie, the way some girls would.' So I told him that, yes, we kissed."

In spite of all my Indian training, my eyes widened at how much fear she felt about revealing a smooch with an ex-boyfriend. My reaction, predictably, made her defensive.

"These things are serious in India, Miranda. I thought he might call off the marriage."

I apologized and wiped the surprise off my face. Geeta wound her plastic straw into a tight whorl. After a while, she looked at me again.

"Miranda . . . do you think Ramesh has had . . . *experiences* in America?"

I wasn't sure what she meant, but the way she emphasized the word *experiences* made it sound vulgar. She lowered her voice.

"He's had a girlfriend . . . so what do you think he would expect on the wedding night? Will he want me to act experienced? Am I supposed to do some Mallika Sherawat moves?"

Geeta had a hint of a smile as she referred to the Bollywood starlet, but I still found it startling, the disparity between her urban, educated lifestyle and her complete illiteracy when it came to the realm of sex. Like most Indian mothers, Geeta's had carefully neglected to explain to her daughter how the body works or what to expect on her wedding night. The fragments that Ramesh had told her about his past—his American-born girlfriend, his lingerie preferences—only served to highlight her deficiencies in both instruction and experience.

I made an effort at a kind smile, but it probably came out looking more like a grimace. I'd enjoyed playing a teasing role as Geeta's sexual mentor and confidante, but now that she was on the verge of marriage, the stakes were much higher. My flippant comments over Old Monks that night in my apartment made me feel a little queasy. What had made me think that I could advise Geeta on an Indian wife's sexual duties? I remembered reading in some Indian women's magazine that if a girl was "too active" in bed, her husband might think she wasn't "innocent." For all I knew, Ramesh subscribed to some version of these pervasive ideas, in spite of his proudly touted Americanism. If I tried to predict his desires or expectations, I'd surely get it wrong.

Geeta had no idea what a bad sexual role model I was. She knew that Benjamin and I had shared a bed, and that, she'd decided, was acceptable only because I'd told her that we planned to get married one day. I still hadn't even admitted to her that we'd broken up, and I didn't want to imagine what she'd think of me if she knew about all my affairs. Recognizing the distance between my sexual morals and hers, I felt suddenly ashamed.

I couldn't tell her how to behave in bed, so I filled the space between us with optimistic platitudes. You'll figure it out, I told her. Sex will hurt the first time, but eventually it will feel good, so you should try to relax. I let most of her unasked questions drift, unanswered, back into the atmosphere. The silence we were left with, underneath the Bollywood pop pumping through the café, was pure and godly and Indian.

On her wedding night, Geeta would be almost as unsullied by the knowledge of sex as her mother and her grandmother had been. I thought of the scene that had played out for centuries in India: the groom peeling off the sequined *lehnga choli,* the bride lying still beneath him like a terrified bird. Now, though, after her groom finishes, the new Indian bride pulls on a lacy thong to cover herself. The bride who bleeds through her imported European underwear: that is today's perfect fantasy of the modern arranged marriage.

CHAPTER 14

The Bride Who Showed Her Teeth

"After marriage, the trouble starts," Radha intoned. She was mincing carrots on the counter with alarming speed.

In the seven months since Pushpa's wedding, Radha's proud references to her daughter's husband, the mobile-in-charge, had disappeared. Taking its place were complaints about "*saas-bahu* tension," the Hinglish phrase used to describe problems between mothers-in-law and daughters-in-law. I'd become somewhat immune to Radha's *filminess*, but this was a phrase I'd heard again and again about new marriages in India.

The difficult in-law relationship is a global phenomenon, of course: It is rarely easy for a stranger to adopt an intimate role in any new family. The relationship is especially fraught in India, where wives almost always move in with their husband's family, creating more opportunities for miscommunication and disagreement. Urban middle-class couples do choose to live separately, but they remain a statistical fraction of the country's millions of families. Even if Geeta would have

liked to join their ranks rather than move in with Ramesh's conservative family, she wouldn't have said so out loud, not even to me.

Warnings about *saas-bahu* tension are everywhere, which made it
hard to believe that any Indian girl could look forward to married life.
The theme forms the entire plot of a top-rated prime-time Hindi soap
opera, the not-so-subtly-named *Because a Mother-in-Law was Once a
Daughter-in-Law* (its Hindi acronym, *KSBKBT,* proves that the Hindi
title is almost as long). The show churned out a new episode every
weekday for eight years; Radha and her daughters had watched almost
every one of them, through the sea of static on their thirdhand TV.
After Pushpa moved into her in-laws' home, though, Radha joked
darkly that her daughter no longer needed to watch *KSBKBT* because
she was living it. The show teaches its audience that new brides are responsible for the bulk of the housework in their in-laws' homes, and
indeed, Pushpa's *saas* had been looking forward to her son's marriage
for precisely this reason. A *bahu* would give her the first break from the
household chores since her own daughter had married and moved out.

Pushpa's *saas* was suspicious of the girl's aspirations to finish high
school, which seemed to her nothing more than an impudent attempt
to shirk her housewifely duties, and decided she needed to crack down
on her. She told Pushpa she could no longer indulge in weekly visits
back to her own family home. This made Radha grumble all the more—
"My daughter is only seventeen!"—but she'd surrendered control of
her when she'd married her off and had to be content with twice-
weekly calls from my landline.

Radha pushed open the door to my room after she finished mopping the floors.

"*Deedee?*"

I could tell what she wanted just from the servility in her voice. I
came out to the living room, and she fished around inside her *choli* for
the scrap of paper—well worn and slightly damp with sweat. It was always the same slip of paper. On it, Babloo had written Pushpa's home
number in his careful handwriting.

After I dialed, Radha took the receiver awkwardly, as though it were a living thing. When a busy signal sounded through the plastic ear-piece, she held it up to eye level and peered at it, as though the instru-ment itself might reveal why she couldn't hear her daughter's voice on the other end. I took it back and dialed again. This time, her face lit up and she pronounced gleefully: "It's ringing, *deedee!*"

When someone picked up, Radha composed herself. Speaking into the telephone was a serious endeavor and required a formal manner. The plastic receiver represented the power of the outside world, a world that her lack of education largely excluded her from. Even if Radha was doing nothing more than ordering milk from the local shop, doing so over the phone imbued the transaction with gravitas. Now Radha asked to speak with her daughter in a low and deferential voice, so I took it that Pushpa's *saas* had picked up. When her voice lifted above its respectful murmur, I could retreat, because Pushpa had come to the phone.

Afterward, Radha came into my office, squatted behind my chair, and waited for me to notice her. I was working with my headphones on, and she didn't announce her presence, so I have no idea how long she was there. This often happened, and I'd always get a start to turn around to find her crouched just inches from my chair.

"Sorry, *deedee,* I just wanted to tell you about my conversation with Pushpa."

There were reddish rings under her eyes that made me think she'd been crying. I didn't want to believe it—surely the restrained and hard-headed Radha would consider it undignified to squat behind me and weep—so I decided to pretend it wasn't so.

She didn't get up, though, and by squatting on her heels directly be-hind my chair, she'd blocked me in. I leaned back so I'd feel less claus-trophobic and waited for her to let out what she needed to say. Then her words gushed out.

"Pushpa's *saas* is very short-tempered, *deedee.* The boy is good, but I don't think the family is. That woman is always complaining, saying Pushpa didn't bring enough dowry. It's not fair! The family themselves asked for cash instead of electronics and furniture. I am going to be in debt for years, *deedee*, and still she is saying I didn't give enough. *Ay bhagwan.*"

Apparently, Pushpa's *saas* carped about the insufficient dowry when she was displeased with her for some other reason—when Pushpa had oversalted the curry, for instance—but couched inside the complaint about the wedding payment, Radha heard something much worse. She heard another mother accusing her daughter of being unable to meet the demands of wifehood. There was really no greater slight in Radha's world. Her children, better educated and worldlier than she, were her greatest source of satisfaction.

Radha also knew that she'd taught her daughter that her sole source of power as a new wife was the moral authority granted by good behavior. She'd warned Pushpa that the best way to win her husband's affections was by being amenable and obedient. Otherwise, he might team up with his mother against his bride, as they'd seen happen on so many episodes of *KSBKBT*. If a girl didn't meet her in-laws' expectations, Radha had told her, she could end up in the burn ward of a Delhi public hospital.

In the photos of Geeta's engagement ceremony, she is poised, unsmiling, on a cushion, her fiancé beside her. A high pile of saris, jewelry, and other gifts stands beside each of them, as though the shot would be used to determine which family had spent more money on the other. Showing me the pictures, Geeta made a point to emphasize that the groom's family is not obliged to bestow wedding gifts on the bride.

"Everyone tells me that I'm lucky to have found this boy. Most brides get nothing from their in-laws—nothing but grief."

Geeta felt lucky in general these days. Since she'd quit her job, she'd been in a blissful prewedding blur. Even Nanima, who was brokenhearted that she was losing her, couldn't begrudge Geeta's happiness. Geeta's skin glowed from good sleep and regular pampering sessions at Madame X. Whenever I saw her, she was either chattering away on her sturdy, made-for-India Nokia about wedding plans, or impatiently waiting for her phone to finish recharging on the wall. Now that she'd dispensed with her job, she spent her days like a true Delhi lunching lady: visiting boutiques, giving away her clothes and furniture, and helping with the wedding invitations—thick envelopes stuffed with five different invite cards, each printed in red and gold on handmade paper.

She stopped by after the salon one day with an offer to share in her wedding joy: She wanted me to be the maid of honor at the wedding. Like other modernized Indian brides, Geeta wanted to adopt the Western concept, even though Hindu weddings include none of the rituals I associated with bridesmaids—no wedding shower, bachelorette party, or ceremonial walk down the aisle. I said yes without knowing what to expect, and soon learned that Geeta expected me to be her celebrity assistant, responsible for her outfits, makeup, and food. I was also to protect her from "negative experiences" during the wedding period and be at her side through as much as possible of her final months of singlehood.

She seemed to think it perfectly reasonable to ask me to come to Patiala a full three months before the wedding. I tried not to snort at the suggestion—my editors wouldn't grant me three months off for my own wedding—the most I could give her was two weeks. Geeta wrinkled her nose in disappointment. Her relatives would be arriving in Patiala weeks before the events began; no one loves to celebrate more than the Punjabis, Geeta reminded me, and there's no better excuse for a family reunion than a wedding, so she didn't understand my reluctance.

By my own standards, two weeks seemed a lot of time to dedicate to a friend's wedding, and Parvati agreed. She cackled that after being assistant to the bride, surrounded by Geeta's family in "Punjabi Wedding World," I'd probably be ready to flee India altogether.

"Sometimes you *feringhees* act as though India is a religion that you have to convert to," she said. "You don't have to prove yourself, you know; you could just go to the wedding for a few days."

Sometimes Parvati was too smart and blunt for my liking. She was right, of course; I did walk around India trying to demonstrate my open-mindedness, as though this would compensate for my great-aunt's four decades of missionary zeal and a century of British colonialism.

Parvati also pointed out a more practical problem: I did not have two weeks' worth of wedding wear in my wardrobe. I owned none of the mandatory silk saris or sequined *salwar kameez* outfits. Even once I borrowed elegant saris from Parvati and glitzy Punjabi outfits from Geeta, I still lacked jeweled heels and extravagant gold necklaces, and was sure to be the most underdressed person there.

Nothing matters more than the outward appearance of wealth at an Indian wedding. In Radha's community, the effect was achieved by soliciting cash from everyone in the neighborhood; in Geeta's community, the relatives showed up with unsolicited envelopes of rupees to slide into Nitin Shourie's palm. He'd pass the envelopes to his wife and fold his hands in gratitude.

He always accepted the offerings. Geeta's wedding was by far the biggest financial undertaking of his life. It didn't matter that his daughter was marrying a stranger; Nitin was determined to create the lavish Punjabi festival he'd envisioned for thirty-one years. There would be legions of uniformed boys doling out quivering curries from massive black urns; freshly baked naan straight out of the blazing tandoori oven; rich desserts that would be the talk of Patiala. Nitin wanted a troupe of Punjabi folk singers in multicolored turbans sitting cross-legged on the cool February grass, their love songs bringing tears to the eyes of the gold-bedecked relatives. When the aunties decreed that Geeta's was the best wedding in family history, Nitin imagined himself smiling humbly. He knew he couldn't possibly achieve all this on a retired bureaucrat's pension. He'd take whatever cash he could get.

Rajiv's jeans-clad leg was pulsing to the Bollywood beats of Red FM as I climbed in beside him on the passenger seat. He was one of Geeta's college friends, and she'd arranged for him to drive me on the five-hour trip north to Patiala.

"Are you ready for pure Punjabi wedding fun, Mirindaah? Are you ready for the times of your lives?!"

For a moment, I wished I'd taken the train.

Until he'd heard the news that Geeta had found a boy, Rajiv thought he'd already attended the last of his friends' weddings. Everyone else he knew had been arranged into matches several years ago; he and his friends had pretty much given up on Geeta. As pleased as Rajiv was about the unexpected opportunity for a reunion, though, he was perplexed by her choice of a match. He found it almost humorous that Geeta would wait this long and then marry a South Indian; surely she'd had plenty of time to find herself a Punjabi boy, and surely that was her preference. I wondered how much Rajiv knew about Mohan. They'd all been friends in college, so I assumed he'd heard about Geeta rejecting Mohan's marriage proposal. I decided that Mohan must not have tried to convince Rajiv that he and Geeta had been "involved," because that would have cleared up the mystery for him.

Rajiv dedicated much of the ride to pondering how the marriage would work—"They are eating such different foods, having such different customs!"—and, more immediately, to how the boy's family would accommodate themselves to a Punjabi wedding. As he put it, "Weddings in South India are pure *puja*. In Punjab, we do ten percent prayer and the rest, pure fun! The boy's family is sure to be having a shock."

I asked whether Geeta's family planned to include some South Indian rituals in the ceremony, and his answer sounded like a warning.

"She's going to have to do things their way for the rest of her life. This is her last chance to be fully Punjabi, and the one chance for the rest of us to show those Bangaloreans how a wedding is *really* done. I hope they're ready."

The irrigated agricultural plains of the Punjab are known as India's wheat belt. When the partition of India divided the state into two parts, Patiala filled with refugees from the Pakistani side. They were Hindu farmers and merchants accustomed to prospering, and as they reestablished their businesses on the Indian side of the border, Patiala began to thrive again. In spite of its relative wealth, though, it feels as depressing as most North Indian towns—dusty streets lined with open-air vegetable markets and the aluminum siding of storefronts.

Ramshackle *bustees* have metastasized across entire stretches of the town, encroaching on the territory of the grand palace of the Patiala monarchs, which once dominated the city. The slums are filled with migrant laborers from poorer parts of India; they cook over open fires and sleep under plastic tarps, just as did the refugees fleeing religious violence sixty years ago.

It was evening when we reached Patiala, and in the air I could feel the shiver of the Himalayan foothills. We passed a delivery boy on his bicycle, a wool scarf wrapped around his hair and looped under his chin like an antiquated head bandage; a Sikh policeman we saw had tied his scarf in the same way over the top of his turban. Geeta met us outside her parents' compound, wearing a heavy cardigan over her *salwar kameez*—another awkward Indian fashion solution for the short winters.

The Shouries' gray concrete apartment block was decorated with strands of white fairy lights and jasmine flowers to announce that there was a wedding in the family. Inside, aunties were flitting about refilling platters with silver-wrapped sweets. Some lanky teenage cousins were watching a cricket game on TV. We said our introductory *Namastes*, and Geeta took me to the room we'd be sharing for the next two weeks. I knew she wanted her bridal assistant close by, but when she pointed to her childhood bed and said the two of us would be sleeping in it with her college friend Anku, I was taken aback at *how* close our quarters were to be.

Geeta was an only child, but she'd rarely been alone growing up—there were always cousins and neighbors around. She'd never understood how I could rattle around in my huge Delhi apartment with only Priya and a couple of part-time maids for company. In spite of her middle-class upbringing, Geeta had the same attitude Radha did to my Nizamuddin palace: I could squeeze many more people into its rooms, and if I did, I would be happier, because I wouldn't ever have to eat alone. On the eve of bidding farewell to her youth, the last thing she wanted was to sleep in a bed by herself.

I tried to form a smile so Geeta wouldn't see my dismay. In my own childhood, I'd rarely shared a room, let alone a bed; like other firstborn brats, I'd fiercely protected my space from the intrusions of my pesky sisters. My parents had made it a priority to stretch my father's academic salary to cover the mortgage on a three-bedroom house. Because my sisters, identical twins several years younger than me, had a bond I couldn't share, I'd decided that if I chose to stick to myself, I'd feel less left out. I played tricks on them and recorded their girlie jabber into my tape player from the closet so I could giggle about it later. When I got older, I slammed my door shut and blasted my music.

Moving to India had only exaggerated this defiant independence. I'd managed to wall myself off in Delhi. In my determination to transform myself into Super Reporter Girl, I'd practically forgotten the pleasures of familiarity and relaxation. Few people other than Benjamin had entered my emotional space, and now he was gone. I was often lonely in India, if rarely alone. There was, of course, the constant background presence of maids, translators, and drivers. Priya was always around—she shared my apartment for a couple of years—and Geeta stopped by several times a week, for meals or just to hang out. My Delhi life also included an oft-changing cast of expat friends: They held dinners and accompanied me to parties.

But none of those friendships—not even those with Geeta and Parvati—replicated the deep emotional bonds I'd had with friends in my twenties, when I'd been more open to the world. Living in Delhi, I'd somehow shut myself off to real intimacy without realizing I'd done so.

Visits with my family were a stark reminder of the effects of all this. In the last few years, I'd started to feel more separate from my parents and sisters than ever before—I hadn't lived in the same country as they in a decade, after all. I made sure to bring work back with me to my parents' house to shield myself from undiluted family time. My default position was to treat our visits as a competitive performance; to demonstrate how amazing my India adventure was, how well my career was going, how happy I was. It took me days to get over it and remember how to be myself and goof around with my sisters.

Geeta wasn't concerned about impressing her relatives, from what I could see. Their affection and ease with one another made me unexpectedly envious. In Nizamuddin, Geeta had learned to accommodate what she considered my American obsession with alone time; she didn't always call before stopping by, but she wasn't surprised or insulted if I told her I was working when she rang the bell. And yet, in spite of my crankiness, she'd brought me into the center of the most important event of her life. Seeing her among her family in Patiala made me realize how far I'd retreated. I took a deep breath and told myself that I should consider the next couple of weeks a much-needed lesson in intimacy.

Oblivious to the soul-searching she'd inspired, Geeta pulled me onto her bed and dumped out a dazzling pile of wedding finery— necklaces, bracelets, and earrings, all in a tangle of antique yellow gold. Geeta said every family she knew had a stash of heirlooms like this in a safe-deposit box somewhere. Indians have long been reluctant to expose their wealth to the state because of high inflation and income tax rates. Instead, they hide it from the tax man by buying wedding finery; an estimated 30 percent of India's economy is locked away in gold. It's a risk-free form of social security the whole family can enjoy.

Geeta experimented with her bridal look—an exotic hairline decoration called a *maang teeka* and a nose ring of heavily filigreed gold. She looked like a painting of a Rajput maharani from the era of real Indian princesses; she also looked uncomfortable.

"How much of this stuff are you supposed to wear?"

"As much as I can manage! This is my only chance to show off the family valuables. After my wedding, it will get locked away again until the next one."

In spite of her mother's strong opinion that she garb herself in the wedding gold, Geeta hadn't decided how much to wear. It had actually inspired another modern-versus-traditional identity crisis.

Ramesh had strong feelings about Geeta's bridal costume, as about many aspects of her appearance, and he'd made it clear that piling it on was not his preferred aesthetic. In the hope of inspiring her to adopt a more American look, he'd bought her a single-strand white gold necklace. Geeta pulled it out of a velvet-lined box on her dresser. It didn't look anything like Indian bridal wear—the design was too simple and it wasn't made of the typical yellow gold. I could tell Geeta was torn. She liked the idea of paring down the bridal look in theory, but she'd antic-ipated being adorned like a princess bride since she was a little girl. Her childhood fantasy didn't parse well with Ramesh, who liked to joke that families smothered their daughters in gold to make sure they couldn't lift their heads during the ceremony.

The marriage-age girl's manual decrees that Indian brides should not appear to enjoy themselves. Since virginal shyness and modesty are their most highly valued attributes, there is a long list of taboo ac-tivities, including smiling, dancing, and lifting their eyes to look at the groom. If this was changing, it was happening only very slowly. Ramesh, who was obsessed with making theirs a somewhat modern wedding, had been asking around for examples of weddings at which the bride had danced. He kept coming up empty-handed. He knew Geeta's par-ents were planning a conventional affair and that his own family would be scandalized by anything else, but he had his American college bud-dies in mind. He wasn't even sure any of them would come, but he couldn't stand to think of them traveling thousands of miles for an event that would cement their stereotypes about third-world people with backward practices such as arranged marriages.

Geeta found it exhausting to maneuver between Ramesh's forceful commitment to a globalized appearance and her parents' time-honored expectations. Just as with her love-versus-arranged marriage conun-drum, she couldn't decide what she wanted herself; and as she had with that decision, she eventually gave in to Ramesh's will. She sat down with her parents and explained that her NRI groom wanted his bride to smile and dance at the wedding, and asked their permission to invite the groom's family to the early wedding events, which are typi-cally restricted to the girl's side. The superstition that the couple isn't supposed to set eyes on each other in the days before the event—which is alive and well in the United States as well as India—has its origins in arranged marriage. It was considered safer for the groom to meet his bride for the first time after the deed was done, perhaps to prevent him from taking a look at her and bolting.

"You should have heard my mother, Miranda. It was so funny." Geeta mimicked Pooja's urgent, high-toned Hindi: "If the bride doesn't maintain her propriety, everyone will talk. They'll all say, 'That girl waited so long to be married, she can't stop grinning!' They'll call you the old bride who grinned and danced like a monkey at her wedding. Everyone knows it, *betee,* a bride should keep her teeth behind her lips."

Geeta was prone in a lounge chair. Her *salwar* legs were hiked up, exposing her bare calves and knees, so the henna artists could paint them with semipermanent tattoos. It was humiliating to lie this way in the vicinity of her father-in-law-to-be, but Geeta had reconciled herself to it. It was simply the price she had to pay to be a modern bride. Typically, the only guests at this public beautification ritual, the *mehndi* party, are women from the bride's family; that the guest list had been opened up to men from both families was Geeta's own doing. They were careful to keep their distance from the outstretched bride, though, instead forming a clot around the bar, jostling elbows as they ordered glasses of Royal Challenge.

Their wives formed an expectant throng around the bride, waiting for the henna artists to take a break from Geeta's skin and turn to painting designs on their fleshy palms. Punjabi women consider the *mehndi* party one of the best perks of attending a wedding; almost every Indian woman I know loves having her hands hennaed. To pass the time while they awaited their turn, the aunties lobbed advice at Geeta. The bride should get her husband's name written inside one of the henna designs, one suggested. It was an age-old strategy to break the ice in the bedroom, she said: Later, alone with her husband on her wedding night, she could titillate him by telling him to look for his name on her body.

Another auntie, another scrap of wisdom: Brides whose *mehndi* designs come out dark on their skin will love their husbands the most. Geeta, who thought she needed all the help she could get in that department, declared that she would leave the henna on her arms and legs overnight, rather than just for a few hours that evening. The dye would seep into her skin and become physical evidence that there was some love in her alliance. The aunties nodded approvingly at her dedication.

I was straining to understand the aunties' Punjabi-Hinglish mixture. My duty for the night was to serve the bride, ostensibly so that she wouldn't blur the wet henna designs by moving her limbs. The Punjabi princess was making the most of it: I scratched her arms and legs when she had an itch, fed her snacks with a plastic fork when she demanded food, and poured *lassi* into her mouth when she announced she was thirsty. Now, seeing her surrounded, I slipped off to find myself a drink. I'd noticed that none of the aunties held tumblers of whiskey, but I hoped that as a *feringhee,* I might be able to break the unspoken rule of Punjabi Hindu weddings—that the men get hammered while the ladies watch.

Maybe not. When a uniformed catering boy sailed past me, holding aloft a silver tray of glasses, he actually veered out of reach of my outstretched hand. Was the hotel staff under orders not to hand out booze to ladies? More likely, he was scared off by the white girl grasping at him, clearly desperate for a drink.

Geeta's prewedding parties have bled together in my memory. Dinner was rarely served before midnight. North Indians are known for late dining, which is only exaggerated at boozy parties and weddings. The men never drink with dinner, so the food's appearance at the buffet signals the end of the night—usually inspiring relief among the hungry aunties and groans among the uncles, reluctant to surrender their whiskey glasses. There were many long hours of mandatory mingling and dancing before dinner.

At one point, I stood watching the crowd and was joined by one of Geeta's female relatives, eager to practice her English.

"You are looking top class in this sari!"

Distracted by the enormous gold necklaces looped across her ample bosom, I was slow to respond.

"Oh, thank you. I borrowed it."

She turned me around to inspect me from behind.

"Best-quality sari. Even the foreign girls can look nice in a sari like this. You must have already done your marriage?"

I responded with a curt yes, hoping to discourage her. No luck.

"And where is the boy?"

I told her he didn't live in India now, and she shook her head: "All alone. You American girls are not like Indian peoples. We are feeling sad even if we eat breakfast alone. But I have cousin in U.S. who says you people are eating your dinner in front of TV!"

She wandered off, still shaking her head. I wasn't alone for long. A male relative of someone lurched unsteadily toward me: "I was seeing you up on the dance floor. You need to learn better the Bollywood moves. Then you will be looking better."

"You're right, Uncle, I certainly have some room for improvement."

"And what about the bush?"

"I'm sorry, Uncle?" I asked, not realizing he'd segued into a discussion of American politics.

"Your Am-*reek*-a president should help us with Pakistan problem. Many terrorists are there! Is the Bush the India friend?"

I backed away, saying I wanted to catch Geeta's debut on the dance floor. I could hear one of her favorite Bollywood numbers, "Bole Chudiya," starting up. I caught sight of her near the elevated platform. A brassy group of aunties was trying to force Ramesh onstage with her. If the bride was to dance at all, they declared, she would do so with her groom.

"I can't dance to this music. . . . I don't even know Bollywood," I heard Ramesh plead. He caught sight of me in the crowd and shouted frantically in my direction, "I'm used to dancing to American hip-hop!"

This only inspired further hilarity among the aunties.

"Hip-hop! Hip-hop! What is this?" they cried.

I certainly wasn't about to call any more attention to myself than I already had, and since none of Ramesh's American friends had come to the wedding, there was no one else to explain the concept. I imagined Ramesh was kind of glad none of his friends were there now, because the aunties seemed determined to humiliate him. As he shuffled stiffly back and forth to the song, his eyes darted through the crowd, on the lookout for the brashest auntie. Twice she dashed onto the dance floor and shoved the couple closer together, to the hoots of the others: "Go on and get close! Get some practice for later!"

You would have thought it was they, not their husbands, who'd been downing whiskey all night.

I was learning that inappropriate behavior becomes briefly acceptable at Punjabi weddings. The bride's female relatives are actually *expected* to flirt with the groom and taunt him about his sexual prowess. Such dramatics are not the norm at the pious South Indian weddings Ramesh and his relatives were accustomed to. I caught sight of Ramesh's older sister watching the spectacle, or *tamasha,* on the dance floor; she certainly wasn't dancing. Her face was a pale, expressionless circle amid the raucous crowd. She and her husband were teetotalers; there had been no drinking or dancing at their wedding, and I doubt she cracked a smile on her wedding day.

Boisterousness has limits at a Punjabi wedding, too. I could tell Geeta was trying not to laugh too much or too loud, her mother's invocation of a grinning monkey surely on her mind. The aunties may have earned the right to act ridiculous after decades of acting the part of well-mannered wives, but they knew where to draw the line. When the wedding photographer tried to take pictures of Geeta dancing, they shooed him away. During the official photo session, I heard them plead with her to stop smiling: "Please, *betee,* try to look like a bride. Look a little shy for the photographer!"

It was late when we got back that night, and it took us forever to untie one another's saris—their time intensiveness is one of the reasons saris are no longer popular as daily wear. Once we were finally ready for bed, though, Geeta still wouldn't let me and Anku go to sleep. She insisted that she had to spend the last night of her unmarried life going through her wedding wardrobe one final time—with us watching. She called her younger cousins in from the other room, and they flopped down on the bed beside us.

Geeta's bridal show had become a regular event during our Patiala evenings. She'd snap open her brand-new suitcases—she loved their satisfying *pop,* I could tell—and pull out a selection of honeymoon wear to model for us. She'd fret aloud about whether she'd made the right shopping decisions and what to wear with what; and then fold it all back into her matching luggage. I swear she took as much pleasure in repacking the clothes as she did in trying them on.

She held up a sundress: "Do you think it's too short?"

"Yes!" the cousins chimed on cue.

Geeta laughed knowingly, as if to say, "Someday, little ones, you too will be buying cute little numbers for your honeymoons."

"Will you be able to wear that in your new home?" asked Geeta's fifteen-year-old cousin Chandni.

"Hardly," scoffed Geeta. "This is just for the honeymoon. Once I get to Ramesh's house, I'll be dressing for his parents. . . . Hopefully they will be nice to me. New brides used to be treated like princesses, but now so many in-laws are making slaves out of their *bahus*. I don't know why it changed."

Chandni had apparently been educating herself about wedding rituals. She piped up about the *churas*—the thick, heavy bracelets that the uncle adorns the wrists of the Punjabi bride with before she is married.

"You better keep on your wedding bracelets after the wedding, Geeta-*deedee*," Chandni told her. "As long as you're wearing them, your in-laws aren't supposed to make you do any housework."

Geeta rewarded her cousin with a luminous bridal smile for her research.

"Believe me, I plan to wear them for as long as I can."

Pooja Shourie's face, taut with anxiety, was the sight that greeted me when I opened my eyes on Geeta's wedding day. I groaned, stiff from a bad night of sleep squeezed three deep on the bed. Geeta sat up beside me, and I could feel her body tensing with adrenaline. Her mother's hands were grasped around her daughter's morning mug of hot milk as she stood over the bed. She reminded her, yet again, that the bride is not supposed to leave the house before the hour of her wedding.

Geeta and her mother had been fighting about this for months. Pooja reminded her almost daily that in the old days, the bride was forbidden to leave the house unaccompanied at all during the entire engagement period. Geeta waved her mother off with an impatient hand; she was happy to embrace some aspects of tradition, but not if they interfered with her primping sessions, and obviously, the salon was essential today. She'd already scheduled two appointments between prayer ceremonies. Since the marriage rites weren't happening until three the following morning—the hour that the *pujari* had deemed astrologically auspicious for the union—she assured her mother there would be plenty of time for it all.

Geeta's mother turned to me and said, in quavering Hindi, "*Betee,* promise you will go with our Geeta. This day, above all days, you must not let the bride out of your sight."

I promised not to leave her alone, consoling myself with the thought that I'd be able to disappear into my book at the salon.

When we got back, Geeta's female relatives were already gathering for the *chura* ceremony. The aunties were a flock of pastel-colored *salwar kameez* outfits, cross-legged on the living room floor, singing a mournful Punjabi folk song. The family *pujari,* in a crisp white kurta, was setting up a shrine in the center of the room. He lit a small fire and laid out offerings of marigold flowers and coconut pieces. Geeta tugged her *dupatta* over her hair and joined the women around the fire.

Her uncle came forward and showed the priest the box of wedding bracelets, in the traditional magenta and white; they used to be made of ivory, but since it is now banned, these were bone. The priest chanted a prayer and purified them by dipping them into a bowl of buttermilk. Geeta's uncle slid them onto her wrists, twenty-one wide bands for each arm. By the time all forty-two *chura*s were on her arms, the women's song had risen to a keening.

"Our daughter is leaving us. She'll never come home again."

The thick coating of makeup on Geeta's face made my skin crawl. I was trying not to look at her. We'd spent at least four hours, maybe five, in the salon, getting our hair and faces done and dressing for the wedding ceremony. My head was pounding from the fluorescent lights, the chemical hair products, and the addling bleep of Geeta's cell phone. It didn't help that the hairdressers had styled my hair in an updo, pulling it so tight on my scalp that my eyes felt perpetually widened. Geeta asked whether she was wearing too much makeup, and I told her, again, that she looked like the perfect Indian bride, which was a tricky way of not answering the question. She knew what I meant, though.

After her first makeup session, she'd insisted they call the manager.

"My fiancé didn't want me to be a traditional bride. He doesn't like this kind of look!"

The manager pretended to be patient, but he basically told her that if she wasn't willing to don foundation, blush, and green eye shadow, she wasn't fit to be married. Even after half a dozen attempts to tone down her makeup, Geeta's face still glittered like a performer's. She'd lost the battle, and we were late for her wedding. The bride was not showing her teeth.

She rapped impatiently on the window of her father's car in the parking lot. Sanjay, the family chauffeur, was curled up in the driver's seat, steaming the windows up with his breath. He jolted awake, wiping the drool from his mouth as he fumbled to unlock the doors. He'd been waiting for hours while we beautified and rebeautified. I wondered whether he'd eaten. Sanjay was wearing one of his two polyester button-downs, the collar threadbare from hundreds of washes. His mother must wash them on alternate days, I thought. In the mornings, the scent of his inexpensive sandalwood soap infused the leather upholstery.

Sanjay had won the affection of Geeta's father because he was clean and respectful, but tonight he was not ingratiating himself with the bride. He kept stealing amazed glances in the rearview mirror at this shimmering incarnation of his employer's daughter. The attention only amplified her irritation. When we slowed to a crawl in traffic, Geeta pounded on the back of Sanjay's seat and hollered at him to find another route. The heavy bracelets clattered unmusically on her arms.

"*Deedee* madam," he protested feebly in self-taught English, "no other road is there. Several-several weddings happening. All guests are in jam."

It was true. The Patiala streets were clogged with wedding-goers. Hindu astrologers had deemed this fall and winter an auspicious time for marriage, prompting families to fast-track potential alliances. On one propitious winter night, the *Times of India* reported, close to ten thousand couples tied the knot in Delhi alone. Geeta sighed in Sanjay's direction and started working her cell phone. Eventually she got hold of Ramesh's cousin, who told her that the groom's party was nowhere close to the wedding venue, either.

Her fiancé was winding his way on foot, in a North Indian marriage procession called a *baraat*. Complete with fireworks, a drumming troupe, and a brass band, grooms' *baraat* processions routinely clog city streets during India's winter wedding season. Ramesh's guests were encircled by a protective constellation of lamp wallahs, a cluster of underfed boys carrying lamps attached to diesel generators that kept the lights and music of the procession going. At the tail end of the *baraat*, Ramesh sat astride a rented white mare, looking the picture of the heroic North Indian groom. In fact, he was miserable—deafened by the celebratory ruckus, his vision obscured by the elaborate headpiece and veil he'd agreed to wear in another concession to Punjabi wedding tradition. In the South, grooms rarely ride horses to their weddings, nor are they expected to don headgear.

The Murthys and their guests were familiar with these rituals only from Bollywood films, but they did their best to go along with them. They tried to dance in the Punjabi bhangra style, arms raised above their heads. The February cold dampened their enthusiasm, though. These were warm-weather Bangaloreans, unaccustomed to the midnight chill of the Punjabi plains.

In the car, Geeta fidgeted with the tassels on her *lehnga choli*. Like the American bride who spends months hunting for the perfect poufy white dress, Geeta and her mother had scoured boutiques in five cities before she'd found one she was satisfied with. The garment she'd settled on was brilliant pink, heavy with embroidery and sequin work; Geeta had joked that she'd lose weight just by wearing it. At this moment, though, she was devoid of a sense of humor.

"Pleeease hurry, Sanjay!" she urged, to no apparent end, since we were sitting in immobile traffic.

"Madams, what can be done?" His face in the rearview mirror was wretched. He would have picked her up and carried her if that hadn't meant abandoning her father's car on the street.

Geeta turned, disgusted, from Sanjay's reflection, and faced me directly for the first time during the ride. We were getting close now: The air was discordant with wedding brass bands, firecrackers, and honking horns. The festive sounds seemed to distress her further. In the half-light of the car, her face was an unreadable shimmer, and her voice was shaking.

"I guarantee everyone else here is a Punjabi marrying another Punjabi. Naturally—we are in the Punjab, and that's what people do. Only I had to be different. My mother always says that there's a reason the traditional arranged marriage worked for so many centuries: If you're going to be with someone for seven lifetimes, you better have a lot in common."

Geeta wasn't trying to be funny. She'd said before that she thought there was nothing more beautiful than the idea of an alliance so perfect that you would be reincarnated together. Now that she was on the brink of formalizing her own marriage, though, she seemed to be considering the seven lifetimes with trepidation, rather than with romanticized glee.

"Miranda, what if I am in love with my boss?"

I drew back in surprise.

"Who—Amit? The married guy?"

Geeta nodded sadly, as though acknowledging an irrefutable truth. I rolled my eyes. I didn't believe it for a minute. Why would she wait until her betrothal was only hours away to raise the possibility that she had feelings for a different man, someone she'd known for years? At the very most, Geeta's relationship with Amit amounted to a few eyelash flutters and flirty comments. She'd just scared herself into voicing the unthinkable, and to the extent that she'd transferred her worries onto Amit, it was probably because he was one of the few men she'd spent any time with at all. I tried to speak sternly.

"You thought he was cute, Geeta; that's not the same."

"No, but . . . it would have been so much easier, because Amit is Punjabi. Automatically we have so many things in common. With Ramesh, I'm going to have to work so hard to adjust. And already there is this imbalance, because he loves me, and I am not sure."

As much as I wanted to dismiss her claim and put an end to the conversation, part of me could sympathize. It was more than just a longing for familiarity and tradition in her marriage; there was something else at the root of Geeta's worries, and I thought I could understand it. I knew by now that she and I shared an overly romanticized view of love and marriage: Hence our mutual connection to Bollywood. She also suffered from the same "I don't care to belong to any club that will have me as a member" syndrome as I did. I'd spent more than a decade dismissing men genuinely equipped for a relationship, falling instead into doomed love affairs with emotional cripples, workaholics, and nomads; during the same decade, Geeta had found fault with pretty much every single one of her parents' Punjabi matches. It was easier for both of us to surrender to the movie version of romance and love than it was to the real thing.

There was no time to ruminate on it now, though—we were pulling into the parking lot, where Geeta's cousins waited in a bright, buzzing clutch. They knotted around the vehicle, and we could hear them shrieking even before they wrested open the car doors.

"Oh my God! We thought you would never get here!"

"Geeta, you look like a perfect doll!"

"Of course the makeup isn't too much, why would you think that?"

The wedding grounds stretched behind them, lit up like a football field on game night. The air was sharp with excitement and generator diesel fumes. Geeta's cousins hurried her toward a reception building, and I scurried along behind, trying not to trip on the folds of my sari. The girls deposited us in a bridal waiting room, with the instruction that Geeta was to stay put until the groom arrived at the gate. They dashed out again, leaving us in the small windowless chamber, whose walls were lined with mirrors. Geeta sat in front of one of them and appraised her bridal avatar.

"What if Amit showed up here and told me he loved me?"

I looked at her, surprised.

"Come on, Geeta, you're really being silly. This isn't Bollywood. You're not being married off against your will to some crooked character; you're marrying an awesome guy you've chosen yourself! It's just wedding-day jitters. Everyone says it happens."

Geeta was still staring at herself in the mirror, as though she couldn't believe what she saw.

"I really didn't want my makeup to be this heavy. I don't know what Ramesh is going to do when he sees me looking like this. He might not even recognize me. Oh my God, what if he doesn't recognize me!"

I snorted, hoping she was joking.

"Well, even if he doesn't, it will be pretty obvious who you are, considering you're the only woman here in bridal gear," I said.

Geeta shifted uncomfortably; if there had been a trace of humor behind her makeup mask, it was gone. I thought of the American friends who'd admitted to having second thoughts before their weddings. One acquaintance back in New York said she had sat shivering in the bathroom for an hour before her mother could convince her to put on her wedding dress; another told me he'd thrown up before entering the wedding hall. But before I could decide whether to repeat these stories to Geeta, the door flew open, and a crowd of plump and bejeweled aunties rushed at the bride. They pulled at her pink head scarf, going *hoo-hoo* to praise her doll-like image. Geeta, who usually loved nothing more than being fawned over, remained stony faced under her mask of makeup.

"Ah, the poor girl is nervous," the aunties told one another.

Some cousins tumbled in, breathless with the news that the groom's *baraat* was arriving. All the ladies were to go off and greet them at the gate. Chandni grabbed my hand.

"This is our most important duty of the evening. It's the ladies' job to get as much money as possible out of the groom before we let them in—it's a time-honored Punjabi custom."

It didn't sound like a very pleasant tradition. I protested that I'd promised the bride's mother that I would stay by her side until she

climbed onto the wedding podium, but they insisted that this trumped
my other duties and dragged me off. When I looked back, Geeta was
still staring at her pink reflection.

Chandni and I joined the other women under a long bamboo trellis.
A red carpet, scattered with rose petals to welcome the groom, led
from the gate to the wedding grounds. The gathered women, however,
were anything but welcoming. They were in a huddle, strategizing how
to best weasel cash out of him. At Punjabi weddings, extortion is the
bride's right. Wedding guests are expected to demand cash from the
groom at several points during the night, starting with his arrival. During the wedding *puja,* the bridal party steals the groom's shoes and
forces his groomsmen to pay up to get them back. Sometimes they even
block the entrance to the honeymoon suite and make the poor man
shell out again before he can lead his prize inside. It's all supposed to
be in good fun, but I found myself worrying about Ramesh, already in-
secure about fitting in to Punjabi Wedding World.

I wormed my way to the front of the crowd at the gate. Ramesh, in
silly headgear and veil, waited on the mare. The two fathers, both in
pink turbans, were holding a formal greeting ceremony. They garlanded each other, embraced, and shook hands, pausing midshake to
pose like politicians for the photographer. The women were deep in
negotiation with Ramesh's brother-in-law, Satish. I heard him boast
in fluent Hindi that he'd learned how to bargain Punjabi style when he
was in college in the North.

"Well, you'll need all your skills to get past us!" shrieked Geeta's
friend Nimrat.

She was nineteen, already longing for a wedding of her own, and
one of several self-appointed protectors of Punjabi culture at Geeta's
ceremony. She swished her shiny hair across Satish's face as she
wheeled around to face the approving crowd of women, chanting, "If
you want in, you'll have to shell out! Otherwise, you can take the boy
back to Bangalore!"

Nimrat made her demand: two hundred thousand rupees, several
thousand dollars. Satish blanched. Although I later heard him bluster

that he had never considered handing over that much cash, he didn't get very far with bargaining down the ladies. I remembered Geeta's words the first day we met, at Ram's vegetable stall: "There is no one more formidable than an Indian woman at cutting a deal." The groom's party was starting to get antsy behind Satish, as the buzz from the whiskey wore off. They'd been there more than an hour. I heard grumbles that they should storm the gate. Eventually, one of Geeta's uncles strode up—an old man who commanded respect in the family. He wagged his finger at Nimrat.

"You should be ashamed! Don't you know that these people are not from our culture? They are our guests, let them in!"

He tugged open the gate, and Ramesh's guests began filing in— timidly at first, and then with more confidence. It took only a beat for the women on Geeta's side to transform themselves from hostile gate-keepers to courteous ushers, folding their hands into respectful *Namastes*. Nimrat couldn't bear it, though. When Satish entered, his arms above his head in a triumphant bhangra dance, she huffed: "These stuffy South Indians have no idea how to do a wedding. We'll get what we are owed."

I made a mental note to keep my distance from the shoe-stealing scene.

I kept picturing Geeta's panicked face and headed back toward the waiting room. I'd missed her, though: She was already up on the stage. My heart pounded. I knew I wouldn't see her again except from a distance. She'd leave in the morning for Bangalore.

The wedding lawn was a tightly packed sea of silk saris and kurtas, the guests lining up to congratulate the couple. I slid through the crowd to catch a glimpse, but there was nothing of Geeta that I could recognize up there. She looked like a pink and gold cardboard cutout, a child princess beside her prince on an oversize wedding throne.

In the early hours of the morning, when we were all cross-eyed with exhaustion, the *pujari* tied the end of Geeta's sari to Ramesh's kurta, and they walked around the sacred fire together seven times. Ramesh stroked a line of red *sindoor* into Geeta's hairline to symbolize that she was his wife. Just before sunrise, she climbed into a palanquin, a covered litter suspended on two poles that I recognized from old photographs of my great-aunt Edith in Kashmir.

Four men hefted the chair onto their shoulders like a coffin, to lead Geeta to the waiting car, and a tragic procession trailed behind. I'd been told many times during my stay in Patiala that it was a Punjabi ritual to make a *filmy* scene when a bride leaves, and indeed, almost everyone there was sobbing. In India, a wedding is considered an ending. In fact, in some parts, the groom's family gives the bride a new first as well as last name. Unlike some brides, Geeta would be able to go back to her natal home to visit—though not very often. From now on, she'd spend holidays with her husband's family.

When she stepped out to say goodbye, I saw that Geeta was crying, too, in great, dramatic heaves. She gripped on to her father. When her groom tried to pry her out of her father's arms, I had to turn my head away, like my mother does during the saddest parts of movies. Eventually, Ramesh shepherded his bride into the car—an imported brand, white, decorated with red roses, and suddenly quite inappropriate for the joyless scene. Geeta was bent over in the seat. Ramesh gestured to the driver, and as they turned out of the parking lot, I caught a glimpse of the groom's face through the back window. His eyes were wide with worry, as though he'd just realized that the two of them were now completely alone.

CHAPTER 15

Any Issue?

The gynecologist's sari flirted open across her stomach, and her *choli* blouse was cut low across her chest. A good sign, I thought, as I sat down in Dr. Kapur's office. The exam table was immaculate and included a roll of table covers, which meant the paper was changed after each patient—a hygienic precaution I'd learned not to take for granted in Indian clinics. I felt a flash of hope that I'd finally found a modern-minded ladies' doctor.

No such luck.

"Are you married?" she asked.

I knew the question wasn't on the form. What Dr. Kapur wanted to know was whether I was sexually active and had multiple partners. In official India, marriage is shorthand for sex—even at the gynecologist's office, the one place that I'd have imagined the word would be acceptable outside the Fitness Circle. This was exactly why I'd been putting off my checkup: I didn't want to have to deal with a doctor nosing her way into the moral dimension of my sexual health.

I considered the question. Was I married? Well, it depended on whom you asked. My maids thought so, as did the gym ladies and the rest of Nizamuddin. Even though it annoyed me to have to lie about it, I'd continued to perpetuate the myth, because surely telling them that I was divorced would be worse than the original infraction I'd tried to cover up, that of having a boyfriend. Though I'd intended to tell Geeta that I wasn't going to marry Benjamin, it hadn't seemed right to confide in her about my breakup during her dizzy months of courtship and marriage. In Patiala, when she'd joked that I should be taking notes for my own wedding, I hadn't corrected her.

I suddenly felt cowardly about my timidity. There was no reason I should care if the gynecologist raised a disapproving eyebrow at my sex life. I was obviously neither a pious virgin nor a pure Indian wife, nor did I especially want to be either of those things. If I felt judged by her, I wasn't sure I could blame it all on India. It probably spoke more to the nagging worry that I was making selfish choices rather than investing in lasting relationships. The doctor might well have asked, "Why are you ashamed of the life you've chosen?" or "Which are you going to choose to be—an independent girl or a married lady?"

I gathered myself. I wanted to talk about birth control, so for the purposes of Dr. Kapur's questionnaire, I decided, I would be married. That wasn't sufficient, though. Her next question caught me off guard, as well.

"Any issue?"

I raised one eyebrow and asked, in a voice that I hoped was dripping with scorn, "What kind of issues are you referring to?"

The doctor looked up, surprised.

"I mean, have you borne any issue yet . . . any offspring?"

The phrase was just an antiquated Britishism and a natural followup to an assertion of marriage. Feeling a little silly, I told her that since my husband and I lived in different countries, we weren't ready to leap into child rearing just yet, and waited for her to move on. But Dr. Kapur drew herself up in her seat and eyed me suspiciously. I was starting to feel the way I imagine Geeta did during her arranged marriage date inquisition with Maneka.

"I see here that you are more than thirty years old—don't you want to have babies? Soon it will be too late."

I stumbled that I thought I still had plenty of time, but before I even got the words out, she jumped in with a monologue in favor of procreation.

"You know, dear, no woman is complete without babies. You'll learn. Look at me—I'm a modern working woman. My husband doesn't make me stay at home and cook all day. But I couldn't be happy without my children. Here, I'll show you their pictures. You'll see how adorable they are."

She pulled out her cell phone and started scrolling through pictures of her kids. I was now longing to get back to the new-patient form. Apparently, since I hadn't leaped to reassure Dr. Kapur that I did indeed want children, I needed to be converted to the cause. This took me by surprise: It hadn't occurred to me that someone might perceive me as a baby-hating crone. Sure, my Delhi friends joked that I was a crazy spinster obsessed with my alley cats, and I sometimes worried that I'd celebrate my fortieth birthday in the same way that I had my thirtieth— with a drunken rooftop party where a friend suggested we stumble back to a more private part of the roof deck to have pro forma sex—but growing up didn't rate top among my concerns.

It was the blessing and curse of being raised by independent intellectuals; I'd always believed I could make the future happen at my own pace. I had plenty of time to figure myself out, I thought, after I'd had my adventures. I assumed it was the same for my friends back in the States. Now, though, I found myself wondering whether I wasn't too far removed from the normal patterns of people's lives to understand my friends' updated plans and dreams. After all, my idea of a committed relationship was a nonmonogamous three-year saga: If my girlfriends were considering adult things such as babies and houses, they weren't likely to confide it to me.

In my fantasy version of this scene, I would have pleasantly asserted myself and informed Dr. Kapur that I was glad to see that she'd achieved perfect balance in her life, but babies weren't my current aim. I wish

I'd reminded her that I'd come to her office to discuss the pros and cons of the Pill and the IUD, and that her baby pictures served no purpose in such a conversation. Instead, I heard myself cooing over her children and thinking bitterly, "Have I proved my maternal instinct yet?" It was all I could do to get her to finish my exam.

I usually saved up stories such as this one to tell Parvati over whiskeys or at the dinner table on trips back to see my family. Anecdotes about crossed cultural wires traveled well, I found. They always got a laugh, and they had the added bonus of making me feel good about the person I'd become while living overseas. I could present my bumbles through India's social conservatism as evidence of the effort I was making to fit into a culture very different from my own. These stories served another purpose, too, of which I was only dimly aware: They helped me separate the person I wanted to be from the person I often found myself being in Delhi. I did my best to tread lightly in India and to be careful in my friendships, but in my stories, I was always a better version of myself. I was never my bitchy Delhi incarnation, Demanda.

Leaving the doctor's office, though, I decided that this one wouldn't make it into my repertoire. If I told Parvati, she'd just laugh at me for caring what some conservative *choot* thought. I didn't want to tell my mother, because she might agree with Dr. Kapur. In the wake of my breakup with Benjamin, I'd noticed that she'd started rather unsubtly reminding me that it *was* possible to keep your independence inside a relationship. My mother apparently didn't need to know Miserable Jen to worry that I'd turn into a lonely, hardened woman.

I had my own doubts too. But I ignored them. Still in Super Reporter Girl mode, I felt anything but prepared for a committed partnership these days. When my girlfriends asked how I was, I'd grin mischievously and say I'd been spending a lot of time in Kabul. Among my expat friends, that was shorthand for having romantic adventures with swashbucklers and wanderers—the only type to be found in Afghanistan. We used to say we loved going to Kabul for the parties, and we weren't joking.

In the years after the invasion, the country filled up with young adventurous internationals—security guys, journalists, and the UN types we cynically called "democracy junkies." They worked in high-security compounds under great strain, and they let loose like nowhere else in Asia. Although alcohol is illegal under the Afghan constitution, everyone ignored that regulation in the chaos of the early years of the war. With foreigners flocking into the country to fight and rebuild, Afghanistan was willing to overlook all kinds of infractions. For years, you could buy cans of Heineken from Kabul street vendors with long beards and Muslim prayer caps.

I was generally pretty cautious in Afghanistan; although I embedded with the military several times, I never followed them into combat. It isn't possible to avoid risk in Kabul, though, and one of the small dangers I was reluctant to eliminate from my life was spending evenings at L'Atmosphère. Owned by Frenchmen and notorious for its late-night boozy pool parties, the restaurant was a perfect target for insurgents. As I waited in the alley on the wrong side of L'Atmosphère's protective blast walls, I couldn't help but think that my headscarf wouldn't help me if the wrong person was to drive past. The sluggish armed guard at the compound entrance moved excrutiatingly slowly as he patted us down for weapons and checked our passports to make sure there were no Afghans among us—they weren't allowed inside places that served alcohol.

Inside was a magical green garden that seemed designed to make you forget the stress of a conflict zone. It was dotted with lounge chairs and hammocks, and there was soccer on the TV and European lounge music in the air. During the winter months, guests clustered around the fire pit with glasses of red wine, and on summer nights, there were couples flirting in the pool. The menu featured foie gras and fish with lobster sauce—items that had their provenance hundreds of miles from the Hindu Kush and required a remarkably complex supply chain to make it there. We had UN and NATO planes to thank for the Frenchmen's extensive wine list, which was better than anything I'd seen in restaurants in Delhi or Mumbai.

Because Afghans were not permitted to indulge in the pleasures of L'Atmosphère, most of them imagined it a den of iniquity; foreigners had already acquired a reputation for depravity among Afghans. My translator, Najib, whispered that his neighbor had seen white women sunbathing naked out in the open. He'd heard that Americans—in Afghanistan, all foreigners are called Americans—held regular sex orgies in their guesthouses. It was hard to know where wild imaginings left off and truth began, because in Kabul, there was something of the lawless liberality of the Roaring Twenties in interwar Europe.

The city was infamous for its "Chinese restaurants," in which food was not the item for sale; these brothels were regularly frequented, we heard, by American security contractors. I don't know if the rumors of orgies were true, but every foreigner in Kabul did seem to be sleeping with every other one; there were stories of unhinged parties, stormy affairs, broken marriages, and high-drama scenes at the airport.

After a couple of months of reporting from Kabul, I found myself even more susceptible to high-drama romances. Recently I'd been indulging in an affair that was all boil and no simmer, to adapt the Indian phrase to my circumstance. Jehan was an Indian-origin guy with a smart-alecky charm that made my knees buckle. When I met him, he'd been working on Afghan economic development projects in Kabul for a couple of years. He seemed sane and less intense than other men I met there, though I guess that was a fairly low standard.

We were both determined to believe that this was more than just another war-zone fling. After a few weeks together at his Kabul guesthouse, we were both telling our parents about each other. I loved the image of myself I saw reflected in his eyes. He thought my sardonic comments were hilarious and my ambitions profound; he described me as adorable and delicate and sweet—not adjectives I'd often had applied to me.

The stream of compliments didn't last. After I went back to Delhi, Jehan visited a couple of times; during each visit, he slipped a little farther off the pedestal. Everything I knew of him had been exaggerated into wonderment by the intense circumstances of our meeting. Now he seemed controlling and closed-minded, and I heard harshness in his voice when he spoke to me—or was I just creating faults where there were none because he was leaving?

Worse than realizing I might be wrong about him, though, was watching myself come crashing down in his estimation. At the end of his second visit, he said something sharp over dinner, and I could tell when he looked at me that his tenderness had drained away. It seemed terribly clear that we'd been fooling ourselves. To my amazement, I was suddenly crying, and we had to abandon our plates of pasta. I remember thinking that our waiter there had a much more sympathetic face than my boyfriend.

Climbing back into the car with K.K. after my appointment with Dr. Kapur, I slammed the door against my knee, giving myself a mighty bruise. K.K. glanced at me, alarmed by the violence in my voice as I let out an ugly Hindi curse. Sometimes when he looked at me in his rearview mirror, I felt as though he could see into my soul, straight down to the most despairing parts of me.

"Okay, Miss Mirindaah?"

I couldn't bring myself to turn up the ends of my mouth into a smile even for my beloved driver.

"No, K.K. Let's just go home."

Married life in India is not complete without the pressure to procreate. Pushpa's *saas* despaired that the girl had crossed the one-year marriage mark without conceiving. Even though her husband lived in another state eleven months of the year, even though she was only eighteen and had many fertile years ahead of her, Pushpa got no reprieve from the duty to quickly bear offspring.

At the Fitness Center, Usha told me that her own mother-in-law had begun dropping hints a mere three days after her wedding.

"At first, she'd just say things like 'I hope my grandson will have your fair coloring.' It sounded like a compliment, but it still made me worry." She laughed nervously, as she always did when she was saying something that could be interpreted as unkind. "That was nothing. When I still wasn't pregnant three months later, my *saas* started to get nasty. She'd moan to my husband, 'What terrible fate to marry you to a girl who refuses to bear me a grandson!' Of course I could hear her, and she knew it. We live in a tiny space."

It was not an accident that Usha's *saas* was specific about the gender of the grandchild she expected. In the words of the Bollywood film *Jodhaa Akbar,* "a marriage is complete only when there's an heir." Until recently, Indian law restricted women's ability to inherit property, and even now, families almost always pass it on to their sons. In a country where the vast majority of senior citizens will never receive a pension, sons represent social security, because it's considered their duty to care for their parents in old age. And, of course, families with sons receive instead of pay out dowry.

India's son preference is actually better described as a daughter dispreference. The latest Indian census data found only 927 girls for every thousand boys nationwide. India is in the center of an epidemic of female feticide, and, strangely, modern technology is to blame. When ultrasounds became available in the 1980s, "doctors" opened private clinics all over rural India that advertised sex-determination tests—a miracle solution to the perennial desire for sons. Low-income villagers were encouraged to take fate into their own hands and abort the fetus if it was female.

The UN says two thousand girls are aborted every day now in India. In some parts of the country, there's such a shortage of marriage-age girls that families are forced to share the same wife among several men or import brides from other states. I reported from one village in eastern India where every other household had a *paro,* or outside bride. Sex-selective abortion is now a crime in India. But although doctors can be imprisoned for revealing the gender of a fetus, they'll offer hints after an ultrasound instead. They will say, "Your child will be beautiful like Lakshmi," if it's a girl, or they'll make a *V* sign for victory if it's a boy.

Once Usha got pregnant, she again annoyed her *saas* by refusing to take a sex-determination test. She'd read enough articles in *Grihshobha* magazine to know that it wasn't practical to keep popping babies out in the hopes of having a boy, as her own mother had. But she said she couldn't have aborted a girl child. Luckily, her "very-very nice" husband agreed that they should keep the child no matter the gender. Usha admitted that she nevertheless felt a pang when the nurse told her she'd given birth to a girl—in spite of herself.

"Not because I think boys are better, *deedee*. I just knew my *saas* would give me more trouble. And it was true: Even before I left the hospital, she reminded me about my duty to bear her a grandson. 'How can I die in peace unless I know that my son has a son to take care of him in old age?' That's the kind of thing she says."

Usha tried to become immune to her *saas's* pleas. Still, when her second turned out to be a boy, she took an auto-rickshaw from the hospital straight to the temple to thank the gods. I was at the Fitness Circle the morning she called. The gym floor exploded with shrieks of excitement, drowning out Red FM. Even though the gym ladies would insist earnestly that the sexes were equal—they'd all seen the Indian government billboards to that effect—it seemed embedded in the culture to feel greater joy at the birth of a boy. For Azmat, the best part about the news was that Usha invited a few of us over for tea to celebrate. Since she spent her days cleaning the floors and waiting for her brother to find her a husband, any excuse to socialize outside of the Fitness Circle was a treat for Azmat.

"Usha hasn't ever been able to invite us over before, *deedee,* because her *saas* is bad natured," she informed me. "She doesn't want Usha to work outside the home, and she thinks we working ladies are a bad influence." Azmat chuckled at the ridiculousness of the notion. "Now her *saas* is handing sweets out to the whole neighborhood and inviting us to visit. She must be out of her head with happiness."

On the afternoon of our tea date, Azmat showed up in an elaborate *salwar kameez* outfit decorated with yellow sequins, which seemed a hot and uncomfortable choice for the cycle-rickshaw ride over to Usha's. Leslie and I were dressed up, too, though, as per Azmat's instructions. We'd brought a ceramic dish set and a chocolate layer cake for Usha's *saas.* Leslie rested the cake box on her knees. This Western extravagance thrilled Azmat: She kept pulling up the lid to marvel at the cake's glistening surface.

Usha met us in the lane outside the cement apartment block where she lived with her husband's extended family. A toothless old uncle was cross-legged in the shade on a charpoy. He eyed us suspiciously: two foreigners and a Muslim girl dressed to the nines. Usha didn't introduce us. She led us up a crooked set of stone stairs, smoothed by decades of wear into a treacherous surface. I felt my sandals slipping and clutched at the wall in the dim light. Others had done so, too: The green paint was smeary with the grease of many hands. Usha said the power had been out for several days. Still, the interior walls, painted pink and mustard yellow, seemed to glow with color. I could make out a portrait of the Dalit hero B. R. Ambedkar on one wall, garlanded with fresh marigolds. Almost every Dalit home in India boasts his image: round face, round glasses, and an inscrutable expression.

Usha's mother-in-law was in a corner on the floor upstairs, cooing at the newborn boy in her lap. In one fluid, wordless motion, she nodded a greeting, gestured for us to sit on the daybed, and ordered Usha to make *chai* at the two-burner stove in another corner of the room. A grudging look of pleasure flickered across her broad, ungenerous face as she received the chocolate cake. She held up the grandson to show him off. He was wrinkled, with sallow skin and eyes lined with kohl. When Usha's toddler daughter wandered over, a shy finger in her mouth, the old woman ordered her to hand out slightly sweet English-style tea biscuits to the guests.

After she'd made *chai,* Usha joined Leslie, Azmat, and me on the bed. She had to step around the plates of her teatime offerings, because the room was too crowded for either table or chairs. I asked where her husband was, and she said he'd started working on Saturdays since their son was born. Even if sons end up being a financial net gain in the long run, Usha explained that they require an early output of cash, in that everyone expects the new parents to share the joy around.

Usha lowered her voice, but her mother-in-law wasn't paying us any attention—she was still *goo-goo*ing into the newborn's face. Usha said that her *saas* had insisted they host a dozen celebratory tea parties like this one; an even greater expense was the upcoming Hindu baby-naming ceremony. Expectations were higher for such an event if it was for a boy. Usha's *saas* had informed her that the family was expected to hand out saris and gold rings to all the female relatives.

"We'll have to take out a loan. It's not that different from having to borrow money to get my daughter married when she grows up. It costs almost as much."

Usha must have been missing the gym-mat chats. Normally hesitant and self-effacing, she was now eager—impatient almost—to discuss her troubles. We shook our heads sympathetically, and Azmat murmured that she'd heard other parents make a similar complaint, but we were all taken aback by Usha's next admission.

"My husband recently suggested that I get the *operation*"—she used the English word—"because we can't afford to have another child."

Leslie spoke first.

"What operation? Do you mean getting your tubes tied?"

"I don't know exactly what it is, *deedee*. The thing that stops you from having babies. My husband says there's a wife version and a husband version. He doesn't want to have it."

India's population more than doubled in the first seventy years of the twentieth century, leading Western journalists and scientists to prophesy widespread famine. The government responded with coercive and forced sterilizations: In the 1970s, officials would round up men with three or more children and herd them off in police vans to "vasectomy camps." Between 1975 and 1976, the government conducted more than eight million sterilizations, more than anywhere else in the world at that time, which means there is still widespread unease about the procedure. A mandatory population control program like China's would never work in today's India; people would simply refuse to abide by it. As India's population swelled to the 1.2 billion of today, many state governments began offering compensation for voluntary sterilizations, though. One especially creative state government plan offers a gun license to men who get the snip.

The compensation from the Delhi state government wasn't quite that exciting. It was the equivalent of twenty dollars, half a month's earnings for Usha's husband. Still, he was "worried that he might not be able to do sex afterwards," Usha said. Azmat let out a bawdy cackle at the English word *sex*, but Usha pretended not to hear; her eyes were fixed on Leslie, the neighborhood health expert.

"My husband found out that ladies get higher compensation than

men for the operation. But will it hurt? Do you think I'll be sick afterward?"

We all turned to Leslie.

"I'm not sure about all the details, Usha, but I think if a woman gets
the operation, it's riskier. You have to go under general anesthesia—
you know, go unconscious. That's probably why the government pays
women a little more."

Usha bit her lip. She hadn't realized she would have to go unconscious, she said. Her husband had already made the appointment.

Geeta was allergic to South India. Six months after she'd moved into
her in-laws' house, she was bloated and spotted with pimples, and she'd
gained fifteen pounds. I hadn't seen her since the wedding. This was
her first trip back to Delhi, and she was staying with me and Priya in
the Nizamuddin apartment. After Geeta got married, Nanima had left
the neighborhood; one of her children had finally taken charge of her.

Geeta sat down on the sofa and looked around as though she'd been
gone for years.

"Wow. I've really been missing Delhi—everything about it. I
wouldn't have expected that! I'm especially homesick for North Indian
food—even Radha's Bihari food that I used to complain so much about—
even that is an improvement over South Indian food. Her chili and oil
is nothing like as bad as what Ramesh's family uses. South Indian food
is so spicy and fattening—I swear, my stomach is constantly upset."

Geeta blamed her ill health and weight gain entirely on the Murthy
family cooking, though after spending a little time with her, I thought
it was probably due to something more than that, since she also
seemed profoundly depressed.

One of my cats wandered in and stared at her. Geeta had never expressed much interest in the scrawny alley cats I'd made my pets—like
Radha, she didn't know why anyone would choose to keep dirty felines
inside the home, let alone shell out money for their food. But now she
held out her hand. The creature turned her back and strutted off, as

though to punish my friend for her history of Brahminical anticat sentiments. Geeta looked hurt.

I was struggling to adjust to the new Geeta, too: a puffy, mellower version of my punchy Punjabi friend, now dressed in a prim *salwar kameez* with her hair neatly pulled back. The miniskirts were obviously gone for good. I wondered whether she'd gotten any use out of her Curves attire, but I didn't dare ask. Her honeymoon was a touchy subject: Ramesh's father had asked them to cancel the trip to Thailand because Ramesh would have been away from the office for too long, so they'd traveled to the more predictable destination of Goa instead. After all her excitement, she'd had a quotidian domestic honeymoon.

Sitting down beside her on the sofa, I wondered whether we would have stayed good friends if we hadn't also been neighbors. Of course, Nizamuddin was the reason we met; and then for a while after that, we'd become so close that it had stopped mattering. Now that we were separated by geography and lifestyle, though, our personality differences seemed to outweigh our bond.

I noticed that Geeta's arms were still decorated to the elbows with wedding bracelets and tried to come up with an appropriate remark.

"You're still wearing your *chura*. I hope they've been treating you as a new bride should be treated!"

She looked back at me dully.

"Yeah, they won't let me do anything. I am like the princess of their household—totally pampered and silent and a stranger."

Being well cared for in her new home should have been the ultimate triumph, but Geeta offered none of the victorious dimpling that should have accompanied such an announcement.

"I have a bad feeling there. It's like they want to keep me an outsider in their household. Like they treat me well to keep me out or something. Bangalore *is* very different to what I know. I feel like a *feringhee* in my own country."

As I'd learned from *KSBKBT,* the TV show about *saas-bahu* tension, mothers-in-law can torture new brides in many ways, most of which, according to the show, involve the kitchen. New *bahus* are sometimes forced to slave away at housework—as in Pushpa's case—and sometimes they are locked out of the kitchen, and therefore the family. In Geeta's new world, it was the latter. Making food was an honor reserved for the better-established women of the Murthy household. Ramesh's mother, grandmother, and aunties competed for space in the kitchen, only occasionally granting his older brother's wife access though she'd been in the family for several years now. The women produced a rotating buffet of traditional fare, all of it rendered eye-wateringly hot with mustard seeds and green chilies. Even at breakfast, there was no reprieve: In Ramesh's house, the South Indian rice cakes called *idly* were served with a fiery morning stew.

A few months after she'd moved in, Geeta asked her mother-in-law for permission to make a Punjabi meal. It is a wife's greatest honor to serve her own food to her husband, she pleaded. It was hard for me to imagine Geeta begging to be allowed to cook, but domestic tasks had taken on a new profundity in her few months of marriage. When she told me that Ramesh's family had complimented her mild potato curry and roti, she looked exultantly proud of herself. Her *saas* had made it clear it wasn't going to be a regular thing, though.

"There was tension every time I went into that kitchen. Some kind of possessiveness, like I was infringing on their territory. I guess that's why they call it kitchen politics." She sighed. *"Ai-yore-ramachandra."*

I smiled to hear her using the elaborate South Indian exclamation.

"Did you pick that up in Bangalore?"

"Ramesh's family all use this expression—just like *'Ay baba'* in the North. See? I'm trying my best to adjust. I'm even using their silly phrases. If I'd heard myself a few years ago, my God, I would have laughed at myself."

Geeta wasn't finished telling me about the food wars, though. After Ramesh specifically asked his mother to make milder versions of the curries for her, the women briefly obliged, she said.

"That's all stopped now. I heard them grumbling about it in the kitchen, but I barely had time to feel guilty before my food tasted the same as theirs again. I know my mother-in-law thinks I'm just having new-wife growing pains, and I should just get used to what they eat."

Geeta tugged her *kameez* over her thighs. "Here's even more proof that I've tried to adapt—I'm looking like a fat housewife after only six months of marriage!"

Geeta had organized the trip up to Delhi specifically so she could see a gastroenterologist. A North Indian doctor was more likely to sympathize with her Bangalorean cuisine issues, she thought, and she'd planned it all out carefully, including the doctor's note she'd bring back.

"I'm hoping he'll give me a prescription for something. Then I can show my mother-in-law that their food isn't good for my system. I want those women to start taking me seriously."

She slouched into the sofa, a weary look on her face. Still perplexing, that Geeta. From the outside, she appeared to be living the Bollywood dream, with a husband who adored her and a family invested in her comfort and safety. I was sure she'd brag about it all when she went back to see her family in Patiala. Yet Geeta was obsessively fixated on her meals, which seemed a minor issue. She also hadn't uttered a word about her former boss—whom she'd panicked that she was in love with on her wedding night—or about her earlier fears about not loving Ramesh. Come to think of it, she'd barely mentioned her husband since she'd come in. I had a feeling she remained as conflicted about the reality of her arranged marriage as she'd been about it in theory.

As we talked over the course of the evening, I realized that the flip side of being pampered in her new home was being watched over and guarded like a fragile and expensive piece of china. Ramesh's father, Keshava, was at pains to defend his daughter-in-law from the dangers of the outside world. He didn't like Geeta to go out shopping on her own, saying that she could be eve-teased even if she was accompanied by a family driver.

"He knows that you lived in Delhi for eight years, right?" I asked.

"Of course. I am always telling him I took care of myself for all those years. But he says my safety is his responsibility now."

Geeta—a lifelong daddy's girl—was eager to represent her father-in-law's smothering as evidence of how much this new father figure adored her.

"It's nice in a lot of ways—I mean, I always know that someone else is taking care of things, so I can relax. We have a special relationship. He told me to call him Appa right away, the same thing his own children call him. When I begged him to let me come to Delhi, he eventually agreed to let me come here on my own, even though he couldn't spare Ramesh from the office. I can tell he trusts me more than my sisters-in-law."

Geeta spent all day every day with the Murthy women, but she didn't exactly paint a picture of female bonding. It was a household of bored women competing for the attention of the patriarch. In the morning, Ramesh, his brother, and his father would leave for the offices of Murthy Electronics Manufacturing, and the women would commence their daily ritual of cooking, cleaning, and praying until the men returned. Geeta, forbidden to do domestic work, was consigned to even fewer activities than the other women: sleeping, eating, and praying.

"Isn't that your dream life?" I grinned.

Geeta shook her head. She couldn't enjoy this life of enforced repose, surrounded as she was by semihostile women who spoke scarcely a word of her language. She said she'd been struggling to learn Kannada.

"Ramesh usually translates for me, but after he goes to work, it's like silence falls. I can't understand most of their comments and jokes. We do *puja* together—Ramesh's mother always says it doesn't matter what language you pray in. Sometimes I feel like shouting, 'You can be bored in any language, too!' I never prayed this much before. These women go straight into the *puja* room for three hours in the morning. They stop only to prepare the meals and go back to it again after they eat. It's as if this is their only entertainment, as if they don't have a TV, as if this is the old India."

A few months before, Geeta had told Ramesh she couldn't stand it anymore and begged him to let her start looking for a job. The decision about whether she could go back to work wasn't Ramesh's to make, though; it was his father's. Keshava's response was that he didn't understand why the girl would want to endure the discomforts of working outside the home if she didn't need to. Perhaps, he hinted, Geeta wasn't aware how humiliating it would be for a well-regarded business family to have the new *bahu* "take a job outside" the family.

"Naturally, people will think that we don't have the money to provide. If the girl wants something to do, I'll find something for her—inside."

A few days later, Keshava came to Geeta with an offer. She wouldn't have to venture out into Bangalore traffic and slog away at a nine-to-five job; she could stave off boredom right in his home office by helping him out with the accounts for Murthy Electronics Manufacturing.

By the time she told me about it, Geeta had resigned herself to the role—this was the best she was going to do.

"It isn't exactly what I'd imagined, but at least this way I can bond with Appa. The thing is—working with Appa isn't good for my relationship with the other women in the house. They're all jealous of me getting close to him. They should be! At least he understands me and knows that I want to do more with myself than just sit around praying all day."

It took us a long time to get out of the apartment. It was just like in the old days—me stomping my feet impatiently at the door while Geeta checked herself over again, to be sure her clothes weren't too tight. She'd settled on a fitted tunic over jeans: a modern look, but modest enough for a married girl out without her husband. Geeta liked to boast that Ramesh gave her a lot of leeway; not many husbands would allow their new bride to take off to another city alone.

By my standards, Ramesh seemed overbearing, though. When Geeta's cell phone rang, it was him again, for the third time in an hour. He kept remembering details to ask about—what she was wearing, how we were getting to the hotel. In fact, Ramesh had made our plans for the night. We were meeting one of his childhood friends, Jayant, so he could give Geeta something "very important" that he'd picked up on a business trip to New York. I was to escort her because it wasn't appropriate for her to be seen with a man she wasn't married to, even if he was her husband's best friend.

K.K. dropped us off at one of Delhi's gaudiest five-star hotels, the American-owned Le Méridien, a place that takes Indian opulence to a new level. Signs at the front desk advertise poolside aroma-oil massages, and the hallways lead to a high-end shopping arcade. I found myself remembering Geeta's coffee date at the Oberoi hotel a couple of years before and how intimidated she had been by the place. Now she strode into Le Méridien's plush upstairs bar looking perfectly at ease with the trappings of the Indian elite. Clearly, she'd become accustomed to a fancier lifestyle in Bangalore.

Jayant stood up to greet us.

"I was right, Geeta! I told Ramesh that if he was nice to his pretty bride, she would plump up like a good Punjabi housewife. I can see he's been nice to you."

I bristled on her behalf, but Geeta just laughed. Comments about weight are standard fare in a country where everything is everyone's business. In fact, Jayant was probably giving her a compliment, because gaining a few pounds is believed to be evidence of a happy marriage. It was a thread of conversation that Geeta wanted to pursue.

"I have become such a good Indian wife, Jayant. I haven't had even a sip of alcohol since I moved down to Bangalore. I pray all day long. I am all the time eating their food, trying to learn their crazy customs."

Jayant was from the North, so Geeta could say such things. He smiled and ordered drinks—beers for himself and me, a soda for Geeta—and when he sat down again made a drumroll on the table.

"Do you know what I have for you?"

"I have a feeling. . . . Did Ramesh make you shop for me in New York?"

"How did you guess."

He was being sardonic. Since Ramesh had exchanged his New Jersey life for what seemed to him an utterly average Indian existence—living at home with an Indian wife—"dressing American" had taken on a new urgency for him. He now refused to wear anything other than Tommy Hilfiger jeans; Geeta said he visited the Tommy outlet at a Bangalore mall every couple of weeks. Ramesh was not impressed with his wife's fashion sense, though. Although she'd worn miniskirts and jeans in Delhi, he thought she suffered from "the Punjabi clothing curse," meaning prioritizing flashiness, sequins, and bright colors in her Indian clothes of choice.

Ramesh had wasted many hours trying to explain the American concept of high-end but simple "lifestyle clothing" to his wife, and trying to impress on her that while ostentatious hotels were appropriate meeting spots, showy attire was not an appropriate fashion statement for the modern bride of an NRI boy. Geeta still didn't see the point in paying a premium for simply designed, high-quality clothes; when she'd bought "Westerns," they'd always been inexpensive, Indian-made knockoffs. But that wasn't going to stop her husband from buying his favorite brands of clothes for her.

Jayant passed a bunch of shopping bags across the table, stuffed with Abercrombie & Fitch T-shirts and Forever 21 dresses. They'd been purchased under precise instructions from Ramesh, after hours of scanning online catalogues.

"Oh my God, there's so much. How much did this all cost?"

Jayant said nothing.

"No, don't tell me. We better call Ramesh. He'll be dying to hear my reaction. He's going to love it—I'll look like I'm on *Friends* or something! How can I wear this stuff at my in-laws' house?"

Geeta had two requests before she left Delhi. She wanted Radha to make her some *khichdi,* Geeta's ultimate comfort food—a mild dish of rice and lentils that they never cooked in the Murthy household. And she wanted to take a walk in Lodhi Garden before dinner, for old time's sake. When we got there, after the late-afternoon monsoon downpour, the park was saturated with color. Geeta didn't seem invigorated by the luminescent green of the lawns the way I was, though. Her pace dragged, and I slowed my step to match hers. That night she was taking the train up to Patiala to see her family for the first time since her marriage. After a week, she had to return to her new life. She couldn't bring herself to say it, but I could tell she dreaded going back to Bangalore.

When Geeta had imagined her life after marriage, it had only been that everything would be easy. And that much was true: Certainly, she was no longer responsible for her own health or safety; her husband and father-in-law not only planned her travel but also bought her clothes. But marriage had brought other, unforeseen, difficulties. Playing the part of the cheery, dutiful *bahu* in her new household took constant effort; she despaired that she'd ever belong among them; and when she wasn't frustrated, she was bored. I can understand the temptation to idealize her life in Delhi, to remember it as a free and exciting time.

"Ramesh was always playing this game," Geeta said out of the blue. "Trying to kiss me on the cheek or grab my hand when no one was looking."

"That's cute!" I said.

"It's silly. He would do it in the car, or when we're at home watching TV, and I was always paranoid that the driver or his aunties would see. But he would say he can't stop himself. He's like that: always saying he loves me—even when I don't say it back—and telling people it's a love marriage."

Geeta looked at me. "One time his grandmother Ajji saw him kiss me. It was so embarrassing. I mean, it wasn't a Mallika Sherawat lip kiss or anything—but still."

An image of Geeta rose up in my mind: clad in the bright red miniskirt that marks Mallika as a loose woman, being caught French-kissing her husband in his conservative South Indian home. I tried to imagine an equivalent humiliation in my world: Perhaps being caught naked by my boyfriend's father or something.

"Ajji spends the whole day doing *puja*," she continued. "She is such a proper Brahmin lady. I thought I would die when she saw Ramesh kiss me. But you know what she said? 'Let him kiss you! How else are you going to bear us any issue?'"

The addition of the aggressively pro-baby grandmother in the scene made it even funnier—despite the fact that this was evidence that the family pressure to have children had now begun for Geeta. If this is a classic experience of newlyweds the world over, the social expectation to quickly create a family is especially extreme in India. I thought of my married friends back home, who said their parents crept around the topic, dropping hints about baby names and good school districts and the like. That seemed the height of subtlety compared to this. Geeta said that Ajji and the other women now brought up the subject all the time.

"Ajji tells me, 'All you have to do is make the babies, and we'll take care of everything after that.' I tell them that I know how it works—I grew up in a joint family, too, and my grandmother basically raised me. Ajji loves saying that I won't ever have to change a single diaper, because there's so many women in this house. It makes me think—if I did have a baby, would I even ever see it at all?"

"It sounds like they've got it all planned out."

"Yeah. I think they expected me to get pregnant immediately, because I'm older than most girls are when they marry. We've only been married six months—I still have my wedding *chura* on, for goodness sake! But these woman act as though it's been forever. And the thing is, I can't help but worry about it a little. I am going to be thirty-two, remember, and everyone knows it's harder for older girls."

It was the first time I'd heard Geeta express anything like regret about having married later than most Indians. When I thought about my experience with Dr. Kapur, though, it made sense. To Geeta, having children had never seemed a matter of choice; she'd always considered it a necessary aspect of womanhood. The thought that she might have actually cut the possibility of children out of her life by marrying late was heartbreaking.

"Perhaps I wasted too much time fussing about finding the right boy. You remember how freaked out I was that I would pick the wrong match."

"Well, it seems as though Ramesh was worth waiting for. Even if you do have problems with his family, it's worked out pretty well."

"True," she conceded. "In fact, even my mother recently said something like that. It was so cool. We were talking about my female cousins, and she said maybe they don't need to get married right after college—that it might not be so bad if they wait a little while and have a job first, like I did."

I grinned. "See, you're at the forefront of an Indian marriage revolution, Geeta. You're leading the charge into the globalized future!"

She gave me a bitter smile that looked as though it belonged more to Parvati than to her.

"Well, I doubt my mother will feel the same way if I don't have kids soon. I guarantee it will be the first thing she asks me about when I arrive in Patiala tonight. When she hears that I'm not pregnant yet, she'll probably panic and assume that it's because I'm too old. The idea that I haven't even started trying yet wouldn't make any sense to her, and I don't know how to explain it."

Geeta paused and then looked up at me with a grin. "She'll probably change her mind and call up my aunt, and tell her to get my cousins married off right away!"

Something about the vulnerability and sweetness in her face as she said that reminded me of how we'd comforted each other during our loneliest days, when we'd first met, years ago in Delhi. Evening was falling quickly now, purpling the bushes with a light that was almost too violent to be real. I smiled and murmured that I was sure she wouldn't have any problems whenever she decided she wanted to try to get pregnant.

"I hope you're right. Appa is always saying that family is everything in India. He says it all the time, and that's where the pressure comes in. Having children is the one thing every Indian is supposed to do well. This is the land of the exploding population, after all. It's like—if you don't have issue, who are you, anyway?"

Geeta picked up her pace. The parakeets were already announcing that evening had fallen, and she had a train to catch.

CHAPTER 16

A Game in Which My Name Was

The driver leaned on his horn, shattering the Sunday morning calm of the neighborhood. I groaned when I saw that Rangeet was behind the wheel of the taxi outside my apartment. K.K. had been on leave in his village for weeks now, so I was stuck with his replacement, whose pores leaked the potent, bitter fumes of cheap arrack at all hours of the day. He drove a white Ambassador, the vehicle that status-conscious K.K. had taught me to disdain. It rattled as though it had been made along with the first batch back in 1948.

As I pulled open the iron gate, I saw that Rangeet, who a moment before had seemed in a great rush to get me downstairs, was now paying obeisance at his tiny windshield shrine. I stood in the street, one hand on an impatiently cocked hip. I already felt silly for ordering a taxi to take me to Lodhi Garden so that I could go for a run there, but I'd found that if I didn't, I spent all my energy dodging beggars and cars just trying to get to the park so I could get my exercise in. Now, an added annoyance: waiting for Rangeet to finish his alcoholic morning invocation before we could make a move. My driver gestured for me to be patient and formed his features into a devout expression as he leaned inside the car, circling a stick of incense around the plastic Hindu gods glued to his dashboard. After a few minutes of chanting, he stubbed it out and stuck the stick back in his pocket.

I climbed in, where the smoke mingled nauseatingly with the booze seeping out of him. I should have just called for another taxi, but my standards for safe driving had fallen substantially in the years since my first night out with Parvati at the Press Club. As Rangeet weaved into the middle of the street, his eyes unfocused and glazed in the rearview mirror, I hoped that the gods had been listening during his moment of piety. At least, I told myself, there weren't many cars on the long stretch of Lodhi Road because it was early on a Sunday morning, but we still needed all the protection we could get.

When Rangeet sailed dreamily through a red light, I shouted in alarm. It was one thing to ignore traffic signals at night. But the day-time streets presented many more dangers. He gave me a rueful stare in the mirror, as though to chide me for shattering his reverent, boozy haze. Then I heard a painful crunch under the tires and a screech of brakes as my face slammed into the leather seat in front of me.

We both looked around, trying to figure out what we had hit. After a long moment, the sticklike body of a teenager unfolded itself from underneath the side of the car, dragging the crumpled ruins of a bicycle up with him. There was a lot of blood on him, and I couldn't tell where it was coming from. I allowed myself a second of relief that the boy could stand, though. I saw it flash across Rangeet's face, too, and transform into anger. He unrolled his window and hollered: "You *behen chode.* What idiot rides a bike like that? You should watch where you're going!"

In a perverted reversal of roles, the perpetrator had made himself into the aggrieved, and the victim of the accident looked desperate to flee the scene. The boy was tugging at the frame of his bike, trying to untangle it from the wheels of the Ambassador. His eyes briefly caught mine through the car window, and I saw that they were dilated black with fear. Something about the boyishness around his mouth reminded me of Babloo, Radha's son, and I felt sadness rise up in me.

This slum-dwelling boy with surely broken limbs and a now-ruined family bicycle was terrified of the man who had hit him, because, as a taxi driver, Rangeet was automatically of higher status than a boy on a bicycle could possibly be.

I heard a burst of shouting behind us and turned to see that several cars had come to a stop in the middle of the intersection. Their drivers were leaping out. For a moment, I thought that they were going to go after the bicyclist, too, but mob justice was on the right side of the law this time. They were coming for Rangeet—and also for me.

Rangeet was rolling up his window more quickly than I'd ever seen him move before, but not fast enough—one of the band of men jammed his fist in the window crack and held it open.

"He's just a boy—how dare you abuse him?" they hollered.

"You're the *behen chode*! You drove right through a red light, you shithead."

When I caught sight of a large Sikh with a baseball bat approaching the taxi, I made my decision before I even knew I had. I opened the car door, leaped out, and dashed down Lodhi Road in the direction of the park, praying that I wouldn't be followed by a stampede of enraged drivers. At least I was dressed for a run.

In India, I had recurrent nightmares about crowds. I've never been an especially paranoid person, but for some reason, I worried about improbable events in Delhi, even after the city became as familiar as anywhere else I'd ever lived. What freaked me out—much more than monkey attacks, market bombings, or insurgent attacks—was getting lost or smashed in a crowd. Throngs, even joyful ones, take on a fervent life of their own in South Asia. I tried not to read the gruesome details of tramplings and smotherings in the paper, but I often couldn't help myself, and then I'd inevitably imagine what it felt like to suffocate in a train car full of pilgrims or to be caught in a crazed swarm of men celebrating a political victory on the streets. That it was unlikely to happen didn't stop me from worrying about it.

Jogging back home along Lodhi Road after a couple of circuits of the park, I saw there was a stream of cars on the road and no sign of the accident. Later, I called the taxi stand, and K.K.'s brother told me that

Rangeet had been beaten up pretty badly. I apologized for having left
him alone to be pummeled by the crowd. What bothered me more was
that I'd never know what happened to the cyclist. Did the other drivers
protect him, did he get away, was he seriously injured? If he'd been
badly hurt, his odds weren't good, because a Delhi boy on a bicycle was
unlikely to be able to afford a hospital visit.

I wished I'd been brave enough to do what I imagined Parvati would
have done. I doubt that she would have called the police, because they
might well have sided with the more powerful and moneyed of the two;
those in positions of power tend to subscribe to the same social hierarchies that made Rangeet feel entitled to yell at the teenager. I could
imagine Parvati cussing Rangeet out and urging the crowd to pummel
him. Then I bet she would have hailed a rickshaw, taken the bicyclist to
a private hospital, and paid his fees.

I was too ashamed to tell Parvati about it until much later. To my relief, when I did, she reassured me that I'd probably done the only thing
I could.

"Who knows what would have happened when they saw that you're
a foreigner?" she said. "That could have made them angrier. They
might have gone after you before you could convince them you were on
their side."

I'll never know whether my presence—an obvious *feringhee* in the
back of the Ambassador—contributed to the drivers' fury after the accident. I didn't look back to see if any of them tried to follow me as I
sprinted down the street. Parvati's words made the possibility seem
more real, though. The incident made me second-guess my own engagement with India. For the first time, I began to seriously wonder
whether my whole enterprise here was flawed. If being a *feringhee* had
crippled me in a situation like this, when I should have been able to do
some good, then something was backward about my life. Surely you
don't belong in a place where the best response you can come up with
is to literally flee.

I'd wanted to connect with India, and largely, I'd done so; but on
days like this one, my involvement with the place felt superficial. My
friends had drawn me close into their lives and I believed I understood

something of India. Yet no matter how well I paid my servants or how many Hindu mythological tales I memorized or how many Indian boyfriends I had, I would always be an outsider. Exchanging niceties with Joginder and the rest of Nizamuddin could scarcely be considered a deep engagement with my community.

And while I'd become pretty desensitized to the misery on Delhi's streets, I couldn't rid myself of the desire to do something about it; hiring untouchables to clean my garbage and giving donations at Hell Corner simply didn't cut it. In fact, tossing rupee coins to the skateboard beggar made me feel like what my aunt Susie would call "Lady Muck," and I didn't exactly like the vision of myself as a do-gooder Victorian duchess handing out alms to the pitiable masses. Working in a soup kitchen back in the States might have given me a little of the same feeling, but at least it wouldn't have been compounded by the sensation that I was also a colonialist intruder. Nothing I did in India seemed honest or lasting.

One consequence of moving around a lot as a child was that I had developed high expectations for being able to fit in almost anywhere. If I made an effort with people, I believed, I should be able to establish bonds and feel comfortable wherever I ended up. Of course, multicultural Western cities are a very different matter, and it was naïve to think this would be true in India.

Delhi is undeniably marching toward globalization, but it shares little with London, New York, or even Beijing, and I doubt it ever will. Given its thousands of different languages and cultures, India has a startlingly strong, unified sense of itself. No matter how many call centers there are in Bangalore, Indian teenagers will continue to eat rice and roti after snacking at McDonald's. Whenever I got worked up about things such as the country's obsession with *Sex and the City*, Geeta would remind me, "India will always be India, Miranda. You don't need to worry about us."

The intrusions of the outside world have also not been uniformly well received in India. It wasn't so long ago that it was a socialist country in which signs of ostentatious wealth were unacceptable. Now, for every teenager glued to HBO shows, there are dozens more who have yet to benefit from the transforming economy. There is palpable rage simmering beneath the shiny surface, which seems especially notable in a place as fatalistic as India. Perhaps the unease about India's urban economic inequality explains some of the anger of the baseball-bat-wielding Sikh on Lodhi Road.

In the months after the taxi accident, the thought of my missionarying aunt's colonial legacy in India would rise up in my mind, the way bile rises in the throat. That morning, I'd acted like a memsahib, guided by my own fear. Edith would have always been treated with sycophancy, and would have always held herself apart in her determination not to be subsumed into the madding crowds of India.

More than sixty years after India's independence, my *gora* skin still inspired complex emotions. While it sometimes drew hostility, my pale complexion was mostly a source of great privilege. Hotel porters and restaurant waiters would straighten up respectfully when they saw me—even though I was usually dressed like a sloppy journalist—and give me the same obsequious treatment they gave to kurta-clad Indian politicians and Delhi ladies in gold-threaded silk saris. Even at the Fitness Circle, Usha would shoo the other ladies off my favorite treadmill when I arrived, no matter how many times I told her not to. Usha and I were friends, but India's underprivileged classes cannot consider a *feringhee* a true peer.

From what I can tell, my great-aunt Edith believed in her British superiority just as profoundly as her servants must have. During her nearly four decades in India, she clung to her Britishness, so determined not to "go native" that she avoided Indian curries and rice, instead teaching the missionary cooks to make shepherd's pie and steamed pudding. In the missionary hospital, Edith made it known that she liked dinner to be served with proper table settings, including starched white damask napkins.

To Edith, the world was starkly divided. There was Englishness, which was just and pleasant, and there was the rest of the world, rather dark and unhappy. There was Christianity, which represented good, and then there was everything else, in which there lurked great, unspecified danger. After Edith moved back to England, my aunt Susie remembers telling her that she'd started going to yoga classes in London. Edith exclaimed in horror, "But yoga is for pagans!"

For all the intensity of her personal belief, Edith and the other lady evangelists didn't have much success in spreading the Gospel in India. Converting to Christianity was rare and dangerous in India in those days, especially where Edith was based—close to Varanasi, one of Hinduism's holiest cities, on the Ganges. Hindu and Muslim villagers who abandoned their religion had to leave their families and move onto the missionary compound for protection.

For the most part, Edith satisfied herself with a quieter kind of evangelism. She worked in the hospital and taught girls to read; she helped finance the education and marriages of some of the children from the missionary orphanage. She hoped her work would speak for itself and translate into awe for Christianity. It only sometimes did. Still, I like to think that her work was appreciated for what it was. Today, many Indians will say that they respect the help that foreign missionaries gave to lepers and untouchables. In the pre-Gandhi era, such people were reviled by most of India.

I wonder how Indians responded to Edith. I know she considered some of the children from the missionary orphanage her godchildren and continued sending them money even after she went back to England. I always assumed that Edith loved India at least as much as I did, but it may not have been so. When I asked my uncle Stephen about Edith's feelings for India, his response surprised me; he probably knew her better than anyone else in the family.

"As far as Edith was concerned, there was no difference between India and Africa," he said. "She didn't care where she was—she wasn't serving India, she was serving her Lord."

Stephen wanted to disabuse me of the notion that Edith was some kind of social humanist heroine, and he was probably right that I had romanticized her to suit the narrative of my own life. But at the very least, her life had been a useful lesson for me in India. If I stuck around for decades, as Edith had, I might always linger on the edges of the place—either wistfully trying to belong, or, like her, rejecting the idea of belonging.

I could already feel myself bumping up against the limits of my friendships with Geeta and Parvati. Of course, all our friendships shift as we change and grow up, but cultural differences exaggerate it. If Parvati had to be an unabashed bitch to shield herself from the judgments of Delhi strangers, it also meant she was sometimes inaccessible to her friends. Her cackle had a harsh ring to it. I'd become less patient with trying to fit into Parvati's idea of the right way to act and be, and I found myself wanting to confide in her less.

After Geeta moved into her in-laws' house, she was scarcely available, either, and her life was changing so rapidly that it was hard for me to keep up. When we talked on the phone, it felt as though we were struggling to suspend our judgments about each other. I couldn't help but wonder about the sacrifices she was making for her marriage and whether we'd soon have nothing left in common. For her part, Geeta couldn't understand why I wouldn't just grow up, go home, and get married.

Breaking the news to Radha was the hardest thing about deciding to leave. I knew she'd see it as a betrayal, even if it had always been inevitable. With Radha, everything was personal; she didn't have space for any other imagining of the world. I'd wanted to find her a new job first before I told her she'd be out of one, but I hadn't had any luck. By the time I worked up my nerve to tell her I was moving back to America, I'd already started packing my things.

How to dispatch your discarded servants is a perennial expat conundrum. Ideally, they can be passed on to the next generation of *feringhee*s. One journalist I know paid his maid's salary out of his pocket for a couple of months after he left Delhi, until his replacement arrived from England. Unfortunately, I couldn't convince the couple moving into my apartment that an illiterate maid with attitude was a desirable asset, and I wasn't willing to become Radha's benefactor in perpetuity. That would have really been an echo of Edith.

As with so many memsahibs before me, my professional relationship with my maid was complicated by the emotional one. I knew I would miss Radha's sharply expressed opinions, her wry humor, and her melodramatic life stories, and I also felt guilty about abandoning her to an uncertain, unpensioned future. In *Out of Africa,* Karen Blixen—writing as Isak Dinesen—developed a strong bond with the laborers on the coffee plantation she owned in colonial British East Africa, now Kenya. Especially close to her heart was an ill-educated tribal boy named Kamante, who worked as her cook. Dinesen couldn't find him another job before she left, and for years afterward he sent her brokenhearted letters, begging his "Honored Memsahib" to return: "Your old servant they poor people now." He said he missed her company, but what he needed, of course, was her employment. That said, the two things were inextricably intertwined.

A few days after I told Radha I was leaving, she made it clear that if it came down to a choice between the two, she was going to miss the money more than me. In the weeks before I left, she'd point out things in the apartment that she'd like me to leave for her, as though she were the blunt grandchild and I the dying grandparent. She unsubtly hinted that she intended to use my "goodbye gift" toward her younger daughter's dowry. I hadn't mentioned anything about a parting bonus, but it apparently went without saying.

Part of me was relieved when Radha restored things to a transactional level. The friendship, if that is what we had, sometimes felt too tangled for me to know how to deal with it. For months I'd been feeling vaguely uneasy around her, ever since she'd caught me having breakfast with a strange *feringhee* man. I wasn't sure Radha had picked up on the fact that there was something romantic going on with this new guy, Ted; there was even a small chance she didn't realize that he wasn't Benjamin, because all *feringhee*s looked alike to her.

Still, I put too much stock in her moral judgments to want to take the risk. When I'd first met Ted, I'd kept him away from my apartment, trying to explain that the shadow of my imaginary husband loomed large in Nizamuddin. It sounded pretty silly to hear myself admitting aloud that I was willing to alter my life to suit my maid's righteous ideas about the world. Ted didn't live in Delhi; he was unaccustomed to the complications of Indian servant relationships. When I met him at an

economic conference, he was in town for several weeks for work. I
asked if I could interview him, and he agreed, saying he'd also like to
take me to dinner.

I carefully prepared a mental list of conversation topics before-
hand, which was my standard protocol for such occasions, so as to
avoid uncomfortable silences. We didn't get to any of my queries about
trade barriers to Indian exports, though. In fact, we barely talked about
work. It was well after midnight when I looked at my watch for the first
time. It quickly turned into another of my ill-considered affairs: an
immediate draw, an impulsive decision, no thought for the long term.
On a whim, Ted extended his stay in India, so we could go to Varanasi
together.

In spite of all that, it didn't feel like a reckless adventure this time.
Ted was different in this way from the swashbucklers who'd defined my
romantic life thus far: He didn't get distant eyed or guarded when I
asked him about his future plans. He came from a tightly knit community in the American South, and he seemed to expect loyalty and kind-
ness from the people he knew. He had a stunning confidence in the
world's ability to become the kind of place he wanted it to be.

We made an exception and stayed at my place one night before he
went back to the States. I wanted to show off my apartment; so accustomed was I to my Indian friends oohing and aahing over my luxury
pad that I hadn't realized that it wasn't really deluxe by American standards. Even after I'd invested in a set of bamboo furniture, it looked
underfurnished when I saw it through Ted's eyes. Although Radha kept
the apartment spotlessly clean, it looked grungy compared to the sanitized, air-conditioned glow that so many American living spaces have.

In the morning, Ted acknowledged that he hadn't slept much. Like
an exhausted Delhi beggar conked out on a traffic median, I'd become
accustomed to the prickly mattress fibers that poked through the
sheets, and to relying on the thin rays of warmth from the space heater
to offset the December damp. I no longer heard the *chowkidar*'s whis-
tle, which had mystified him and kept him up all night.

I got us up early, for fear of hearing Radha's key in the lock. We were sitting down to coffee and an omelet when she walked in. I greeted her in what I hoped was a jaunty voice: "Oh, hi! My friend just came over for breakfast." Radha pulled her *dupatta* over her head, as she did in front of anyone of the opposite sex, and nodded a shy *Namaste*. I doubt it occurred to her that he'd been there all night.

She was distracted by something else: the smell of eggs in the kitchen. She gave the omelet pan an exaggerated sniff for my benefit and looked at me reproachfully, as though I'd left her the detritus of a roasted pig. Relieved that this was her only gripe, I told her I'd wash the pan. She gave me a look to say, "That's right you will!" and moved on to the sweeping.

I could tell that Ted was uncomfortable, sitting like a colonial governor at the breakfast table while Radha made her way around us with her broom. We paged our way through the stack of newspapers. After a while, I heard a strangled laugh and followed his gaze to the tangle of dust and cat hair she'd swept up in a corner. Floating on top of the pile was a blue condom wrapper.

Clearly, I would not ever achieve Radha's moral approbation without changing my life in ways I wasn't willing to. In spite of my guilt-driven attempts to fit in with her idea of how I should act, I knew I'd never fully succeed. Nevertheless, watching her walk with a straight back through her small world had taught me something about pride and principled behavior. I felt as though Radha had helped me realize something important about myself. I couldn't put my finger on exactly what it was; maybe it doesn't have a name.

After I made it clear I planned to give Radha a few months' salary as her final bonus, she started to consider me with affection again. In the weeks before I left Delhi, we'd stand around the kitchen with Maneesh, reminding one another of funny things that had happened in the apartment. The time Radha discovered that one of the cats had clawed the seat off the toilet, which she took as absolute confirmation that the feline was a filthy untouchable; the day that Maneesh saw a gecko scamper into my hair as I leaned against the wall, and I'd scrabbled frantically in my scalp, sending the thing flying across the room. These silly stories had the same familiarity and tenderness of family tales.

Neither of them asked me what my life would be like in America. Maybe neither had any context for it; or maybe the future, like the past, was an irrelevant blur to Radha and Maneesh. I didn't want to imagine their lives after I left, either. I couldn't stand to think that things might be harder without my meager patronage, any more than I wanted to think of Delhi continuing without me.

I kept turning to *Out of Africa*. At the end of Dinesen's days in British East Africa—the adopted country that she left against her will, to go back to Denmark—she felt as though the place was actually retracting from her, as if to show her its full beauty: "Till then I had been a part of it, and the drought to me had been like a fever, and the flowering of the plain like a new frock."

Dinesen knew she'd never come back to Africa, and she wanted to imprint herself on it, to claim it as her own.

"If I know a song of Africa, of the Giraffe, and the African new moon lying on her back, of the plows in the fields, and the sweaty faces of the coffee pickers, does Africa know a song of me? Will the air over the plain quiver with a color that I had had on, or the children invent a game in which my name was?"

If India had been a man, we would have had a very unhealthy relation-ship indeed. The place overwhelmed and infuriated me; sometimes, after a hot day of frustrations, I felt as though it was taking blood from me to feed itself. In the mornings, though, waking up with India beside me, I was a girl newly in love. I'd lie very still, blinking into the bright white light. I could hear Radha moving around in the apartment, and I'd pray that she wouldn't intrude. I liked to let the outside cacophony wash over me, as though it was part of my dream. If I lay perfectly still, I imagined, it would stay with me for the whole day.

The temple drumming and rickshaw traffic that had once echoed strangely in my ears now sounded like home. Ram, the vegetable seller, with his dusty tomatoes and tiny hard lemons, calling out a deep-throated "*Sub-ziiii!*" as he tried to drown out the guava and mango boys with their competing carts. The screeching breaks of the trains in Nizamuddin Station and the pigeons flapping and cooing against my windows—they all seemed part of me. In Delhi, I'd grown into myself. However halfhearted my belonging could be, this city had taken me in, a stranger, just as it does so many millions of impoverished Indian migrants, and made me part of its rhythm. Now I felt as though my own daily clatter—the smell and breath of me, my hopes and thoughts—had been subsumed into the city's crazy hum. That was the closest I would come to conquering India, and it was enough.

K.K. picked me up in the middle of the night. A tousle-haired boy with a cleft palate followed him in a van. I'd sold my bamboo furniture back to my landlord and given many of my belongings away, but I still had a dozen Indian army–issue canvas bags filled with books and *salwar kameez* suits to take back to America. My feral alley cats were in an airline-approved steel cage. To judge from their yowling, they were not happy about being relocated to the land of plenty, but I wasn't about to do a Holly Golightly in the film *Breakfast at Tiffany's* and throw them out of the taxi. I was determined to commit myself to something.

As we loaded up the vans, the neighborhood *chowkidars* paused on their rounds to watch us with the dull interest of the perennially exhausted and bored. Any kind of activity attracts a crowd, I thought—even at three in the morning. It was strange to meet the watchmen in person for the first time now, after years of hearing them banging and whistling through Nizamuddin's night streets. All three were tall and lean with serious expressions, their gray uniform caps cocked sideways on their heads. I tried to memorize their faces and then thought: It doesn't matter. It's time to go.

Climbing into K.K.'s van, I remembered that Radha's husband had once worked as a *chowkidar* in Nizamuddin. That was before he contracted "brain fever" and before I moved to the neighborhood that I now considered mine. Eventually these watchmen, too, would die or move on, and new ones would replace them. The landlord would take down the brass plaque with my name on it, and Radha would find another house to work in. The hot season would come, the rickshaw drivers would curse at their customers, and still the crows would pester the monkeys in the trees. Nowhere would the children invent a game in which my name was.

Two years after I left Nizamuddin, I woke up to the *han-ji* wallah announcing himself on his bicycle with his drawn-out call. In an unlikely turn of fate, my old apartment was empty of tenants, and the landlord offered to let me stay in it for a couple of weeks. Being there exaggerated the sensation of drifting, specterlike, through my past. In Nizamuddin market, the cobbler and electrician were still industrious in their stalls. The press wallah stared at me from her perch on her charpoy as I walked past her that first day, unsure whether it was me or a different *feringhee.* She'd lost more of her teeth, so her lips were pulled flush against her gums. Her daughter, still as thin as a stalk of bamboo, was old enough to take care of the ironing herself now. She leaned the weight of her body on the coal-filled iron, pressing down onto a man's white cotton shirt. Steam sizzled up in a shield shape. A mound of clothes behind her lit the hut with color and spoke of how much work they had to do before evening.

The air of the market was thick with the smell of raw sewage, released by the recent rains. It mingled with that of freshly cooked chapatis and chickpea stew at the little local food stall. Several rickshaw drivers stood beside it, hastily gulping a morning meal to sop up their arrack-induced hangovers. A dog panted in a corner of shade—protruding ribs, dull eyes—too sapped of energy to beg for scraps. All was right in the world, except that the sign outside the Fitness Circle was gone and the door was sealed with a wire lock. I went over to inspect it more closely. The lock was wrapped with gauze and, ridiculously, covered with a wax seal, as though that made it impenetrable; clearly it was the work of the Delhi government.

The city authorities had been on a rampage recently of enforcing their widely ignored building codes. Like many small-business owners, Leslie didn't have a commercial license to operate out of her basement space, but she'd never been especially worried about it. India's government had neither the resources nor the will to consistently implement its rules, and city building regulations were ambiguous, filled with loopholes and opportunities for bribes. One day, though, without any notice, the city authorities showed up at the gym and declared they were locking the equipment inside.

With the Fitness Circle gone, it was hard to track down the gym ladies. None of them had cell phones—neither did Radha or Maneesh, for that matter. India may have lurched into economic success, but it had brought neither technology nor stability to my friends in the neighborhood. In fact, in a fast-changing, cheap-labor economy, their lives were even more vulnerable to sudden transformation than they would have been a generation ago. Now slums were routinely knocked down to make way for new hotels and malls; the upwardly mobile were getting rid of their own servants and transferring into new buildings with professional maids and garbage-collection services.

I spent days searching Nizamuddin for them all. I lurked outside the house where I'd heard Maneesh had been hired; I perched myself on Maniya's charpoy waiting for Radha to appear; I wandered around the Muslim *bustee* hoping to run into Azmat. Eventually I saw her brother, Mehboob, on the street. He gave me the number for the family cell phone, and I called it until Azmat picked up. She sounded positively giddy about reuniting with a former gym lady and promised she'd be over as soon as she changed into an outfit appropriate for afternoon tea.

I found it comforting to see that Azmat's clothing tastes had not mellowed. She was wearing a hot pink *salwar kameez* outfit, the sleeves hung with beaded tassels. With evident pride, she handed me a gift of a handkerchief on which she had hand-painted her name and an orange flower: "So you will always remember me." She said she missed the Fitness Circle so much that she couldn't walk past the building anymore. Her loyalties to the ladies were astoundingly deep. If she'd come from my world, Azmat would have been president of the college alumni club.

"It's bad to lose the income, but that's not the worst part. It's that it's so much harder to keep up with what all the ladies are doing. It takes me days to find things out now! I hate it."

Nevertheless, Azmat had an impressive stockpile of gossip about each of the ladies I could think to ask after. She'd been spending time with them again, because Leslie had started holding aerobics classes in her living room. The class was packed; she'd had to move the furniture into the front yard to make room for them all. Leslie had asked Usha to help, and they were now offering living room gym classes a couple of times a week.

"I'm glad to have something to fill my time," Azmat said. "I still haven't done my marriage, *deedee,* and that means I have a lot of time to sit around. No good boy has arrived."

The only prospect who'd "arrived" for her was a boy who worked on a ship. He'd expressed interest through a mutual friend, but when Mehboob had discovered that the boy could be gone for up to a year at a time and that he had no family to speak of, he'd nixed him. In the meantime, a good boy *had* arrived for Azmat's sister—not for the older sister, Rhemet, but for the youngest girl in the family, Khushboo, who was only eighteen.

Azmat called her sister's suitor a "boy" because that's the appropriate way to refer to an unmarried male, but Khushboo's suitor was at least fifteen years older than she was. His family was cagey about his exact age, either because they didn't know it or because they wanted to disguise it; Leslie suspected it was the latter. Despite that drawback, and the fact that ignoring sibling chronology and marrying off Khushboo first could seriously impair the older sisters' chances, Mehboob didn't feel he could turn down the only acceptable proposal that had come in for any of them. Azmat seemed sympathetic to the decision: "She's prettier and younger, so it was easier to find her a match."

I was impressed, again, by her ability to not hold a grudge. Azmat was truly good-natured, I thought; a great catch for any boy. She no longer seemed to believe so herself, though. In the last year, Azmat told me, she'd suffered a serious setback in her marriageability.

"See these black spots on my face? They are from my uterus. I bought some skin-lightening cream, but still the spots aren't going away."

I'd forgotten that discussing matters of health with the gym ladies required a different vocabulary. It took some effort to assemble the facts. Eventually I made some sense of it: Azmat had been ill with a high fever for weeks, and she'd paid a visit to the local *bustee* homeopath. He'd told her that she would never have children.

"I went black," she said, apparently referring to both her physical and mental state: She'd never get married if word got out that she was infertile. One of the gym ladies took Azmat to a real doctor, who gave her an ultrasound and told her that the homeopath was right—she had cysts on her uterus, which meant it should be removed. This doctor had agreed to allow Azmat to delay the surgery for a year, in the hope that she'd get married and pregnant before then. In the best-case scenario, he said, she'd be able to have only one child. Given the slow pace of her husband hunt so far, even this seemed optimistic.

The medical verdict sounded awfully extreme, but who was I to contradict the word of an Indian ladies' doctor. When I talked to Leslie—the neighborhood health expert—about it, she said she'd given up trying to work out the facts; it was too frustrating. Instead, she said, she tried to focus on Azmat's positive attitude about what was surely the worst crisis an Indian girl could face.

"When she was sick, she'd joke that at least she was losing weight without working out. She has a good perspective on life. You know, when I was feeling depressed a couple of years ago, she told me that she was sure that life would turn out well for me because I'd helped people in the neighborhood. It didn't matter whether it was true so much as that she believed it. But I wish the same could really be true for her."

It took more than a week to get to Radha. I was pretty sure she was playing coy with me, either still annoyed at me for leaving or trying to prove that she didn't need me anymore. I asked Joginder and three shop delivery boys to send her messages before she finally told one of them she'd meet me. In the rising heat of a September midday, she and Maniya were seated cross-legged on the charpoy in the alley. They eyed me affectionately as I walked toward them. Maniya's boy was still playing cricket in the park, using a bigger stick for a bat now.

"It's been such a long time, *deedee*. I didn't think you were coming back." She and Maniya were both smiling, or at least as much as I could expect them to—they looked pleased, in an understated, weary way. Radha's voice was gruff as I sat down. "I had to take up two jobs after you left, *deedee*, because these people aren't paying me well."

She wanted to establish right off whether I was moving back into my old apartment. When I told her I wouldn't be staying in Delhi for good, she informed me she only had a few minutes: "I'm glad to see you again, but I can't just sit around and chat." Babloo and Sujla would be waiting for her to make lunch.

She agreed to give me a quick update on the family essentials. First off, she informed me that Pushpa wasn't yet pregnant. I absorbed the information with the solemnity with which I'd learned to treat all of Radha's news.

"The girl has been trying," added Maniya. "But still, no child has come."

After a moment of silence for the lack of a grandson, Radha's face brightened. Babloo was almost finished with his two-year college degree, she said. She'd send him over to my apartment to see me.

I probably wouldn't have recognized Babloo on the street. He looked as though he was eating more than one slum meal a day now. His complexion was ruddy, and he'd grown a soul patch under his bottom lip, as was fashionable among Bollywood heroes of the moment. He was decked out in the familiar outfit of the aspirational middle class: an Indian knockoff button-down shirt, bearing the logo of some unknown company on the breast pocket, and tight jeans. As he sat down at the table where I'd once taught him English, he filled the empty apartment with the fragrance of a sharp, inexpensive cologne that made me sneeze. Gone was the scent of hair palm oil that I'd always associated with him.

Babloo brought me gifts, a strange collection of things: an Indian-made tube of moisturizing cream—"I think it is a very good brand, madam"—a pencil holder stamped with the logo of an Indian company, and a package of sweets tied with twine. The oil had seeped through the paper wrapping, creating a dark square.

"Things must be going well for you, Babloo."

"Yes, madam, very good!"

He looked at me, waiting for me to direct the conversation.

I gave him a sari for Radha for Diwali and asked him not to call me madam—I wasn't his teacher anymore. It was a silly thing to say, because the other options—my first name, *deedee,* or auntie—were designations too familiar for a *feringhee* who had employed his mother for five years. He smiled politely.

Once Babloo warmed up, though, it became apparent he was much more comfortable in the world than he had been a couple of years before. His English was pretty much fluent now. His comfort with the language had allowed him to transcend his class and make friends who spoke English socially—middle-class friends. If it wasn't for the slum cut of his jeans, he could have been one of them. Once he graduated, Babloo told me, he wanted to get an MBA somewhere—he was even thinking of applying for a passport, because he had dreams of doing it overseas. He wanted me to help him figure out how to do that.

It seemed an almost impossible leap within one generation. Radha couldn't have pointed to India on a map; she wouldn't even know what a map was. When Babloo asked for my email address, it took me a moment to recover from my stunned silence and write it down for him. He gave me a funny look, informing me that he regularly "did the email and the Google" at Internet cafés. As he gathered up his notebooks, he asked, with studied casualness, "Shall I show you a snap of my GF?"

I didn't know what he meant, but he said the acronym with so much freighted meaning that it almost sounded like a teenage dare.

"Of who?"

Babloo stroked his soul patch self-consciously, determined to keep playing it cool.

"You know, my GF! She's a girl in my college. A Brahmin girl."

He pulled up an image of a girl on his cell phone; she was wearing a fitted, knee-length, modern *salwar kameez*. I complimented her in a way I hoped sounded appropriate, and he seemed gratified.

"I wish you could meet her sometime. She is wanting to meet you, madam. Don't tell my mother I have a GF, though. Okay?"

I told him I'd never do that and tried to overcome the temptation to ask whether he planned to marry the girl. I didn't want to undermine the confidence between us. The grown-up Babloo wanted to align himself with me—the sole *feringhee* he'd ever met—and prove himself a globalized citizen of the world. He wanted to leave behind the restrictive ways of his illiterate mother and the old India.

There was no way for me to ask about marriage and not also be asking, as a Bihari auntie would, "Are you protecting the girl's innocence?" I was quite sure that Babloo had plenty of aunties asking him questions like that, and not enough people complimenting him for making the leap into the educated class. He was dedicated to advancing himself so that he could get the kind of job his mother had always hoped for for him. He said he'd promised his younger sister that he wouldn't let her be married off before she finished high school, as Pushpa had been. In any case, since he'd carefully mentioned his GF's high caste, I was pretty sure I knew the answer to the aunties' question. Of course he planned to marry the girl.

. . .

"I've let my hair go!" Parvati said as she hugged me hello.

The dusting of white over her thick black braid was an arresting sight. In India, both women and men much older than Parvati consistently dye or henna their hair to cover the gray. Not doing so was practically a political statement.

"I'd been dyeing it for years, but I'd always said that I would go natural when I turned thirty-five. Kind of a depressing way to celebrate a birthday, isn't it?"

I climbed into the car, and Vijay leaned back from the passenger seat to shake my hand in his odd, formal way.

"Her gray hair actually has a useful function," he said. "Now when she argues with aggressive *haramis* for trying to rip her off in the market, they assume she's a crazy woman and get away from her as fast as they can. She doesn't even have to yell at them."

Parvati rolled her eyes at me in the rearview mirror as she started the engine. Since she'd been promoted to a managerial position at her job, she said, Vijay had been making fun of her for ordering people around and wearing what he called "power saris."

"It's a pain to put on a sari every day, but I decided it's worth it for the respect I get at work when I do. The boss isn't thrilled about the gray hair, though. I'll probably have to dye it again. *If* I stay in my new position, that is. I'll tell you about my plan over a drink."

The Press Club looked cleaner than I remembered it. Vijay said that there'd been an influx of new members from the fast-growing ranks of TV correspondents. These journalists were young, good-looking, and well mannered—nothing like Vijay's cuss-mouthed, hard-drinking newspaper friends. More women had joined, too. I could tell because the outhouse that served as the ladies' room had been upgraded—now there was a lock on the door and a working flush.

As we sat outside on the club patio, my eyes stung and my throat burned from the particulates in the air. I laughed that after two years in America, I'd become too delicate to handle Delhi's atmosphere, but Parvati said that the pollution had become much worse in the last couple of years. There were cranes stretched all across the city's low horizon, constantly expanding the business district and the outskirts, as well as the Delhi Metro. Rising incomes meant there were more cars and scooters on the streets now, too.

"It's disgusting—when I blow my nose at night it comes out black and my throat is sore all the time," she said.

Given the pollution, it seemed strange that the Press Club had decided to drape white tablecloths over the outdoor plastic tables. Parvati said it was the work of one of the beverage companies that had started doing promotional events there in an effort to ingratiate themselves with the club's new members. If Smirnoff was setting up shop at the Press Club, times certainly had changed, I thought. I'd never seen the patrons of the place drinking anything other than Indian-made beer or whiskey.

A chubby twenty-something kid was dispatched from the Smirnoff booth to our table. He offered us cocktails in an American-inflected English unmistakably learned at a call center job. Parvati dismissed him with a flick of her hand: "No one here wants those chickenshit drinks." The boy retreated, and she called for Dev, her regular Mao-suited waiter, and ordered us Seagram's Blenders Pride and Royal Challenge for Vijay.

Vijay wandered off with drink in hand to greet some other friends. Parvati leaned toward me intensely, as she was wont to do over whiskeys at the Press Club.

"I don't want to grow old here, Miranda. All the new money has changed the city. Look at these poseurs with their vodka drinks. And there's much worse. Delhi has always been aggressive, but petty crime is rising fast now. There's so much anger—I don't think it's safe here anymore. Recently, a car full of men chased my car along the highway at night, and I was thinking that anything could happen."

Parvati said she'd recently gotten together enough money to buy an inexpensive plot of land in the Himalayan foothills, not far from the village where she was born. She wanted to save enough to build a house there, so that she and Vijay could quit their jobs and leave Delhi for good.

"It's in an isolated place, outside the village. Hopefully we'll be left alone."

It was hard to imagine Parvati anywhere other than Delhi. I asked whether she'd miss it, and she looked at me sharply.

"Delhi *is* a village, Miranda. It just pretends to be this urbane place, when in fact it's all the worst things about a village. The idea that you can be anonymous here is bullshit—you know that. Everyone in Nizamuddin knows everything about you. The only thing for us is to leave. It's the only way to escape the past. I don't want Vijay to keep feeling like he has to hide his wife and her baby from everyone. It's just tiring, you know?"

Vijay returned to the table then, accompanied by a meticulously dressed older man with a comb-over and the slightly uneven walk of someone affected by polio as a child.

"Parvati, Miranda, this is Dilip-*ji*—you know, the respected senior journalist."

The gentleman straightened his back at Vijay's introduction and folded his hands in a *Namaste* gesture.

"I am so pleased to finally meet Vijay's *dulhan*. Welcome, welcome."

His Hindi was formal and slightly drunken. Parvati offered him a plastic chair. Dilip did not want to take a seat, though. He wanted to extend the social flourishes for as long as possible, effusing praise on Parvati. My Hindi was a little rusty, but I was pretty certain that he had referred to Parvati as a "revered bride." Her stunned expression made me think my translation was correct.

Parvati was in a good mood, though, so she was willing to play the part that this gentleman expected of her. Her patience started to give out only when Dilip-*ji* tried to press money into her hand, a symbolic gift of a hundred and one rupees. He kept insisting that the money was "to bring good luck for the new bride." Vijay had stopped talking, and his head was in his hands. Finally Parvati placed the money on the tablecloth and turned to me. "Come. I have to go to the toilet."

I was happy to oblige. My head hurt from trying to follow what was going on. We stood outside the door to the ladies' outhouse, where the branches of a bodhi fig tree hung low in the courtyard, the leaves coated with a layer of desert dust.

"It is bloody ridiculous. Did you hear him? That old fool thinks I am Vijay's new bride. For God's sake, I have gray in my hair!"

"What makes him think you guys just got married?"

"I don't know! I guess he just assumes it because he's never seen Vijay with me before. He's tipsy and overexcited. I was trying to be nice, but God, did you hear the flowery language he was using? I thought I was going to puke."

"I was pretty impressed at your ability to play along with it," I told her. "I don't think I've ever seen you be so accommodating."

"I know. Even I am impressed with myself. Did you hear me promise to cook for him, like a good Indian wife? So funny! But when he tried to give me that money, it became too embarrassing. I mean, Vijay is married to *another woman*. Ugh. I can't go back there. Maybe Vijay will work up the nerve to inform that fool we're not married. Let's just sit here awhile."

It sounded like a grand idea to relax underneath the wide canopy of the fig tree in the courtyard of the Press Club, even if we were actually sitting on browned-out grass beside a reeking bathroom. I tried not to inhale through my nose and reminded myself that Buddha achieved enlightenment under a bodhi tree in Bihar. Thinking about Buddhism made me realize that Parvati had mellowed a lot in the last couple of years. As we sat listening to the traffic on the street outside, she seemed to find some inner calm. When she looked at me, I saw that the tense lines around her eyes had loosened.

"It's comical, isn't it? This kind of thing still happening when I'm in my thirties? It must seem strange to come back to this city of crazy conservative *choot*s!"

I laughed. Parvati knew that situations such as this were inevitable in the life she'd chosen. She'd rejected the easy destiny of a village girl, and what she'd gotten instead wasn't really all that bad.

In Geeta's married world, the streets smelled of spicy fish curry and were lined with violet-blooming jacaranda trees. The Bangalore street vendors sold pineapples and coconut water from their wooden carts, rather than the guava and squash hawked from carts in Delhi. Moving away from her in-laws seemed to have stirred the long-dormant homemaker in Geeta. As we pulled through the gate of her one-story rented house, I saw that the driveway was decorated with intricate blue and pink chalk designs that are popular in South India. Fresh blossoms floated in a ceramic pot of water outside the door.

The house she and Ramesh lived in was light and airy, with white marble floors and fans whirring overhead. There were two large bedrooms, which immediately made me sure that they were still trying to have kids; I knew that Geeta, the consummate bargain hunter, wouldn't pay for an extra room unless she planned to use it. The sounds of the neighbors floated in from both sides: a woman singing a romantic old movie tune as she moved about the kitchen, and a breathless news anchor announcing the day's headlines in the Kannada language. Geeta was quick to advertise the advantages of her new place, although I'd never seen her in-laws' house.

"Even when Ramesh is at work I don't get lonely," she said. "I can always hear people around me. Of course, my in-laws don't believe me. They think it's miserable that I am here by myself during the day."

I put my bag down and sank into a black leather couch, which seemed an uncharacteristically flashy touch for a middle-class Indian home; I wondered whether Ramesh's father had bought it for them. A small Sri Lankan mask was hanging on one of the whitewashed walls of the living room, and I recognized it as the gift Ramesh had given Geeta on their first date, when he'd told her he wanted to marry her.

They'd moved out of the Murthy household just three months before, after two years of trying to make it work there, and the decision seemed to suit Geeta: her skin glowed as it used to, and she'd lost some of the weight that she'd blamed on Ramesh's parents' diet. In fact, with her hair curled up in the humidity and her face dimpling with pleasure at seeing me, she looked like herself again, very different from the dissatisfied Punjabi housewife she'd been last time I saw her in Delhi. Nevertheless, the decision to move out of the Murthy household was apparently still raw, because Geeta wanted to explain.

"I feel bad about leaving Ramesh's parents, but living there was too much. I have different expectations. And then I thought—why should I have to do this? This is the new India!"

"Wait—so it was your idea to move out?"

I didn't know any of the details. Our contact had been limited to occasional emails since I'd moved back to the States, and I realized, with a flash of shame, that our correspondence had been much more about me than it had been about her. There was a reason for my self-involvement, though: When I'd told Geeta I was undertaking a real marriage—to Ted, the *feringhee* I'd met in Delhi—she'd been so thrilled that she didn't want to talk about anything else.

She'd helped me organize the ceremony, making sure it had plenty of Indian touches. We'd talked about little other than my wedding jewelry for months. She'd designed a necklace-and-earring set for me and had it made for me in Bangalore, all of which required a great deal of deliberation, debate, and haggling. As she'd often reminded me, the bride's jewelry sends an important statement about whether she is modern or traditional. We'd eventually settled on a modern design—Ramesh-approved—in the traditional yellow antiqued gold, making me a "modern-cum-traditional" bride. I wore it with a red silk dress, because after living in India, I didn't want to get married in white, the color of widowhood.

Geeta couldn't make it to the wedding—which we held in Dublin, where my parents lived—but our first dance was in her honor—the love song from the classic Shah Rukh Khan movie *DDLJ*.

Now that I was emerging from my bridal absorption, I realized I had a lot to catch up on. Geeta had always been an advocate of the extended family, and I'd assumed she would do as her mother advised and adjust to her new in-laws. I was surprised that she'd had the gumption to "do a nuclear" and leave the joint family home. Geeta fixed us a jug of *nimbo panne,* that refreshing lemon drink I'd missed. Ramesh retreated to their bedroom with his, and Geeta started at the beginning.

"The spicy food was only part of the problem. My in-laws are kind of dirty also—there is always laundry and children's toys scattered around—and that drove me crazy. And, I had no independence. They were always in my business, asking what I was doing, and always, all day long, praying. There was no relief."

As Geeta had feared, working in Appa's office had ratcheted up the tension with the Murthy women to almost unbearable levels. She became paranoid and would keep Ramesh up at night, whispering about what she thought she'd overheard his aunties saying and what they might be plotting. Eventually he decided that he had to work up his nerve and tell his father that he and his wife were too modern to live in an extended family.

"Appa nearly had a heart attack," Geeta told me. "He said they'd do anything to make us stay—even remodel the top floor for us to live on. But even if we had a separate kitchen, it still would have been hard." She sighed. "The family means so much to Appa, and he feels like he failed with us. That part makes me sad." She looked around at her little house, as though reminding herself of the satisfactions of a private space. "But the thing is . . . a joint family sounds better than it is in reality."

Geeta was relishing the simple freedoms she'd regained: shopping excursions with no escort other than the driver, and walking in circles around the neighborhood at dusk for exercise, which Appa had deemed unsafe. Best of all, of course, was escaping the oppressive spice of the Murthy family cuisine. Geeta had now completely sworn off hot South Indian food. When we went to the Murthy house for dinner, she'd pick at her plate and make *paranthas* when we got home. She cooked Punjabi food most nights, which Ramesh seemed to have gotten used to. Occasionally, he would prove his globalized mettle by cooking pasta, or by insisting that we eat at Domino's. We went out for pizza three times in the two weeks I spent there.

"We want to show you the best of Bangalore," he'd say in explanation.

It seemed pointless to remind him that I could have pizza at home—to Ramesh, that was just it. He wanted to prove that Bangalore was just as "advanced" in its global cuisine as Washington, D.C., where I was living.

Geeta had also asserted her independence by scaling back her *puja* to an hour a day. That still seemed a lot to me, since, to my knowledge, she hadn't prayed at all when she lived with Nanima in Nizamuddin. Here she kept coconut pieces and fresh flowers in the refrigerator to use as offerings. It was mostly out of a sense of obligation: She said her mother-in-law quizzed the maid and driver sometimes about how much time she'd spent praying. But I could also tell that it wasn't purely a desire to be accepted by her new family; she got genuine satisfaction out of these elaborate South Indian prayer rituals.

Geeta had set aside a separate *puja* room in the new house and brought in a wooden shrine that held a dozen idols of Hindu gods, including a turquoise plastic Hanuman, the monkey god, inexplicably dressed in what looked like a pink diaper and seated on a swing. When I picked it up and chuckled, she narrowed her eyes at me.

"It isn't what the gods look like that matters, Miranda. You should know that by now. I see how contented Ajji looks while she is meditating, and how peaceful the whole house becomes. Praying is one of the reasons I've become happy here."

Some nights, Geeta would wander over to her *puja* room before she went to sleep, switch on the fluorescent tube light, and stand there for a few minutes in silence, just looking at the idols. It made me wonder what she was thinking. Was she communing with the gods in some way, or just checking that all was in order and the flowers were fresh in case her mother-in-law stopped by?

Ramesh's family still provided the shape to their married life. They hadn't had a chance to make friends in Bangalore, Geeta said, because they spent all of their free time with her in-laws. When her brother-in-law had minor laser surgery, Ramesh's father instructed them to join the rest of the family in the hospital during the operation and recovery. I entertained myself while they spent a full two days in the waiting room.

The following weekend, the in-laws bustled in unannounced one morning before any of us was dressed. Geeta, sleepy eyed in a pair of pink sweatpants, was unenthusiastic when her mother-in-law instructed the driver to unload a trunk load of watermelons, cantaloupe, and dates for them. Then she lied and told her that we'd already had toast and *chai* for breakfast.

"I need to prove to them that I can take care of my husband myself," she said after they left. "If I'd told my mother-in-law that we hadn't eaten yet, she would have sent the driver off to bring us a cooked breakfast from their house. It's ridiculous—they treat us like babies and then constantly hint that we should be having our own kids."

She slammed a pot of water on the stove to make Ramesh's tea.

When we were alone, I asked whether Ramesh's family was still bugging her to get pregnant.

"Of course they are. It's been two years since we got married. I am practically middle-aged by Indian standards. They bring it up all the time. My sister-in-law says things like 'You should have babies before Ajji dies.' She partly means that it will be easier for me with Ramesh's grandmother around, because I won't have to lift a finger for the baby. But she also means that Ramesh and I owe it to Ajji to give her a great-grandchild before she dies."

Geeta sounded annoyed, but she was also more temperate than she'd ever been about her in-laws before. Even though dealing with them was still a daily challenge, moving out of the Murthy household had obviously been the best thing for her relationship with them.

"The thing is—we're working on a different schedule to most Indians. We wanted to take some time for ourselves before we had babies. But there's no way to explain that to them. How could they possibly understand? It doesn't make sense in the traditional Indian context."

I could sympathize. Now that I was a married lady myself, I was experiencing it, too: Indians across the board were anything but shy about reminding me that I should be with child. That was my next task in life, and by not fulfilling it I seemed to make people suspicious. Within minutes of greeting me, Radha and Maneesh had both asked why I hadn't had a baby yet. Even the lady who used to teach me Hindi acted a little strangely when I said I planned to wait a while before trying. It seemed to make me suspect, just as being single in Delhi once had.

Of course, I felt the pressure back in the States, too. My friends and I laughed that there was a widespread expectation that we would swiftly reproduce—even in the land of older marriages, IVF, and childless professional couples. One of my good friends in New York admitted to me that she was terrified she wouldn't be able to get pregnant in the months immediately following her wedding. "I would feel like such a failure," she said.

Still, Geeta was right when she said that she imagined it was more acceptable to hold off having kids in the States than it is in India.

"There's no models for people like us in my family or Ramesh's," she said. "In fact, what Ramesh's parents keep saying is that we've both had plenty of time to ourselves. His mother tells me that because I waited so long to get married, I've already had my selfish time; now it's time to stop thinking of ourselves and give her some grandchildren. Like it's my duty to get pregnant." A half second later, she added, "Really, they are right, though. It is my duty."

Geeta, like everyone around her, considered having kids to be the natural follow-up to marriage; she felt compelled by tradition, family, and timing to do so. Still, it was complicated for her. Geeta's modern self rebelled against being pushed into motherhood, just as much as it did against the idea that her new family dictated her decisions now.

I could see how Ramesh's family would make Geeta feel claustrophobic, even after she and her husband had "gone nuclear." And yet—I had to admit that a life defined by family didn't seem so awful to me anymore. The idea of living in the same country as my boyfriend had once filled me with terror, but that had changed. When I'd left Delhi, I'd moved not just to the same country but into the same apartment as my new boyfriend. Mingling my books with Ted's on his shelves felt like the greatest expression of intimacy I'd ever made.

What if we forget whose are whose? I remember thinking.

Now I was a part of his family. While it sometimes felt like more responsibility than I was prepared for, what stood out to me was how light it could be. We spent the Christmas before we were married in Ted's conservative southern town, a place as foreign to me as India once was. I made mince pies for their Christmas dinner, the way my mother always had. Ted's mother had a stocking knitted for me and hung it up on the mantelpiece with the rest of the family's. A few years before, matching Christmas stockings would have made me want to run screaming from the room; now, seeing them on the mantel, I felt tears come to my eyes, and realized that I felt grateful and proud.

In Bangalore one night, after Geeta cooked a heavy Punjabi meal, we went for a digestive wander around the neighborhood. The moon was almost full, and in its light the white marble houses shone like temples. Our voices set off the stray dogs, but we ignored their howling. The air, rich with the fragrance of jasmine and freesia, felt soft and freeing. Geeta asked Ramesh to tell her the South Indian names of the flowers and trees as we passed them. She always sounded impressed by his answers.

"I never used to notice nature before—but here women use flowers all the time. They put them in their hair and decorate their houses with them. I do it, too. Every morning, I pick white jasmine from the bush in the driveway for *puja*—never the blossoms on the ground, only freshly picked ones."

She ran over to a shrub hung with graceful greenish white blossoms.

"Look, Ramesh! This one I know. We have it in the Punjab. We call it *raat ki rani*—queen of the night—because its fragrance comes out only after dark. A sweet smell. It reminds me of home." She looked at Ramesh, and they both smiled as she corrected herself. "My first home, that is."

Acknowledgments

The women in the book were my friends long before I imagined writing about their lives; they trusted me with their secrets not because I was a reporter but because I was a friend. Both Geeta and Parvati understandably felt some discomfort about the project. My greatest thanks go to them, and to Azmat, Maneesh, Radha, and Usha. Because their stories are sensitive and their lives are fluid, I have changed Geeta's and Parvati's names and altered some identifying details to protect Geeta. Several other names have also been changed.

The list of those who helped me make sense of India over the years would be many pages long, but I especially need to thank Binu Alex; Bhavna, Kajal, Kiran, and Kuku Bhardwaj, who made Nizamuddin sing; Praful Bidwai; Sadanand Dhume; Vinod K. Jose; Poornima Joshi; Aunohita Majumdar; Anosh Malekar; Chandana Mathur; Janis McClinch; Jawed Naqvi and his clan; M. P. Nunan; Amit Sengupta; Kalpana Sharma; Rakesh Sharma; Leslie Weightman; and Aanchal White.

My agents, Gail Ross and Howard Yoon, saw the shape of this book before I did and challenged me to find it. Susanna Porter at Random House saw it, too, and I am lucky to have as sensitive and engaged an editor as she, and such a wonderful team in her colleagues.

Thanks to Ted Clark and Loren Jenkins at NPR, and to Karen Lowe and Julie Small at *Marketplace,* for their support to me as a reporter; and to Lynda Blake, Rosemary E. Duncumb, Jocelyn Gordon, Stephen Tyrrell, and Win Waters for graciously sharing their memories of Edith and missionary life.

I am grateful to the mentors and friends who helped me with the manuscript: Susan Cheever, Hillary Frey, Rob Gifford, Jordana Hochman, Richard Lehnert, Wyatt Mason, Nandan Nilekani, Matthew Power, John Schidlovsky, Erik Shonstrom, and Madhulika Sikka.

My forever thanks go to Jessica and Megan Kennedy, Emily Noelle Lambert, Diane Spear, and Susie Tyrrell. And above all, to Ted Jones, for believing in Bollywood.

Select Bibliography and
Suggested Reading

Adiga, Aravind. *The White Tiger.* New York: Free Press, 2008.
A shocking vision of India as we've rarely seen it rendered in English; the Booker Prize–winning novel about a modern country that tramples over its lowest castes and classes.

Bumiller, Elisabeth. *May You Be the Mother of a Hundred Sons: A Journey Among the Women of India.* New York: Ballantine, 1990.
One of the very few books in English about women in India, written by a *New York Times* reporter, is a sensitive rendering of their lives.

Chopra, Anupama. *King of Bollywood: Shah Rukh Khan and the Seductive World of Indian Cinema.* New York: Warner Books, 2007.
An insider's view of India's movie world, written by the wife of one of the biggest producers in the industry, Vinod Chopra.

Dalrymple, William. *City of Djinns: A Year of Delhi.* London: HarperCollins, 1993.
This travelogue is one of the most evocative and hilarious portraits of New Delhi ever written.

———. *Nine Lives: In Search of the Sacred in Modern India.* New York: Alfred A. Knopf, 2010.
A beautiful exploration of the religious heritage of the subcontinent.

Das, Gurcharan. *The Elephant Paradigm: India Wrestles with Change.* New Delhi: Penguin India, 2002.
A treatise in favor of globalization, written as part memoir and part economic analysis by a prominent Indian economic thinker.

Debroy, Bibek, and D. Shyam Babu, eds. *The Dalit Question: Reforms and Social Justice.* New Delhi: Globus, 2004.
A collection of essays on caste in modern-day India.

Desai, Kiran. *The Inheritance of Loss.* New York: Grove/Atlantic, 2006.
A novel that switches between the narration of a sixteen-year-old girl coming of age in tumultuous times in India and that of an illegal Indian immigrant in the United States.

Dinesen, Isak. *Out of Africa.* New York: Random House, 1938.
Magical stories of expat colonial-era life on a coffee plantation in Kenya.

Doniger, Wendy. *The Hindus: An Alternative History.* Penguin, 2009.
A fascinating popular history of Hinduism by one of the world's foremost scholars of the religion.

Ghosh, Amitav. *The Hungry Tide.* New York: Houghton Mifflin, 2005.
A luscious novel set in a far corner of India, where the mangrove forests and Bengal tigers teach us something of the consequences of globalization.

———. *Sea of Poppies.* New York: Picador, 2008.
An adventure story set in nineteenth-century Kolkata.

Guha, Ramachandra. *India After Gandhi: The History of the World's Largest Democracy.* New York: HarperCollins, 2007.
An intensely engaged, highly readable survey of a fascinating period in India's history, as it grows into the proud, independent nation we know today.

Ilaiah, Kancha. *Why I Am Not a Hindu.* Kolkata: Samya, 1996.
A manifesto of the Dalit caste, this book is laced with fury and sarcasm.

Jadhav, Narendra. *Untouchables: My Family's Triumphant Journey Out of the Caste System in Modern India.* New York: Scribner, 2005.
The searing tale of a Dalit family determined to escape the rigid confines of the bottom of the caste system.

Jhabvala, Ruth Prawer. *Out of India: Selected Stories.* Washington, D.C.: Counterpoint Perseus, 2000 (first published in 1957).
A fascinating collection of stories by a German writer who spent most of her life in India.

Kakar, Sudhir. *Indian Identity.* New Delhi: Viking Penguin, 1996.
Three deeply revealing studies from India's best-known psychoanalyst.

Khilnani, Sunil. *The Idea of India.* New Delhi: Penguin India, 1997.
Trying to make sense of India's founding principles in light of its fast-changing attitudes.

Kipling, Rudyard. *Kim.* London: Macmillan, 1901.
A novel written from the center of the British Raj in India.

Lahiri, Jhumpa. *The Namesake.* New York: Houghton Mifflin, 2003.
A tale of the struggle to belong, told through a family of Indian immigrants to the United States.

Luce, Edward. *In Spite of the Gods: The Strange Rise of Modern India.* New York: Doubleday, 2007.
A careful look at the contradictions of a fast-globalizing India from a *Financial Times* correspondent.

Mayo, Katherine. *Mother India: Selections from the Controversial 1927 Text, Edited and with an Introduction by Mrinali Sinha.* University of Michigan Press, 2000.
A furious and well-considered rebuttal to the controversial book *Mother India,* which was written in 1927 by an American journalist to attack the idea of Indian self-rule.

Mishra, Pankaj. *Temptations of the West: How to Be Modern in India, Pakistan, Tibet, and Beyond.* New York: Farrar, Straus, and Giroux, 2006.
Essays on topics as diverse as jihad and Bollywood by one of India's most interesting contemporary writers.

Mistry, Rohinton. *Family Matters.* London: Faber and Faber, 2002.
An illuminating novel set inside a love-torn Mumbai family.

Naipaul, V. S. *India: A Million Mutinies Now.* London: William Heinemann, 1990.
The final volume of Naipaul's brilliant trilogy of nonfiction travelogues exploring the land of his ancestry.

Nilekani, Nandan. *Imagining India: The Idea of a Renewed Nation.* New York: Penguin, 2009.
An argument for the policies needed to help India continue its remarkable growth story.

Omvedt, Gail. *Dalits and the Democratic Revolution: Dr. Ambedkar and the Dalit Movement in Colonial India.* New Delhi: Sage, 1994.
A history of the untouchable leader and lead author of India's constitution.

Peer, Basharat. *Curfewed Night: One Kashmiri Journalist's Frontline Account of Life, Love, and War in His Homeland.* New York: Scribner, 2010.
A heartbreaking account of one of the world's least-chronicled conflicts.

Roberts, Gregory David. *Shantaram.* Melbourne: Scribe, 2003.
A sprawling novel that makes its declaration of love for India from inside the country's slums, drug gangs, and jails.

Rushdie, Salman. *Midnight's Children.* London: Jonathan Cape, 1981.
A way to experience viscerally the history of the subcontinent.

Sen, Amartya. *The Argumentative Indian: Writings on Indian History, Culture, and Identity.* New York: Farrar, Straus and Giroux, 2005.
An erudite exploration of India from a winner of the Nobel prize in economics.

Sharma, R. N. *Manusmrti.* New Delhi: Chaukhamba Sanskrit Pratishthan, 1998.
A translation of the Sanskrit text of the first recorded Hindu law book, *The Laws of Manu*.

Srinivas, M. N. *Social Change in Modern India.* Berkeley: The University of California Press, 1966.
A groundbreaking text about the rules that guide India.

For five years, MIRANDA KENNEDY reported from across South Asia for National Public Radio and American Public Media's *Marketplace*. From her base in New Delhi, she covered the conflicts in Afghanistan and Pakistan and other major stories across Asia. She wrote extensively about women, caste, and globalization in India, and her stories have appeared in publications like *The Washington Post*, *The Boston Globe*, *The Nation*, and Slate. Before she moved to India, Miranda was a magazine editor and public radio reporter in New York, where she covered the September 11 attacks. On returning to the States, she moved to Washington, D.C., to work as an editor at National Public Radio's *Morning Edition*.